William Bradshaw and a Faint Hope

By

Arthur Daigle

Publication Information

This novel is entirely a work of fiction. The names, characters and places portrayed in it are the work of the author's imagination or are used fictitiously. Any resemblance to actual people living or dead, events or locations is entirely coincidental.

William Bradshaw and a Faint Hope

by

Arthur Daigle

Cover illustrated by Vanette Kosman

ISBN: 978-15118855877

This book is dedicated to my family, who still puts up with me after all these years.

About the Author

Arthur Daigle was born and raised in the suburbs of Chicago, Illinois. He received a biology degree from the University of Illinois Urbana Champaign, and has worked in such diverse fields as zoo intern, research assistant, fisheries intern and grading essay tests. In addition to his writing, Arthur is an avid gardener and amateur artist. This book was almost inevitable since the author has been a fan of science fiction and fantasy since he was old enough to walk. William Bradshaw and a Faint Hope is his second novel, with more on the way.

Acknowledgements

There are many people who deserve credit for helping with this novel. As with my first book, my inspiration came from the works of the filmmaker and puppeteer Jim Henson and the British artist Brian Froud. I hold these men in the highest esteem for their creativity and humor. I owe a debt to the Millennium Writers' Group, which I belonged to for many years prior to the group folding in 2009. I received helpful feedback from them, and I greatly miss their company. I must also give credit to my family, who helped me improve my book and provided constant support.

William Bradshaw and a Faint Hope

by

Arthur Daigle

Chapter One

A highwayman waited patiently next to a dirt road while reading a copy of *Banditry for Beginners, An Introduction to Wealth Extraction* (a best seller for evildoers new to the trade). He was tall and thin, wearing threadbare clothing and a cloak, and was so dirty from weeks without bathing that the smell coming off him wilted flowers and panicked birds. It was early in the morning, and he'd been hiding behind an old oak tree for hours waiting for a victim to pass by, blissfully unaware of the humiliating defeat he was about to receive.

It wouldn't be the first time he'd been beaten. Being so far away from a settlement wasn't a good place to find victims, but a rival gang of thieves had pushed him away from the nearest city. A very determined Girl Scout had driven him even further away. He'd also been chased five miles by a rabid groundhog, an event that was the source of recurring nightmares. But that happened weeks ago, and he had a good feeling about his chances here.

The highwayman's patience was rewarded when a young man walked down the road. The man had brown hair and gray eyes, and wore a green shirt, black vest, black pants, black gloves with green fingers, a black hat with a green ribbon sewn in the base, and a cape, black on the outside and green on the inside. His clothes weren't the height of fashion, but they were in good condition. The highwayman smiled. Anyone dressed well had money.

Waiting until the young man was close enough to touch, the highwayman leapt out from behind the tree. With a triumphant yell he reached into his grubby cloak, drawing out a battered long sword with one hand and a rusty dagger with the other. Pointing the sword at his victim's chest, he shouted, "Hands in the air!"

To the highwayman's surprise, the man seemed to be more amused by this than frightened. "Hi there, William Bradshaw, King of the Goblins. And who are you?"

The highwayman stared at him, dumbfounded. "What are you doing?"

"Introducing myself," his victim replied casually.

The highwayman put his dagger away and took out his book from behind the tree. "You're supposed to try to run away or hand over your money when you meet a highwayman. It says so in chapter two, right after the part about selecting a good ambush site and not being eaten by wildlife."

Will pointed a finger at his attacker. "You're a highwayman?"

"Yes, and a dangerous one at that!"

Still smiling, Will said, "This is a bit of good luck. Do you have something to write on?"

Confused, the highwayman said, "There are margins in the book. It says you can use those for taking notes."

"That should do," Will said. "I've been living in these parts for a few months, and the road conditions are terrible. There are wagon ruts deep enough you could lose a cow in them, and the potholes are even worse if you can believe that."

Puzzled, the highwayman asked, "Potholes?"

Will nodded. "I know Ket Kingdom is strapped for cash, but if the roads are in bad shape then farmers and merchants can't get to market, and that's going to cut down on tax revenue. Plus there's road kill everywhere and nobody's picking it up. That's a nasty job, believe me, I know, but it has to be done."

The highwayman waved his book. "I don't think you understand. I'm a highwayman."

"You already said that."

"That doesn't mean I work for the highway department." The highwayman held up his book and explained, "A highwayman is someone who robs people as they go from one place to another. I am, in fact, robbing you."

"You're a robber?" Will asked.

"Yes," the highwayman explained patiently, "I am a robber."

Will scratched his head. He glanced at the tall grass along the road and saw shapes moving through it. Here and there a head peeked up and a small, goofy looking face stared at the highwayman. Will wanted to keep the highwayman's attention on him, so he asked, "What's it like?"

"Oh, it's grand! There are plenty of advancement opportunities, you get lots of fresh air, travel to new places, and you get to meet the most interesting people and see what's in their pockets. Speaking of which, empty them out."

Will did as ordered. The contents of his pockets included a bottle cap, a handkerchief, a handful of lint and a brochure for Eddy's All You Can Eat Rib Roast Restaurant. The highwayman looked at the meager offering and gave Will a suspicious glare. "You're joking. That can't be all you have."

"Sad but true," Will replied.

"You said you were a king!"

"Yes," Will said slowly. "I'm the King of the Goblins. I'd like you to think about that. Do goblins generally have anything worth taking?"

The highwayman rubbed his chin. "Um, no, but you being a king I was hoping for something better than the shiny rocks you'll find in a goblin's pockets."

"I'm sorry to tell you that's not the case," Will said. "The kingdom is flat broke. The only reason we're not in debt is the fact that nobody was crazy enough to lend us money in the first place. You can have the lint if you want."

"No, you don't get much for lint." The highwayman was stymied. He had weapons and a victim, but no loot. This didn't come up in the book, or at least the parts he'd read. He wished he'd bought the advanced burglary books or finished the one he had. Then he saw something shiny hanging from Will's belt. A scepter! "All right, I'll take your scepter. Hand it over."

"This?" Will looked at his bronze scepter set with fire opals, a prize he had no intention of losing. He glanced around and saw more shapes drift through the grass. They weren't very big, but there were a lot of them and they were all moving toward Will and his attacker. They'd need a few seconds to get into place. He had to stall the highwayman for a bit longer. "You do realize this is a fire scepter, right? I can turn it on pretty fast, and turn *you* into 180 pounds of well done steak."

"You can? Oh, it's magic! Yes, I heard about those, very good resale value. Uh, let's see...I've got it! You don't move at all, and I'll take the scepter from you and won't stab you. Sound fair?"

"Now that you mention it, no," Will said. "You're sure you want to do this? Robbing a king is a bad career move."

The highwayman laughed. "You said it yourself, you're the King of the Goblins. Those dirty little things aren't much of a threat."

"If there's only one of them then you're right, they're normally not a threat," Will conceded. "But they do have two things going for them."

Curious, the highwayman asked, "What's that?"

"They're very quiet when they want to be," Will said as a mob of thirty goblins dressed in rags or miniature WW I German infantry uniforms poured out of the tall grass and ran at the highwayman. "And there's never only one goblin."

The mob hit the highwayman from behind. Two of the taller goblins struck him in the back of the knee and tipped him over backwards, and he fell screaming into the mob. Goblins flowed over him like water, piling on him, stealing his weapons and pinning him to the ground. The entire mob began babbling now that they didn't need to be quiet.

"Tie him up!" one goblin shouted.

"Kick him in the shin!" yelled another.

"Take his wallet!" said a third one.

"It's not supposed to work like this!" the highwayman cried out from under the pile of goblins. The goblins were weaker and smaller than him, but their numbers more than made up the difference. Within seconds the highwayman was hog tied and set on the ground next to Will.

"That was nicely handled," Will told them. He could have dealt with the highwayman with his fire scepter, but there was no need to kill the man. "Leave him where the authorities can find him."

"You got it, boss," a goblin with tusks said. They dragged the protesting highwayman away and left Will to continue his walk home.

William Bradshaw headed back to his kingdom as he did this time every morning. He had to get breakfast in the nearest human town, the only place for miles with edible food. With breakfast over he was expected to go back to ruling his subjects, a teeming mass of short, stupid and moderately crazy goblins living in what would be called a landfill if you were being charitable.

His life wasn't always like this. Will wasn't even from the world of Other Place. No, he was from Earth. He'd applied for a management job advertised by the law firm of Cickam, Wender and Downe, and was interviewed by an irritable and possibly insane lawyer named Twain. Will had learned too late that the job was to rule the goblins of Other Place. It was a world filled with men, elves, dwarfs, dragons, wizards and goblins, and a near total absence of common sense.

Will had been stuck here for five months, during which time he'd inadvertently started a war with a human king called Kervol Ket. Everyone, goblins included, had believed Kervol would win easily, despite the fact that the man was so dumb he could lose a battle of wits with a doorknob. Will and his followers had won the war, somehow, but that didn't get him home.

Will walked through grasslands and young trees, through canyons and around rock outcroppings. It was a pleasant autumn day, cool enough that he didn't work up a sweat when he exercised. The air smelled sweet from wildflowers growing on the side of the road. Bees buzzed around him, but thankfully the mosquitoes were gone with the cooler weather. Not far away, farmers harvested their crops and gathered hay for the coming winter.

On the way home he came across four goblins chasing pixies. Will didn't understand their hatred for pixies, tiny pale skinned flying creatures that looked like people with butterfly wings, but everyone he'd met felt the same way about them. The four goblins threw rocks and knocked most of the pixies out of the air, but one got away. The surviving pixie was still laughing at them when Will took out his scepter and turned it on. FOOM! A white-hot blast of fire swallowed up the pixie. The goblins cheered and clapped.

With that done, Will continued on to the Goblin City. The decrepit metropolis had the distinction of being not only the capital but also the only city in the kingdom. In its heyday it was home to thousands of miners, craftsmen and merchants working hard to dig iron ore from the ground. When the ore ran out so did they, leaving the huge walled city behind. The wall had a lot of graffiti scrawled on it, including the message *'Logic has no place in the Kingdom of the Goblins or in elected office'.*

The city had decayed after decades of storm damage, occupation by goblins and most recently it endured a war. Signs of the war were still present. There was a crater a hundred feet across and fifty feet deep in front of the city, where Will's followers had set off a bomb to drive off the attacking human army. The city wall had a gaping hole fifty feet wide courtesy of an enemy catapult.

Goblins were running all over the place. They were bizarre, and no two looked alike. They stood two to four feet tall, and their skin color ranged from red to gray to blue to tan, with a few light skinned like Will. Some had horns, others stunted wings, some were furry and others bald. Many of them had exaggerated features like huge ears, noses or feet. As a rule they were crazy, stupid and delighted in causing mischief.

Outside the city was a cluster of tents belonging to the lab rat goblins. Their workplace was originally underground, but during the war they'd brought it outside to work on the bomb that made the crater outside the city. Once the fighting was done they'd decided to remain on the surface. The lab rats were a constant source of explosions and were rated as the best form of entertainment around.

BOOM! One of the tents exploded, sending up a plume of smoke. Nearby goblins laughed and ran for cover as broken lab equipment rained down on them. The falling debris included a goblin thrown in the air. Will grabbed the little fellow before he hit the ground.

"My Liege," the goblin said once he recognized Will. It was Vial, goblin alchemist and leader of the lab rats. He was a little goblin with short red fur and dressed in a white lab coat and black pants and glasses, resembling a warped version of a university professor. Vial was a master of alchemy, which was equal parts chemistry, mythology, guess work and blind luck. He took great pleasure in blowing things up, and if there was an act of massive destruction in the kingdom it was a sure bet Vial was responsible.

Will set Vial down and dusted him off. "Hi, Vial."

"Sorry to drop in unannounced. My fellow researchers and I were testing a new formula, and it proved a tad more potent than expected. It was definitely a learning experience. It's just as well we met, as I have solved your problem."

"Which problem is that?" Will asked.

Vial pointed to the crater outside the city. It was his bomb that made it, and he was as proud of it as a new father. "You've been asking goblins to fill in the pit."

"Yeah, with garbage from the city," Will said. "I figured we could fill it in and clean up the place at the same time. Of course that's kind of hard since I can't get anybody to do it."

Vial smiled and nodded. "Goblins are more interested in making messes than cleaning them up. They can't stay focused on a job that boring for more than a few hours. But I've come up with a way to fix the problem."

Curious, Will asked, "How?"

"It's quite simple," Vial began. "We made the crater with Big Bertha, our biggest and most powerful bomb ever. It occurred to me that all we need to do is make a second bomb of equal size and set it off next to the crater. At least some of the dirt should fall in the pit and help fill it up."

Exasperated, Will said, "That leaves us with another crater."

Vial smiled broadly. "That's where the third bomb comes in!"

"No blowing stuff up," Will said. "Just keep making cement."

Will looked at the damaged section of the city wall. Over the last few weeks the goblins had made some repairs to it, but like filling the crater they didn't stay at work for more than a few hours. They couldn't stay on task for long if there wasn't an instant reward for their work or the promise of future mayhem.

Will pointed to the damaged wall. "When I left there were builder goblins working on that. They wandered off again, didn't they?"

"Right after I made the second delivery of cement," Vial said.

"Then it's hardened in the buckets and useless!"

Vial waved his hands. "Not so. The builders took the cement with them to the maze. No doubt it was put to good use."

Next to the Goblin City was the maze. At one time it had been a part of the city, but the goblins converted it into the largest maze on Other Place at the request of a previous king. Months earlier, Will had convinced the goblins to repair the maze and then enlarge it. It kept a lot of them occupied and out of trouble, granting Will some much needed peace and quiet. Goblins loved the maze, so it was no surprise they'd rather work on that than the city wall.

"I suppose they're not going to cause me trouble whether they're working on the wall or the maze," Will said. "Keep them supplied with cement wherever they are. For the time being no more bombs, just cement."

"As you wish. If you should change your mind, I have come up with an exciting variation of the Big Bertha bomb. I call it the Mother In Law of All Bombs, and it can—"

"Just cement," Will repeated. Still smiling, Vial went back to the tents.

Will walked into a city that was little more than a motley collection of featureless stone boxes. The entire place was falling apart. Buildings were crumbling and the streets were covered in trash after decades of neglect and goblin abuse. A tangled web of vines covered the walls, which was probably the only thing holding them together. Underneath the city was a network of tunnels, natural caves, old mining shafts and rooms carved by the goblins. Needless to say, they were half wrecked like everything above ground. The goblins didn't care about the wretched state of the city, and they broke out laughing every time Will suggested they repair the place.

Will wandered through the city until he found a small house in an alleyway. The house was coming down like the rest of the city, but it had a good roof. He reached inside and took out a poorly made chair and woodworking tools, then sat on the ground and filed down one of the chair legs. He'd been building the chair in his few spare moments for the last two weeks, and would likely be at it for another two until it was finished.

"When bards sing of the great deeds of kings, furniture making usually doesn't come up," a squeaky voice said from behind him.

"Hi, Domo," Will said as he looked up at his friend. Domo was a small goblin with gray skin and ratty black hair, and was as close as the goblins had ever come to having their own leader. He wore yellow robes and carried a gnarled walking stick. He and Will didn't get along at first, but they were friends now. Domo often provided information about Other Place and suggestions how to avoid being hurt or humiliated.

Domo walked around the chair and studied it. "What's this?"

"This," Will said proudly, "is what we humans call a chair. It's the latest fashion where I come from."

"That was either sarcasm or proof you shouldn't do standup comedy," Domo said. He poked the chair and watched it wobble. "Doesn't look like woodworking is your thing, either."

"No, but if I want a chair this is the only way I'll get it. I can't get one from the nearby human villages, what with me being broke and them expecting money for doing work."

"Scandalous the way peasants behave these days," Domo said. "We do have our own carpenters, you know."

Will filed down the leg some more and tried sitting on the chair. The legs still weren't even. "I thought of that. I asked four goblin carpenters to make me a chair. I wanted a bed to replace the pile of rags I have to sleep on, but I figured I'd start by asking for something small."

"And?" Domo prompted him.

"Chairs shouldn't have more legs than centipedes."

The four dysfunctional chairs Will had received (and burned as firewood) weren't proof that the goblins hated him. Quite the opposite, they liked and even respected him. That didn't change the fact that goblins were stupid and crazy. When asked to make something as simple as a chair, they felt the need to make improvements. While he couldn't actually sit on the chairs, and they'd looked like they were dreamed up by an impressionist painter and built by a one-eyed, drunken chimpanzee with arthritis, Will could at least take comfort in knowing there was no malice involved.

"So this wobbly, splinter ridden thing is your handiwork?" Domo mused. "I figured you'd be looking for a way out of your king contract."

"As a matter of fact I am." Will filed down a different leg. "As we speak my king contract is in a pot of boiling tar. King Arnold the Belcher escaped his king contract by eating it, so I figured I'd look for novel ways to destroy mine. So far it's survived being eaten by a cow, rotting under a moldy log, burning by my fire scepter and dissolving in acid."

There was a faint 'poof' as Will's king contract appeared in front of him and drifted to the ground, as it did every time he destroyed it. It was whole again, proof that somewhere hidden in its thousands of lines of fine print was a clause that protected it from boiling tar. The contract kept him here until he could find a loophole in it. Cickam, Wender and Downe had tricked 47 other men into being King of the Goblins and they'd escaped. If they could get home then Will could too...eventually. The problem was that each time a king escaped that loophole was closed, making it that much harder for the next king.

Will picked up his contract and studied it for a moment. *Article 53, subsection 2, paragraph 18, line 1: The King can't escape his contract by turning it into a paper hat. He also can't use it for napkins, origami or wallpaper, and definitely can't use it for toilet paper (which is gross).*

"So much for that," Domo said. "Have you tried asking Vial to blow it up?"

"No, and thanks for the suggestion."

"Boss!" Mr. Niff the goblin shouted as he ran up to Will. Mr. Niff had blue tinted skin and wore black clothes, and had his Swiss army knife out ready for battle. A warrior goblin, Mr. Niff was fiercely protective of his King and thought nothing of running to Will's aid. He did that even when he was hopelessly outmatched, or when Will wasn't actually in danger. "I heard you were attacked. Are you hurt?"

"I'm fine. The goblins took care of the guy," Will said.

"Was it one of King Kervol's men?" Mr. Niff asked. Hopping from foot to foot, he demanded, "Was it Galrithas of the Ruined Land, slayer of armies and wielder of the sword *Reaper of Tears*?"

Puzzled, Will said, "No, just a robber. Why would that other guy be after me?"

"I just assumed," Mr. Niff replied.

Domo stepped in front of Mr. Niff and said, "Don't scare him like that. You know Galrithas sells insurance these days."

Galrithas might not be after Will, but plenty of other people were. Over the last few weeks some men from Kervol's army had tried to take revenge for their humiliating defeat. After the first attack, Mr. Niff had organized a bodyguard of goblin warriors to keep an eye on Will when he went for his meals. So far they'd beaten up three knights, two archers, a foot soldier, five insurance salesmen and today they added a robber to the list.

"You should take the troll brothers with you next time you go," Mr. Niff said. "Better yet, take an army. I can get a thousand guys ready in no time."

Will sat on the chair. It still wobbled. "That would make more trouble than it would solve. All the extra goblins would end up making mischief in the town. Those people have been good to me, and I don't want to give them any grief."

"Speaking of the trolls, they said another minotaur showed up today," Domo said.

"That's the fifth one this month," Will replied. A steady stream of hopeful minotaurs had shown up ever since the goblins began fixing and then enlarging the maze. Half bull and half man, the powerfully built monsters preferred to live in mazes, and there were precious few to go around. This made the goblins' maze hot property. "Does this one look like he'll stay?"

Domo shrugged. "Don't think so, but who can tell? London and Brooklyn told him you were having breakfast and asked him to wait."

"Where are the boys, anyway?" Will asked.

Mr. Niff pointed outside. "They're playing poker by the maze. When you're ready they can introduce you to the latest applicant for maze monster."

"I might as well take care of that," Will said. He put the tools and chair away and headed out of the city with Mr. Niff and Domo. They found the trolls London and Brooklyn waiting by the maze and deeply involved in a game of cards.

The trolls were as tall as Will and far stronger. They had fine scaly skin, ears like fish fins, serious under bites and were built like professional weightlifters. Both trolls wore only cotton trousers. Brooklyn was slightly shorter and had lighter colored scales, but otherwise they were identical. The trolls had lived in the kingdom for years, acting as enforcers for several kings before Will got the job. They didn't ask for pay, which was a blessing given that Will was broke, and instead considered the opportunities for violence that came with the job as its own reward. When they saw Will coming, London put the cards in his pocket and they headed over to greet him.

"Morning, boss," London said.

"Hi, guys. Domo said we had another minotaur show up. Where is he?"

Brooklyn pointed at the entrance to the maze. "He went to look around."

Will peered into the maze and shuddered. It covered five hundred thousand square feet on the first floor, a mind-boggling arrangement of high brick walls that formed blind corners, small rooms, dead ends and cunningly hidden traps. Goblins were busy building a second floor consisting of platforms scattered across the maze, connected to each other by elevated walkways and to the first floor by stairs, and included even more traps. It never ceased to amaze Will how goblins, who were so stupid they thought cheese was a vegetable, could make such a daunting challenge.

"Lead me to him," Will told the trolls. They went inside with the goblins in the lead to spot and either disarm or avoid the many traps they would surely run across.

The maze was a beehive of activity with builder goblins adding onto the maze, extending the second floor or adding traps to the floor and walls. A fair number of goblins just milled around pretending to work. Many of the goblins had stopped for breakfast.

Goblins had a very broad concept of what qualified as food. If something had been alive in the last few decades, it was considered edible. After that it fell to the particular goblin's taste. Today the goblins were feasting on old belts, cattle bones and a disgusting concoction called goblin stew that became dangerously unstable if it wasn't eaten within hours of being cooked. Goblins boasted that they could survive anywhere, and it was true, usually by living off other people's garbage.

Mr. Niff paused in mid-step and declared, "Space is warping. Cover your head before something covers it for you."

The air over the maze began to ripple and smelled musty. Having so many goblins close together created another problem. All the races of Other Place could do magic, but goblin magic was based off their innate craziness and stupidity. Put enough goblins together and their craziness and stupidity would reach critical mass and warp space. Goblins could barely control the warp effect and usually didn't bother trying. Nearby objects could be warped to a different location, while at other times objects were warped in from across the universe. This last effect provided a steady stream of junk the goblins used or ate.

Will ducked under a ledge for protection and waited for space to warp. "What do you think it's going to be this time?" he asked.

"Apple corers," Domo said as the air rippled faster.

"Dog biscuits," London said.

"Stuffed woodchucks," Mr. Niff said. "I'm betting a small green frog on that. Any takers?"

The air rippled like a pond hit by a stone. Fingernail trimmings, loose hair and wilted flowers rained down from the sky. The rain of debris lasted only a few seconds, and when it was done the air returned to normal. With the threat of potentially heavy or slimy objects falling on their heads gone, Will and his followers continued on.

They found the minotaur inspecting a pie throwing trap. The minotaur was seven feet tall, heavily muscled, had short brown hair and curving horns on his bull head. He wore cotton trousers and held a double-headed steel axe that looked like it weighed more than Will.

"Good morning, William Bradshaw at your service," Will said as he shook the minotaur's callused hand. "I understand you're looking for a maze to live in."

"Yes," the minotaur grunted. "I heard you were expanding the original maze. I wanted to take a look around and see if there was a place for me."

"Good to hear it," Will said cheerfully. "There's always room for hard working people around here, especially because we don't have very many of them. So, what's your first impression of the place?"

"The layout is good, but I don't understand the trap design," the minotaur confessed. "There aren't any falling rock traps, or walls that come together to squish intruders."

Will nodded. "A lot of minotaurs say that. We don't have many visitors. To be fair, we've only had one, and he just wanted a dry place to sleep. We figured if we killed the few visitors we got then we wouldn't get any more. Add in lawsuits, angry relatives and workplace safety rules, and we decided to go in another direction. We have chutes that drop people from the second floor to the first, walls that turn to block passages, pie throwing traps and things like that."

"No death traps?" the minotaur asked dubiously.

"Sorry, no." Will replied. "The closest we come is a catapult that flings visitors into a pond outside the maze. We're more into traps that annoy and humiliate instead of crush and destroy."

The minotaur frowned and rubbed his chin. "That could take some getting used to. It's traditional for a maze to be filled with deadly traps. The maze I grew up in could have destroyed an army without my parents lifting a finger."

Will patted the minotaur on the back. "I know it would be a big adjustment, and I don't want you to work somewhere you won't be happy. If it makes you feel any better, none of the other minotaurs took the job. Tell you what, take a few days to think it over, and if you decide this is the right place for you then come and see me."

"Okay," the minotaur rumbled. He walked away shaking his head.

"We won't see him again," Brooklyn said.

"It's his choice," Will told them. "Better he says no than be miserable for years to come."

Before they could leave, a ragged band of humans came around the corner and ran toward them. London and Brooklyn ran to the attack with Mr. Niff a step behind. The man leading the charge raised his hands and cried, "Stop!"

Will stepped in front of the trolls to stop them and demanded, "What are you doing here? For that matter, who are you?"

"We're knights with King Kervol's army," the man said. On closer inspection the men were filthy, had scraggly beards and had thrown away or lost most of their weapons and armor. All of them were on foot. "We followed some goblins into the maze during the war, and we've been trapped here ever since."

Exasperated, Will said, "Oh come on, that was months ago."

"It's true," another knight pleaded. "We've been stuck here the whole time, eating whatever we could find and drinking rain water. The goblins avoid us and we can't catch one to show us the way out. Please, we just want to go home!"

"Okay, we'll get you out of here," Will said. He took another look at the knights and frowned. "Hold on, if you're knights then where are your horses?"

The knights looked down shamefully. "They, uh, they ran off when we discussed eating them."

"You what?" Will shouted. "Niff, what's the fastest way out of here?"

Mr. Niff pointed to a side passage. "Down here and take a left."

"Get out of here and go home," Will ordered them. The knights cheered and ran off. Will shook his head. "Eating their own horses!

What's wrong with them? Wait a minute, we didn't take that way to get in."

WHAP! The air was filled with terrified cries as the knights were thrown high into the sky and out of the maze, landing outside with a splash. A chug-chug noise followed as the catapult automatically reset itself for its next victim. Will turned around and looked at Mr. Niff, who said, "You asked for the *fastest* way out."

Will shrugged. "So I did."

"On a related note, there's a problem with the maze," Domo said.

"What's wrong?" Will asked.

Domo pointed at the builder goblins working on the second floor. "The guys have reached the limit of how much more they can add. They can't cover the entire maze with another floor without blocking out the sunlight."

"That *is* bad," Will said. Expanding the maze was hard work that employed a thousand goblins. If they finished they'd be bored in a hurry. There was no telling how much trouble they'd cause, and a lot of them would start hanging around Will. He didn't hate goblins, but they were hard to be around for long periods, and dealing with them would eat up a lot of time he'd rather use trying to escape his contract.

"Plus a hundred guys show up every week since we beat Kervol," Mr. Niff added. "We've been sending most of them here to help out."

"Point made," Will said. He paced back and forth as he thought. He didn't notice the goblins gathering around him and watching him intently. "Okay, what about tunnels? We could have them dig tunnels under the maze that connect different parts of it, maybe add an entire floor under this one. Is that possible?"

"Maybe," Domo said. "That would keep them occupied for months, maybe years."

"We could build more traps," a builder goblin said excitedly. "Like chutes to drop people from the ground floor down!"

"Or springboards that toss them back up!" shouted another.

"We'll need digger goblins for that," a third said. "Wow, a three story maze, what an incredible idea! Three cheers for King Will!"

The assembled goblins ended up cheering four times, too enthusiastic to bother counting. Some of them ran off to recruit digger goblins into the project while others grabbed paper and pencils to draw up plans. They likely wouldn't follow those plans, and might even eat them, but Will took it in stride.

"That should keep them busy for a while," Will said. "Let's leave before they start tearing up the floor."

Will and his friends left the maze and headed back to the city. Will wanted to finish working on his chair and make another attempt to destroy his king contract. Between that and going out for lunch and supper, his day was going to be pretty full.

"Aha!" someone yelled. Startled, Will looked around and saw four humans, two men and two women, running around the bomb crater toward him. Well armed and carrying themselves with a degree of professionalism and competence Will rarely saw, the group stopped and their leader pointed a scratched and nicked sword at Will. The trolls got in front of him while Mr. Niff drew his knife and Domo scurried away in search of help.

Will smiled. He'd talked his way out of some of dangerous situations since coming to Other Place. Whoever these people were, he had them outnumbered and could get a lot more help in a hurry. Chances were good they wouldn't start a fight. "Hi there, William Bradshaw, King of the Goblins. What can I do for you?"

The leader of the group stepped forward. "I am Sam Jarvis, adventurer and treasure hunter without peer. My allies and I have traveled far to get here."

"I can't imagine why," Will said.

Sam Jarvis raised his sword high into the air and declared, "We have come for the Bottle of Hope!"

Chapter Two

Confused, Will asked, "You want what?"

"The Bottle of Hope," Jarvis repeated. He was a handsome young man with blond hair and a mustache, wearing leather armor and armed with a sword and shield. He also had a bow and quiver of arrows strapped to his back. "It's one of the fifty most powerful magical devices in all of Other Place, and we will have it!"

Mr. Niff slapped his hand over his face. "Oh brother, here we go again."

"Who are you nutcases?" Will demanded.

Jarvis struck an impressive pose and answered for his team of four. "We five are the renowned Jarvis' Looters, a team of adventurers without peer."

Will looked around. "Wait a minute, five of you?"

Sam ignored the interruption and kept talking. "I am Sam Jarvis, leader and former imperial guardsman. Under my leadership we five looted the Ancient Tower of Evil, we plundered the Dungeon of Lost Thoughts, we raided the lost and found department at the Bridgeton Hotel, we almost broke into the Infinite Library and most recently we searched the Sewers of the Mad King Ludwig. I got a nasty ear infection in those sewers."

"First I've heard of you," Will said.

Jarvis scowled. "Thanks a lot! Just because we didn't bring home piles of gold or kegs of jewels doesn't mean we didn't try hard. All that sifting through rubble to find a few coins is over. We've tracked the Bottle of Hope here."

"What are you talking about?" Will demanded. "I don't have anything like that."

"Yes you do!" Jarvis insisted. "Helena saw it."

Jarvis pointed at one of the women traveling with him. She was young with blond hair and wore a gray dress with a hood and cape. The woman didn't carry any weapons, but what drew Will's attention was that she wore a blindfold over her eyes.

"I can't believe she'd see anything with her eyes covered," Will said.

"She's a seer," Jarvis explained. "You know, a blind fortuneteller, sees all, knows all."

Will gave her a skeptical look. "No kidding? What's my high school locker combination?"

"4-10-20," Helena said. "You left a bag lunch there the last day of school. The mold that grew on it became so big it achieved sentience and declared war on mankind. Then the janitor sprayed it with disinfectant."

"Lucky guess," Will said. "Listen, whatever this thing is, I don't have it."

Helena raised her hands and waved them around as she spoke in a spooky voice. *"I can see through the mists of time and space, finding treasures lost and abandoned.* Mostly it's loose change and lost baggage, *but this time my blind eyes have seen the most precious of treasures, the legendary Bottle of Hope. In these accursed lands, where the laws of space are bent by the minds of goblins, where a man not of this world rules as king, here can the Bottle of Hope be found."*

Will leaned up against the outer wall of the maze and pointed at Helena. "She's good. That's one of the better fortuneteller acts I've seen. I mean the voice alone must trick a lot of people into believing you."

Jarvis angrily shouted, "She's not a fraud! Helena helped us find a lot of treasure over the years. She's the only reason we're not broke."

London counted Sam's team. "He said there were five people."

Brooklyn nodded. "That's what I heard. And who are the rest of these yahoos?"

Sam rolled his eyes. "Fine, I'll finish making introductions. My friend and sworn companion is Thumac the incontinent barbarian, and that's Christina Dredmore, master swordswoman."

Will took a second to study Jarvis' other followers. Thumac was taller than the troll brothers and noticeably heavier, but the extra weight was all muscle. His brown hair was long and tangled, and he had a thick beard. Adding to an already intimidating appearance, Thumac wore badly tanned animal furs and carried a sword as tall as he was. He growled at Will, but suddenly looked worried and ran off into the bushes.

Like Jarvis, Dredmore had leather armor and a sword. She was also very pretty and had long black hair tied into a ponytail. Will smiled and approached her, his hand outstretched. "A pleasure to meet you." In response, she took a dagger from her belt and lashed out at him. Will stumbled back to Mr. Niff and the trolls. "Why is it all the pretty girls I meet want to hurt me?"

"I think it's instinctive," Domo answered him. He was back with fifty warrior goblins. More goblins were coming in fast, some in the WW I German army uniforms of warrior goblins, others in leather clothes, and more dressed in rags and tattered clothing cast off by far larger races.

"So where's number five?" London asked.

Nervously, Jarvis said, "That would be Renault, our master thief. He's doing five to ten years in a maximum security prison for armed robbery, but he's still part of the team, and we'll welcome him back with open arms once he breaks out."

Domo shook his head in disgust. "Has anyone told chuckles that we don't have the Bottle of Hope, or that an army of elves searched for it and came up empty?"

"We heard," Jarvis said, "and we don't believe you. Helena hasn't been wrong once in the years I've worked with her. Two weeks ago she saw the Bottle of Hope in your kingdom and how it was overflowing with power. Can you imagine how much money it's worth?"

Will shrugged. "Honestly, no. I haven't got a clue what it is, what it looks like or where to find it."

Jarvis pointed an accusing finger at Will. "I'm not buying your bumbling idiot act. You led this bunch of losers to beat King Kervol. Admittedly Kervol is a first class idiot, but he's a first class idiot with an army. You're not as dumb as you look!"

"He is so!" Mr. Niff protested.

"Does anyone listen to me?" Will asked. "Jarvis, I am being totally honest with you. I don't have this thing you want. I never had it. I don't particularly want it. If I did have something that powerful I'd use it to smack you around for a couple of minutes. And since it hasn't occurred to you, I'd like you to look around."

Jarvis and his followers did as instructed, and found over a hundred goblins surrounding them. The goblins were armed with clubs, rocks, bowling pins and other blunt objects, and they looked annoyed.

Will smiled. "That's right, you're badly outnumbered. I could defeat you with the trolls alone, which I'm sure they'd enjoy since they haven't beaten up anyone in days."

"Weeks," London corrected him.

Will looked surprised. "Weeks? I need to let you two out more often. Jarvis, there are only two ways this can end, with you attacking me and losing or with you walking away. You don't win either way, but the second option spares you a lot of pain and humiliation. So do us both a favor and go home before this gets ugly."

Jarvis looked at his followers as Thumac came back out of the bushes. "Plan number four."

Dredmore smiled. "Done."

The four adventurers launched into battle. Dredmore waded into the goblins and kicked them aside. Helena attacked a different group of goblins, swatting them to the ground, obviously not bothered by her blindfold. Thumac lumbered toward the trolls as he hollered and swung his sword. Jarvis went straight for Will.

"I keep trying to be reasonable, and it gets me nowhere," Will said. He unhooked his fire scepter from his belt and pointed it at Jarvis.

"Go ahead," Jarvis taunted him. "You turn that thing on and I won't be the only one to burn."

Jarvis was right. The fire scepter was enthusiastic even at the best of times. If Will turned it on, it would fry Jarvis along with thirty or forty goblins that were standing near him. Jarvis put his hands on his hips and laughed contemptuously. Will swung his scepter and hit Jarvis on the hand.

"Oh, that's the way you want it, huh?" Jarvis swung his sword and missed Will's head by inches. The next swing sliced through the edge of Will's hat. Will swung his scepter again, but Jarvis easily blocked it with his shield.

Next to Will, London and Brooklyn fought Thumac. The barbarian swung his huge sword and missed, burying it halfway into the ground. The trolls slammed into him and forced him back. Thumac roared and brought both fists down on London. London slipped aside and punched Thumac in the stomach, which didn't seem to hurt the barbarian at all. Thumac grabbed his sword and pulled it from the ground, but before he could attack he looked scared and ran off into the bushes again.

Puzzled, London asked, "Are we supposed to wait until he's done going to the bathroom?"

Brooklyn backed away. "I'm not going in after him."

Nearby, Dredmore swung her sword and forced back the unruly mob of goblins. She was a competent warrior and parried every attack against her. While she was fighting back against a goblin armed with a piano leg, she pulled out her dagger with her other hand and threw it at Will. The dagger would have hit, but Mr. Niff jumped up and grabbed it by the handle.

"Hey, give that back!" Dredmore demanded.

Mr. Niff tucked the dagger into his belt and thrust out his chin. "Make me."

Dredmore leaped at Mr. Niff and swung her sword at his head. Mr. Niff ducked under the sword and then grabbed onto her leg. Dredmore tried to kick him off, but the tenacious goblin hung on. Then a second goblin grabbed onto her leg and another on her arm. Soon a dozen goblins clung to her, slowing her down. More goblins piled on until Dredmore collapsed under their weight.

Thumac came out of the bushes again and pulled up his trousers. London and Brooklyn pulled back their fists, only for the barbarian to look worried again and run back into the bushes. Brooklyn shouted, "If you're not going to do this then let us fight someone else!"

Helena faced off against Domo and a mob of goblins. Unarmed, she slapped and kicked them aside. She knocked Domo down and forced several more goblins back.

"You can't win this," Domo told her as he got up.

"I don't have to win. I just have to keep you busy until Jarvis captures your King," she said as she knocked another goblin aside. "Then you have to give up."

The air rippled and took on a musty smell as the goblins began to warp space. The goblins were so numerous and excited by the fighting that they were warping space faster than normal. Bent nails, worn down sandpaper and sawdust appeared around Helena and fell to the ground. Domo smiled at her and said in a nasty voice, "Enjoy your flight."

The goblins' attention was focused on Helena and so was their space warp. She tried to jump away, but was caught and warped fifty feet into Thumac as he was coming out of the bushes again. She slammed into him with enough force to knock them both to the ground and keep them there. Domo waddled over and asked, "Didn't see that coming, did you?"

"Saw it," she mumbled. "Couldn't do anything about it."

The goblins and the troll brothers converged on Will and Sam Jarvis. The two men were trading blows, and Will was coming off the worse for it. He wasn't as strong as Jarvis and he couldn't match the adventurer in skill. Jarvis swung again and chopped off a piece of Will's sleeve.

Breathing hard, Will lunged in and grabbed Jarvis' sword arm. He dropped to his knees, forcing his scepter and Jarvis' sword into the air. Pointing the scepter straight up, he turned it on. FOOM! The scepter shot a jet of white-hot flames that vaporized Jarvis' sword. Will wrapped his arms around Jarvis' left leg and stood up, tipping Jarvis on his back. He pointed his scepter down into Jarvis' surprised face.

"If I turn it on now, only one person is going to get hurt," Will said.

"We surrender," Jarvis said reluctantly.

Will kept his scepter aimed at Jarvis. "How very generous of you. Guys, take their weapons and tie them up."

"You didn't have to melt my sword," Jarvis protested. "Do you have any idea how much those cost?"

"I don't know, your sword was kind of beat up," Domo said. "I can't see you getting more than four gold coins for it. Of course replacing it with a new one would cost twenty."

"Unless he bought a used sword," Mr. Niff said as he took Jarvis' shield. "There's a good market for used weapons. I bet he could get a sword for ten gold coins."

Domo nodded. "Yeah, but you never know what you're getting when you buy used. There are a lot of lemons out there cleaned up to look nice."

Will hung his scepter on his belt as goblins swarmed over the adventurers and tied them up. "Okay Jarvis, I didn't get through to you before, so I'm going to try again. This bottle of whatever —"

"Hope," Domo prompted him.

"Thank you, Bottle of Hope, I don't have it. It's not here. I'm going to have London and Brooklyn take you across the border and drop you off. Once you're there they'll untie you and give you your stuff back. If I see you again for any reason there's going to be trouble. Do we understand each other?"

"The bottle *is* here," Jarvis said stubbornly.

"If it is you're not getting it." Will nodded to the trolls. They grabbed the adventurers and dragged them off while four goblins followed carrying their weapons. Will didn't notice Mr. Niff slip the dagger he'd taken from Dredmore into his belt instead of returning it "Well that's a first, being robbed of something I didn't have."

"It's not new for us," Mr. Niff said. "This happened before."

Domo nodded. "Treasure hunters and adventurers came here looking for the Bottle of Hope back when we were led by King Irving the Cheapskate, who stole the towels and candy dish when he escaped his king contract. Adventurers messed the place up a bit looking for the bottle, but it wasn't too bad. Then the King of the Elves showed up with an army so big it made Kelvol's army look like a foxhunt. They brought wizards, tame griffins and lots of magic weapons. They stayed for weeks digging up the place, pawing through our stuff like deranged raccoons, even tearing down buildings looking for the bottle."

"You mentioned that when I was first brought to Other Place," Will said. "Nobody found it then, so why come back?"

Domo threw his hands in the air. "Who knows? That loopy broad with the blindfold thought it was here and led those losers to our door. If there are others like her who think the bottle is here, even if it isn't, we could be looking at another invasion."

Will looked at the Goblin City, still damaged from the last war. The wall was only half fixed and there was still a crater in front of the city. They'd won the war by the thinnest of margins. But if they were invaded again, they'd be facing forces much stronger and better armed than what Kervol had brought against them. Would they be so lucky a second time? "I can't let that happen. Come on, guys, we're going to talk to Gladys."

Will and the goblins went deep under the Goblin City into the network of tunnels carved by both miners and goblins until they reached the throne room. The name was misleading, as there was no throne, only a room roughly cut from the rock with empty crates to sit on. Against the back wall was Gladys the magic mirror. The mirror was as tall as Will and consisted of a bronze frame and backing, with bronze feet that looked like eagle's claws that gave Gladys some mobility.

When she was built, Gladys could see anything she wanted to over the entire planet. Unfortunately, her last owner crippled her in an act of petty vengeance. Gladys could now only see the world by looking through scarecrows the goblins had set up. In spite of that she saw a lot of what went on in the kingdom and was a valuable source of information in general.

"Good morning, Gladys," Will said as he marched in. Gladys' pouting figure appeared in the mirror, an overweight woman with blond hair, wearing way too much makeup and a garish yellow dress with orange dots. All in all, she couldn't be farther from the stereotype of a magic mirror.

Gladys yawned and rubbed her eyes. "Hey, Will, what's up?"

Will sat down on a crate in front of the mirror. "I just had some people with swords try to mug me. The thing was, they wanted something I didn't have, a little wonder called the Bottle of Hope."

"Oh come on!" Gladys said as she rolled her eyes. "We already went through that with the elves."

Mr. Niff smiled. "On the plus side, before the elves left we were able to swipe some nice stuff from them."

"People, focus," Will said. "I don't know anything about this bottle. Can any of you tell me what it does or what it looks like?"

A bookcase appeared behind Gladys in the surface of her mirror, and she took a book out. Paging through it, she said, "There's a lot of stuff written about it. The Bottle of Hope is one of the fifty most powerful magical devices on Other Place. Its original owner was Nathaniel Lightwell, the most revered holy man in the last five hundred years."

"First I've heard of him," Will said.

"Not surprising," Gladys replied. "He was righteous man, a champion to the poor and powerless. He taught that people should help one another and treat each other fairly regardless of race or nationality. Pretty much everybody agrees he was wise and just, and they do their best to ignore everything he said."

Will frowned. "I guess some things don't change no matter what world you're on."

"Got that right," Gladys agreed. "Anyway, good old Lightwell was a renown healer in his day. They say the power of God flowed through him like a river. There are all kinds of stories about him healing sick people, fighting against injustice, winning against overwhelming odds, stuff like that. He once turned back an invading army with nothing but a sermon, a walking stick and a bag of peppermint candy."

"Why candy?" Will asked her.

"The guy had a sweet tooth like you wouldn't believe. He could go through a two pound bag of mints in a week."

Will waved his hand. "Okay, go on."

Gladys held up the book, showing a picture of a shiny copper water bottle with the word 'HOPE' stamped on it. The bottle had no other designs and looked to be about the size of a one-liter soda bottle. "This is it. According to the stories, Lightwell bought it in a city and kept it with him. There was nothing special about it back then. After he died some jerk stole it off his body. Two days later the bottle showed up in a hospital, no explanations how it got there. Anyone who drank even a drop of water from it was healed of all injuries and disease no matter how serious."

Will rubbed his chin. "Nice. I can see why people would want it."

"There's more," Gladys said. "The hospital used the bottle until it was empty. The next day thieves broke in and stole it, only to have other thieves take it from them. Since that day there have been stories of the bottle being found all over the planet. Each time the bottle is full of healing water and nobody knows how it got there. The new owner uses it to heal the sick and injured, even curing entire plagues. Best guess is each time it's discovered someone steals it and then loses it. Maybe they hide it and can't come back for it, or they get robbed or lose it in an accident. Nobody holds onto the bottle for long."

"Hold on," Will asked, "there's something I don't get. How did it get so powerful in the first place?"

Domo sat down on a crate before explaining. "There are two ways to make a magic item. The first is the way dwarfs do it. They use magic to merge two things together, like with your scepter. They took a fire salamander and merged it with the bronze scepter to make a weapon stronger than the sum of its parts."

Will held up his scepter. Horrified, he asked, "You mean a living thing was killed to make this?"

"He's not dead, bozo," Gladys said. She had a sharp tongue and didn't suffer fools at all. "You can see the little guy in the largest fire opal."

Will studied the gem and saw the tiny bright salamander inside. Will waved to him and he waved back. "Is he happy in there?"

"He went in voluntarily," Gladys said. "Fire salamanders only live about ten years in the wild. Nobody bothers them since they can generate their own fire, but that kind of magic wears them out. Dwarfs search for old ones and offer to join them to a magic weapon. Most fire salamanders agree because they can live for centuries inside a fire scepter or burning sword. They can't be forced into accepting the deal."

Will looked at Gladys. "That means you..."

Gladys shrugged. "Yeah, it's the same deal with me. I signed up to live in here. It seemed like a good idea at the time. Be a magic mirror and see the world."

"Back to the topic at hand," Domo said. "The other way to make magic items is called spillover. Start with a person who's incredibly powerful, a noble king, a wizard, a hero or a holy man. These guys radiate power. They can't help it; they give it off like body heat. If they carry something with them long enough it soaks up some of the energy. A hero's sword becomes unbreakable, a king's crown warns him if someone lies to him and a holy man's water bottle gets the ability to heal illness and injury."

Will got up and started pacing. "The fortuneteller said she saw the bottle, and Jarvis said they'd come a long way to get here. If she saw it then so could other people, and they could come from far and wide to take it just like Jarvis and his crew."

"That's what happened last time," Domo said. "Hundreds of people sensed it was here. Holy men, wizards, fortunetellers, they were drawn to it like moths to a flame. More people came following those guys, either working with them or trying to steal it once they found it. The King of the Elves heard the bottle was here from his wizards and brought an army to take it."

"Oh boy." Will stopped pacing. "How long do we have until another army invades?"

Gladys closed her book. "Last time this happened it was less than a month from the first treasure hunter showing up to the elves invading. And since none of you bozos thought of it yourselves, there are people a whole lot meaner than the King of the Elves who might come with an army in tow if they think they can get the Bottle of Hope. We might even get a couple armies invading us."

"But we don't have the bottle!" Domo shouted. "We didn't have it last time, either."

Will stood still, lost in thought. "Maybe it is here."

"Boss, I don't mean to be disrespectful, but you weren't here last time," Mr. Niff said. "The elves searched the kingdom top to bottom. If it was here they would have found it."

"Maybe, maybe not," Will said. "Gladys, I need you to scan the kingdom and see if you can find the bottle. Domo, Niff, I want you guys to organize search parties to look for it. If it's here we need to find it and get rid of it before an army comes to take it."

"I'm on it," Mr. Niff said proudly.

Will went back to pacing. "Maybe one of the goblins found it but didn't recognize its value. Ask around if anyone has the bottle or remembers seeing it."

Domo raised his walking stick and said, "This is a long shot, but it might be in the treasury."

Surprised, Will asked, "We have a treasury? Why didn't you tell me?"

Domo shrugged. "It didn't come up in conversation."

"Oh come on!" Will shouted. "If I knew we had a treasury when King Kervol came I could have bought him off instead of fighting him."

Mr. Niff smiled and said, "Boss, you got to understand, what men value isn't what goblins value. The bottle might be in there, but there won't be jewels or bags of gold."

Will nodded. "Okay, we'll stop there first, then organize search teams. We've got to do this fast or we could be flooded with treasure hunters like Jarvis and his gang. There's no telling who else is on their way."

A thousand miles away was a marsh, and hidden deep within the marsh was a cave with long stalactites dripping from the ceiling like the teeth of a ravenous predator. There was a table and chair in the corner of the cave, and a backpack filled with the tools needed to survive in such a formidable place, snares to catch game and pans to cook it. Water jugs and earthenware plates completed the furnishings.

The cave was a dreary place, but outside was far worse. The marsh contained many towering trees, all of them dead, their bark rotted off and the wood underneath beginning to soften from decay. Here and there clumps of tough grasses and ferns stuck up from the mud, but they too were dead and blackened. The swamp was empty of all animals, even the tiny gnats that normally infest wet places. Indeed, the very water was dead, empty even of microscopic life if one bothered to look.

Dismal as it was, there were worse things in the marsh, things hidden deep in the mud. On the surface there were yellowed bones sticking up from the muck. If someone was foolish enough to dig through the mire they would find the ground filled with the bones of countless animals, far more than could ever have lived here.

A tall man marched toward the cave. He'd been hunting and foraging in the parts of the marsh that still supported life. The man was old and had a beard streaked with white, but he was still strong and healthy. He wore black robes and a cloak, and a black enamel mask that covered his face from the upper lip to his forehead. Four pixies flew obediently behind him.

The man walked with the aid of a staff. It was ivory white and made from the skulls of many small animals fused together, topped off by a human skull missing its jaw. As the man walked through the marsh, the trees rotted even faster as he and the staff approached. One great old tree finally gave out under the staff's malignant influences and fell to the ground. The man took no notice of it as it crashed down behind him and splashed water and mud high into the air.

The man had lived here for years with the staff, biding his time and trying to go unnoticed. There was little danger that he would be discovered. Few people came into this decaying land to begin with, and fewer still stayed due to the negative atmosphere. Those who did tarry within this dismal place rarely left, for both man and staff wanted no witnesses to their presence.

The man almost reached the cave entrance when he stopped in mid-step. He was tired from a long day of foraging in the wild, a job made harder by the growing region of death and decay his presence generated. He had to go farther each week to forage in lands he hadn't despoiled. Tired as he was, there was an exultant expression on his face as he looked up into the sky before directing his attention to the staff.

"There! I felt it, too. It finally came back." His voice was smooth as a slithering snake, as soft as the silk in a spider's web. The staff made a noise in reply like dozens of voices all speaking at once. It should have been impossible to understand the chaos coming from the staff, but the man heard every word clearly. "Yes, you were right. You're always right. We just had to wait long enough and it would show itself."

The staff spoke to the man in its many conflicting voices. He smiled in return. "It's the perfect place. There's no one there to stop us, no one who matters. No armies or meddlesome heroes can stand in our way this time!"

The staff spoke again and the man nodded. "You're right. It will call others to it, fools who will defend it. It always uses others to fight its battles. We have to move quickly and strike before it's ready."

The man lifted the staff high into the air. The human skull glowed brightly and its discordant voices grew louder. The bones buried in the mud began to quiver and rise to the surface. Pinpricks of red light appeared across the swamp, a veritable sea of lights, followed by rasping cries. The man smiled, a smile tainted by evil and madness. "We shall find the Bottle of Hope...find it and kill it."

Chapter Three

"I can't believe you guys never told me we have a treasury," Will said as he followed Domo and Mr. Niff through the winding, garbage strewn tunnels underneath the Goblin City.

"Be fair, you never asked me if we had one," Domo replied. "None of the other kings we had wanted to take a look at it."

"Did you tell *them* about it?" Will demanded.

"Since you asked, no."

Dwarf miners had made most of the tunnels here decades ago. They were straight, neat and well made. After the dwarfs dug out every last speck of iron ore, the goblins moved in and added onto the tunnel network. The result of both races digging was a confusing network of passages leading in all directions. Side tunnels and rooms split off the main passageways, twisting around like a web made by a drunken spider. After only three minutes underground, Will had taken so many turns and side tunnels that he was hopelessly lost and completely dependent on the goblins for directions.

Like the city above, the goblins had made a mess of the place. There was garbage on the floors and graffiti scrawled on the tunnel walls, including the message, *'Are you disturbed, mad, completely out of your mind? If not, we can help'*. Goblins ambled down the passages on their own business, although a few of them saw Will and decided to tag along.

"The treasury is a holdover from the old days when they mined iron here," Domo explained. "The dwarves used to keep all their money above ground in a bank. One day robbers broke in and stole a week's payroll for the miners. After that the dwarfs converted an old mine chamber into a treasure vault to hold the workers' pay."

Mr. Niff smiled. "It was a clever idea, except a month later a couple dwarfs tunneled into the vault and stole another week's payroll. Those dwarfs are very industrious miners."

"Charming," Will said. "That's the sort of larceny you usually only see in organized crime or state government."

"There's not always a lot of difference between the two," Domo replied.

"True," Will said. "What's in the vault, anyhow?"

They stopped before the vault doors. The twin doors were made of solid rock mounted on steel hinges and held shut with an elaborate steel lock. Two goblins guarded the vault, both armed with swords and wearing pieces of human sized armor much too large for them.

Domo pointed his walking stick at the vault doors. "In there is all the treasure of the Kingdom of the Goblins. Everything we value, everything that truly matters to us, can be found in that room."

Will walked up to the door and found his path blocked by the goblin guards. "Halt! This place is off limits to everyone who is a goblin and everyone who isn't a goblin. If there are goodies you want put in the vault then leave it with us and we'll add it to the piles of loot."

"Hi, guys," Will said. "Listen, there could be something in here that's very important, and we need it to save the kingdom."

"Ha!" the guard said as he tried to keep his helmet from slipping down over his eyes. "I have guarded this vault for twenty years, give or take a decade, and I have never let anyone inside. I have turned back all manner of thieves and scalawags who sought to plunder our riches. So you can take your 'very important', and your 'save the kingdom' and you can shove them where the sun doesn't shine, because I ain't falling for it!"

"I am your King, you know," Will told them.

The guard studied him. "You're King Stanford the Imbecile?"

The other guard shook his head, rattling his helmet as he did. "No, he got away by selling the kingdom at a church bake sale. Happened a long time ago. This here must be King Albert the Penitent."

"The man who introduced baked beans to our kingdom?" the first guard asked. "No, he had yellow hair, terrible breath, too. If he's not Stanford and he's not Albert, might he be King Floyd the Drummer?"

"No, I'm William Bradshaw," Will told them.

The guards looked at him and then glanced at one another. "Him, a king? I don't buy it. He must be some loony who walked in off the street."

"Has to be," the second guard said.

"But I have the uniform and the scepter!" Will protested.

The first guard struggled to lift his sword high enough to point it at Will. "You probably stole them off the last guy. I bet a house fell on the real king, you saw it happen, and suddenly you're richer by a scepter and some old clothes."

"That's enough of that," Mr. Niff said. He marched up and grabbed both guards by their pinky fingers. They yelped as he dragged them away from the door. "Sorry about these two. They got dropped on their heads too often. Go on in"

"What about the lock?" Will asked.

Squirming, the first guard said, "Uh, we lost the key around twenty years ago, give or take a decade. But it was unlocked at the time, so no worries."

Will pushed the doors and they swung open with a creak. He stepped into the vault with Domo and Mr. Niff. The other goblins following Will filed in, ignoring protests by the two guards.

The vault was fifty feet wide and thirty feet deep, with an arched ceiling twelve feet high. The walls had the same rough chiseled look as the rest of the tunnels. There were old iron gates meant to hold out thieves, but they were open and unlocked. The tunnel dug by the dwarf thieves so long ago had been bricked over and filled in.

Inside the treasury was the biggest collection of junk Will had ever seen. There were piles of worthless quartz crystals polished smooth. A bucket of mouse skulls sat in the corner. Off to one side was a display case with a sword handle and no blade. Against the back wall was a small bookcase with a few tattered paperback books written by goblins. Bushel baskets filled with bird feathers sat next to the bookcase. A 300 pound bronze statue of a wombat dominated the center of the room. Filling out the vault were bags of fools gold (clearly labeled as such), a collection of boar tusks, a small green jar, mounds of unidentifiable material smothered by dust and a rag doll on a wood pedestal.

"This is the treasury?" Will asked in disbelief.

"All our most valued possessions are here," Domo said reverently.

Will walked between the precariously stacked piles of junk, careful not to knock anything over. "You'll have to explain to me how any of this is valuable."

Domo swept his arms over the vault's contents. "When you led us to victory over King Kervol it was a history making event. Before that every group around bullied us. If we somehow got out hands on gold or silver, it was a sure bet someone was going to hunt us down and take it. It was too hard to get riches or keep them. Besides, where would we spend it? There's not a town or store in existence that welcomes goblins."

The little goblin scooped up a handful of sparkling quartz crystals and let them slip between his fingers. "But long ago we realized a great truth. Fools gold is as pretty as the real thing. Quartz shines just like diamonds. Nothing here is expensive, since it would be stolen if it was, but it's still pretty. The rest of the items here are trophies of our few accomplishments."

"So there's nothing here worth money?" Will asked.

"There used to be a bag of coins we swiped from wishing wells," Mr. Niff answered. "We gave that to Cickam, Wender and Downe. They wanted a fee to bring you here. It was the coins or the bucket of mouse skulls, and there was no way we were giving that up."

Will took a closer look at the sword handle. The blade was gone, with nothing left except a melted stump. "Hey, wait a second, this is King Kervol's sword, the one I melted."

Mr. Niff smiled. "I picked it up after the battle and brought it here. It's not every day we humiliate a human king. I took it as a reminder."

The rest of the goblins gathered around the rag doll on the pedestal. The doll wasn't much to look at, beaten up, stained and missing a button eye. But the goblins acted like it was something holy. One of them tried to touch it, only to have another goblin slap his hand away.

"What's the story with that?" Will asked.

"That's some of Mr. Niff's handiwork," Domo explained. "Ten years ago he was out in the woods when he heard a little girl crying. She was lost and it was getting dark. She asked him for help and he led her to the nearest human village. Once she was there she saw her house and her family looking for her. Before she ran home, she hugged Niff and gave him her rag doll as a reward."

"It wasn't nothing special," Mr. Niff said bashfully. The other goblins glared enviously at him.

"It's our greatest treasure," Domo said. "Will, goblins have been bribed many times, and on rare occasions actually paid for doing something, but that was the first time ever a goblin was rewarded."

Will nodded. "More precious than gold."

The two goblin guards tugged on Will's sleeve. "If this sightseeing tour is over, can you all be on your way? It's most improper to have people wandering around touching priceless artifacts."

"Maybe you can help us," Will said. "We're looking for the Bottle of Hope, and we think it might be in here."

"That trouble magnet, here?" the guard sputtered. "May the day never come again that we are so cursed! The elves, may they all be kicked in the shin and afflicted with athlete's foot, forced their way in and ransacked the place. We told them it wasn't here and none of those pointy eared critters would listen."

"I thought you said no one ever broke in?" Will asked.

The guards looked at one another nervously. "Uh, well, we were on our coffee break when the intrusion occurred and other guards were on duty, so in a technical sense *we* never let anyone break in."

"They didn't take anything," the second guard added. "So if nothing was taken then obviously there was no break in."

The first guard nodded, rattling his helmet again. "You should listen to him. He knows what he's talking about."

Will studied the mass of keepsakes. "Are there hidden compartments in here?"

"I shouldn't think so," the first guard replied. "This vault is dwarf made, and they don't bother with tricks like that."

"Are there other vaults, ones that may have been made after the second payroll robbery?" Will asked the guards.

The second guard shook his head, rattling his helmet again. "No, the second robbery was three months before the mine closed. There wouldn't have been enough time to make another vault. What you see is what you get."

"Okay," Will said. "To be on the safe side we're going through this place top to bottom. Be careful not to break anything."

Searching the vault took three hours and turned up nothing. Will left and headed back to the surface with Mr. Niff and Domo. It was almost lunchtime, and Will needed to go to the nearest human town for food.

"While I'm gone, I want you guys to ask around if anyone's seen the bottle," he told them. "After that we need to organize search parties."

"What do we do with it if we find it?" Mr. Niff asked.

"Raffle it off?" Domo suggested as they came out of the tunnels and onto the surface.

Will twirled his scepter around as he considered the question. "You know, this could be a good thing. The bottle can heal hurt or sick people. Do we know anybody who needs healing?"

Domo shook his head. "Goblins are a hardy bunch. We'll recover from anything in a few days if it doesn't kill us outright. You might find some humans in Kervol's kingdom that need help, but using it there creates a problem."

"If people find out I have it then someone could try to steal it from me," Will said. "Yeah, I thought of that. I figure if I take it out of the kingdom then at least there won't be armies rampaging through the place looking for it. Do you think my king contract will allow that? It doesn't let me leave the kingdom for long."

"Fair question, and one I have no answer to," Domo replied.

Vial and his lab rat goblins came back into the city bearing empty buckets, finished making their latest cement delivery to the maze. "Ah, My Liege, I understand there was a problem earlier today with some adventurers trying to rob you."

"Yeah, four of them, and more on the way," Will said. "Vial, things could get ugly over the next few weeks. Cut down on the cement and start making bombs again, something small and portable."

Vial smiled and opened his lab coat. There were three rows of pockets on the inside of the coat, and all three held bottles of fizzing liquid bombs. "I am armed and dangerous as we speak. Give me a day and you will have all the explosives you need."

Curious, Will asked, "Is it safe to walk around with those in your coat? I mean, what if you fell over and they went off?"

Vial raised an eyebrow. "You know, it's never come up before. I shall have to run an experiment about that. Oh it will be a learning experience!"

"Another time, Vial," Will said.

The troll brothers returned with a smile, dusting their hands off. "Got rid of those losers who attacked you," London said proudly.

Brooklyn's ears twitched and he turned around. He pointed out the city gate and said, "Looks like we're back in time to deal with another one."

Not far outside the city a slender man ran toward them. The man wore tight fitting clothes dyed black and was armed with two swords, both still in scabbards strapped across his back.

"Another treasure hunter?" Will asked.

"Has to be," Domo said. "Nobody else would bother coming here."

Will pulled his scepter off his belt in case the man wanted a fight as the trolls got between him and the intruder. London snorted and said, "Ah come on, it's an elf already!"

The intruder came to a halt in front of Will. He was tall and graceful, and had pale skin that sharply contrasted with his black clothes. He looked young in spite of his silver hair. The elf had pointed ears, and eyes that were the brightest blue Will had even seen. "Salutations."

"I think he said hello," Domo said.

Will smiled. "Hi there, William Bradshaw at your service. I am the latest fool to get tricked into being King of the Goblins. So, is this a social call or is there an army not far behind you?"

"Army?" the elf asked. "Why would I have an...oh, you think I'm with that simpering inbred idiot that rules the Kingdom of the Elves. I'm proud to say I have no affiliation to that mockery of a true elf leader."

"Good, because we aren't quite ready to host that many guests." Will smiled but kept his hand on his scepter. "So, what's your name?"

Haughtily, the elf replied. "You may call me Thistle, as my true name is unpronounceable in your language." He looked down and added, "It's also unpronounceable in my language."

Surprised, Will could only manage to say, "Huh?"

Thistle clenched his fists and shook ever so slightly. "It's my parent's fault," he said, his voice dripping with hate. "They picked my name out of a history book. They said it was the name of an ancestral hero. My name is 87 syllables long and has no vowels!"

The elf slipped by the trolls and grabbed Will by the shoulders. With a look of anguish on his face, he stared Will in the eyes and said, "I can't pronounce it. No one can. I spent twenty ghastly years being called 'hey you' by everyone around me! What kind of parents would do that to their child? In desperation I finally ran off and took a false name!"

Thistle broke down in tears and sobbed on Will's shoulder. Will had no idea where this came from or why it was happening to him. Awkwardly, he patted the elf on the back and said, "Uh, there there, it'll be all right. Domo, are there therapists on this world?"

"There used to be, but they went extinct from pollution and habitat loss."

The elf stepped back and got control of himself. "Sorry, very sorry about that, it's just every so often I have to let that out. I'm fine."

"Well, um, glad I could be of some help," Will said.

Thistle wiped his eyes on his sleeve. "Actually, I came here for another reason. I search for the Bottle of Hope."

"Isn't everyone?" Domo asked.

The elf regained his composure and looked Will in the eye. "Even you must know the value of such a device. With it's power I could attract followers and form my own kingdom, one far superior to that abysmal mess run by the so-called 'Elf King'. I could rule the lesser races with the dignity and graciousness he lacks! I learned of its existence from a blind fortuneteller who said it could be found here. Cost me quite a bit of money."

Will rubbed his eyes. Blind fortuneteller, now didn't *that* sound familiar? "Was this fortuneteller by any chance a woman with a blindfold and a gray dress?"

Excited, Thistle asked, "You've met her?"

"Sadly, yes."

"Is the Bottle of Hope here?" the elf demanded.

"I'll tell you what I told the last group of people who came looking for it. I don't have it, I don't know who does and I have no proof it's here at all."

Thistle studied Will's face. "You're telling the truth. I doubt a man with a face like yours is even capable of telling a believable lie."

Will wasn't quite sure how to respond to that. "Uh, yeah. Listen, I don't mind you being here. I'd appreciate it if you can find the bottle and take it before armies show up looking for it. You're welcome to stay as long as you like, provided you don't hurt any of my followers."

"Hurt them?" the elf asked in shock. "Please, sir, my name may be a joke, but my reputation is good. Only the most uncultured thug would harm inferior beings like you and your goblins. I thank you for your help and courtesy, and bid you good day."

As the elf ran off into the wilderness, Will asked, "Hey, why did you name yourself after a weed?"

Thistle called over his shoulder, "Because no matter how hard you try to get rid of me, I keep coming back!"

Will stared at the elf and asked the others, "When we were talking, did he insult me? I can't tell."

Mr. Niff nodded. "Yeah, he did. A couple times."

"The thing with elves is he probably didn't think he said anything wrong," Domo added. "They treat everyone like that, and treat other elves a lot worse. We don't take it personally. Neither should you."

Will shook his head. "I don't care if he's rude as long as he stays out of our way. I'm going out for lunch. When I get back we're going to try and take care of this mess before it gets any worse."

It took an hour to reach the human town where Will went for his meals. He had to make these regular visits because he couldn't stomach the things goblins ate. If nothing else taking meals outside the kingdom gave him a chance to get away from his followers for a little while and socialize with other humans.

It was a nice town, too, a farming community with fields of wheat, orchards, barns and cow pens. There were about a hundred buildings clustered around a general store, inn and blacksmith's shop. Clean, well built and cared for, the town was technically on King Kervol's land, but for tax reasons they pretended to be in the Kingdom of the Goblins.

Will walked down the dirt road and nearly reached the town when he saw how much trouble he was heading into. He stopped in his tracks and said, "Oh come on!"

The town was decorated with banners and streamers. There were stalls set up along the main road and vendors selling all manner of goods. Their customers were a horde of bounty hunters, thieves, adventurers, explorers, magicians and someone who looked like a museum curator. They came equipped with a bizarre collection of weapons, armor and gear, no two of them alike.

Will hastily sneaked into the town's inn and took a table near the back. It was a nice place with good food and very popular with visiting merchants. Many farmers stopped in for a meal, too. There was a collection of old signs nailed to the wall above the bar, each one with a different message. The innkeeper, a hulking man with a grizzled beard, came over to take his order.

Weakly, Will said, "Uh, hi. Couldn't help but notice the armed goons out there."

The innkeeper nodded. "It started yesterday. A couple guys came to town looking to buy supplies and ask questions about your kingdom. This morning even more of them showed up, so the townspeople set up stalls to make money off them."

"At least they're getting something out of this," Will said. When King Kervol had brought his army through a few months back, locals had made a fortune selling food and equipment to his soldiers. It was no surprise that they were willing to take advantage of this situation as well.

Will ordered his food and sat back. This was terrible! There was going to be an army of treasure hunters and mercenaries roaming through the kingdom, and the crowd outside was only a preview of what was to come when neighboring kingdoms came in force to look for the bottle. Worse yet, how was he supposed to take his meals here with so many adventurers in town? Sooner or later one was going to think Will had the bottle and try to rob him. He had to get rid of the bottle fast.

"Hey there, friend," a man said as he walked up to Will's table. The man wore leather armor and was armed with a sword and crossbow. He looked tough and likely hadn't shaved for days.

"Do I know you?"

The man smiled. "No, but I can guess who you are. Not too smart coming to town in your work clothes, Your Majesty."

"It's this or nothing," Will said. Blast it, the guy knew who he was. This couldn't end well. "I don't want to be rude, but I'd appreciate it if you found another table. I'd rather be alone."

"Don't like talking when you're eating? Your mother would be so proud." The man looked Will up and down. Back at the bar, the innkeeper frowned but did nothing. "The guys outside don't know who you are, not yet anyway. That means you've got a golden opportunity to fix this mess before it gets worse."

"Kind of late for that," Will said as he gripped his fire scepter.

"No, it's not." The man's smile disappeared, and he pointed his crossbow at Will's chest. "I heard how you beat up Jarvis and his gang, so I'm not taking any chances. Drop the fire scepter. If you use it in here you'll burn half the inn anyhow. Yeah, that's right, I did my homework on you."

The other patrons saw the weapon and froze. No one came running to Will's aid, but he couldn't blame them. These were farmers, not soldiers, and in a town as peaceful as this one they didn't travel armed. A few people backed away from the treasure hunter as the rest watched in horror.

This was the third time in one day someone had threatened Will's life, and he'd had about as much of that as he was going to take. He stared at the crossbow for a few seconds before glaring at the treasure hunter.

"Okay, I know somewhere in that wad of sponge cake you're passing off as a brain this seemed like a good idea, but I want you to give it a second thought, assuming you had one to begin with. You're threatening a king. Not a very good king, I'll admit, but a king nonetheless. The odds of this turning out well for you are very small, while the odds of you waking up tomorrow with a splitting headache and wondering, 'why did I do that, and how did I end up in Nome, Alaska?' is pretty high. Bottom line, you really don't want to do this."

This statement wasn't likely to end the standoff peacefully, but Will got sarcastic when he was under stress. In all honesty this trait was responsible for many of his problems, but he couldn't help himself.

The treasure hunter scowled. "Yeah, that's right, make fun of me. Once I have the Bottle of Hope I'll be rich enough to buy my own kingdom. Then nobody will laugh at me again, not if they want to live. Now drop the scepter or I put one in your arm."

Will set his scepter on the floor. "I don't have the bottle."

"Sure you don't," the man sneered. "You and I are going back to your kingdom. Your goblins are going to bring me the bottle and I'll leave. I don't think I have to tell you what's going to happen if you try to be brave. I get the bottle and you get rid of these losers when they discover it's gone. Everybody wins."

The innkeeper walked over to Will's table, coming up behind the treasure hunter and moving very quietly for such a big man.

"There's got to be fifty people outside, and all of them want the Bottle of Hope," Will said. "At least half of them want to question me, take me prisoner or at the very least sell me a time share. Do you really think they won't notice you marching me off with a crossbow pointed at my back?"

"We're going out the back," the man said. He gestured for Will to stand up. "Come on, we—"

Wham! The innkeeper's first punch knocked the crossbow out of the man's hands and clear across the room. It fired in midair and the crossbow bolt buried itself in the floor. The man went for his sword, but the innkeeper's next punch was already coming. He sent the man flying into the wall and knocked him out. The rest of the patrons stared in surprise. The innkeeper grunted and pointed to one of the dozens of signs posted above the bar. This one read 'No Panhandling'.

"Thanks," Will said as he retrieved his scepter. "I'm so sorry about this. I didn't mean to cause you any trouble."

"I know," the innkeeper replied. He walked to the bar and came back with a large leather bag. "Here. Beef jerky, hardtack biscuits, dried apple slices and powdered soup mix. This should hold you for a while so you won't have to come back until these guys have moved on."

"Thanks. What about him?" Will asked and pointed to his attacker. "He's going to be mad at you when he comes to."

The innkeeper smiled. "There are a lot of guys outside who might buy a sword and crossbow. I figure that and all the money he's carrying will make up for him pulling a stunt like that in my place. You'd better go out the back."

Will took the bag and headed out the back way, fleeing the town before anyone else recognized him. Not far off he ran into a mob of goblins waiting for him outside town. One of them asked, "What's wrong, boss? You're back early and out of breath."

Will looked back at the town and the treasure hunters who'd soon invade his kingdom. "Come on, we're going home. I don't think we'll be able to come back here for a while."

Back in the Kingdom of the Goblins, Will found his followers in a state of excitement. They were scurrying around and all of them were carrying weapons, mostly clubs and rocks. Mr. Niff ran up to Will and said, "Boss, we've had ten more treasure hunters try to sneak in the city looking for the Bottle of Hope, and that's just since you left."

"I met one of them in town. The place is crawling with them, and at least some of them aren't nice people."

Mr. Niff nodded. "Tell me about it. They tried capturing goblins and forcing them to say where the bottle is. Lucky for us the jerks were all working alone. We managed to overpower them."

Suspicious, Will asked, "Overpowered them and did what with them?"

"Took their stuff, painted them with clown makeup and dumped them outside the kingdom," Mr. Niff said. "What else would we do with them?"

"That's okay...I guess." Will looked around the crowd of goblins and asked, "Did you ask the guys if they've seen the bottle?"

"Yeah, and so far nobody knows where it is. I got a few guys still asking around, but with these loopy treasure hunters all over the place it's going to be hard for them to reach everyone."

Will twirled his scepter as he walked toward the Goblin City. "Has Gladys seen the bottle?"

Domo waddled up to them and said, "No luck there. We've put up a record number of scarecrows for her to look through, and she hasn't turned up anything but more treasure hunters coming over the border. It's happening just like last time."

"Maybe, but it's going to end differently," Will said. "If Gladys can't see it and nobody has it, then we're going to have to send our own people out to look for the bottle. The groups will have to be big enough to defend themselves if treasure hunters attack. If we put a lab rat goblin with each group and arm them with Vial's bombs, do you think they'll be okay?"

"That should be plenty of firepower," Mr. Niff said.

"There aren't too many lab rat goblins, so we may need to put London and Brooklyn on teams to bolster them," Domo added.

Will twirled his scepter. "Okay, get Vial out here. I need to know how many lab rats he can spare. And somebody find the trolls."

Goblins hurried off to do his bidding. Will opened his mouth to say more when he grabbed his forehead and winced in pain. Domo and Mr. Niff ran up to him, and Mr. Niff asked, "Boss, what's the matter?"

"Migraine headache," Will said as he rubbed his head. "Oh man did that come on fast! Uh, guys, does something feel wrong to you?"

"What do you mean?" Domo asked.

"I don't know. The second the headache came on I started feeling weird, like something's wrong but I don't know what."

Domo winced and rubbed his head. "Ah, that's what you're talking about. Just hit me. Nasty!"

Will grimaced and tried to pinpoint the cause of his discomfort. Everything looked normal enough, well, normal for the Kingdom of the Goblins, anyway. There wasn't a cloud in the sky except for one large cloud far in the distance. Strange, that cloud was black as pitch and seethed like a storm cloud. The cloud's appearance wasn't the only thing odd about it. Nervous, Will asked, "Is there a reason why that cloud is moving against the wind?"

"Human elemental magic," Domo said. "There's a wizard up there who's got enough control over wind and water to make a magic cloud to carry him around. That's a big cloud, so he's a powerhouse."

"It shouldn't be black," Mr. Niff said. He didn't sound concerned, but instead a little angry. "I've seen magic clouds, and they're puffy white to blend in. That cloud shouldn't be black."

London and Brooklyn ambled out of the city with Vial. The cloud came closer, boiling and writhing. It soon dominated the sky. London pointed at it and said, "That can't be good."

Will gripped his scepter tightly. "If anyone has a suggestion, I'd love to hear it."

The goblins stopped scurrying around and stared at the cloud. They were being hit with the same pain and sense of foreboding as Will. Several goblins complained of headaches. Some of them took cover under trees or behind rocks. Most of them stood their ground and whispered to one another. They began huddling into groups.

The cloud descended until it was a hundred feet in the air. It floated for a few seconds, smoky tentacles reaching out beneath it, then began to break up. It formed fifteen smaller clouds, each one a hundred feet across and maintaining their shape and size. Fourteen of the clouds raced off and dropped down across the kingdom. One cloud fragment, the largest one, came down in front of the Goblin City.

As the cloud landed, a tall man walked out of it. He wore black robes and carried a bone white staff. The man looked around, his expression hidden by a half mask. Four pixies fluttered around him. When he spoke, he had a soft voice filled with derision.

"Such filth. To think that there is an entire kingdom given over to goblin vermin. It is a blight upon this world, a blemish that should have been removed long ago. That this place even exists is proof that this corrupt world must be cleansed."

Goblins backed away from the man. Will took a few steps closer and said, "You're not the first person to talk about my goblins that way. The last guy was a king, and we sent him running home."

The man snickered. "I'd heard of that disaster. There was a time when mankind was a force to be reckoned with and could have dominated this world, but they wasted the opportunity and sank into decadence and debauchery. Mankind has grown so weak and degenerate that even goblins can defeat them. When the time comes they too shall feel my wrath."

"Get a load of this guy," London said.

Brooklyn nodded. "Personality like that I bet he gets invited to all the parties."

"He *is* human, right?" Will asked his followers.

Domo nodded. "Yeah. He's a wizard, and they've got powerful egos. He's going to look down on everybody."

The wizard strolled toward Will, calmly studying his surroundings. "I have traveled the length and breadth of this world, observing the largest and most ancient cities, holy places and academies of learning. I have seen the so-called 'natural wonders', the relics of our world's past and the accomplishments of this generation.

"Junk. All of it is worthless and wretched. Each time I travel to a new place I think perhaps it might have some value, some tiny bit of worth, but it never does. Everywhere I go is another disappointment.

Each time I think this world can't sink any lower, become more vulgar and distasteful, I find a place like this that proves me wrong."

"Charming," Will said. Now that he was closer to the wizard, he saw a ring of dead grass around him. Plants withered and died wherever the wizard stepped. "You really ought to use deodorant. You got a name, or should I just call you magic cloud guy?"

The wizard lifted his staff high into the air. Now that he was closer, Will could see that it was made of small animal skulls and topped with a human skull minus the jaw. The large skull glowed and filled the air with a disturbing sound of many voices talking at once, impossible to understand. "I am Evander Hollow, and I wield the Staff of Skulls! I am power incarnate, magician without peer. Tremble before my might, and know that there shall be no mercy!"

"Okay," Will said, "that statement pretty much rules out the two of us being friends. I'm pretty sure I know what you came for, and you know what? You're not getting it. You're going to get back on your cloud and float out of here. And if you don't, my friends and I are going to kick your wrinkly white butt out of the kingdom. Isn't that right, guys?"

Will turned around. The goblins were looking at Evander like he was twenty feet tall. Many of them backed away from the wizard or held their heads in pain. The only exception was Mr. Niff, too courageous and too stupid to recognize he was way out of his league. The little goblin stepped in front of Will and drew his knife.

"You can't come here and threaten our King just because you're unimaginably powerful!"

"Unimaginably powerful?" Evander asked. "That doesn't even begin to describe the Staff of Skulls. With its might I shall cleanse this world of the weak and incompetent. I shall burn away the chaff that holds us back, destroying you lesser beings that do not deserve to live. You would stand in my way? Fool. Behold that which I have created, that which you yourselves shall soon become!"

Evander struck the staff against the ground. The cloud behind him evaporated, leaving behind a hundred skeletal animals. They were the animated bones of boar, deer, wolves and a few bears. They stood swaying gently and pawing the ground, a hateful red glow coming from their eye sockets.

Mr. Niff's fists trembled, not in fear but in rage. He wasn't the only person to react that way. Everyone went from being afraid to looking like they were going to go berserk. The troll brothers uttered swear words in their own language so foul that if translated into English would blister paint off a wall. The goblins, regardless of guild, size or age, looked like they'd suddenly gone rabid. Will felt an overpowering feeling of disgust just looking at the skeletal animals.

"Necromancer!" Domo spat. "He's a necromancer!"

Will pulled his fire scepter from his belt. It rattled so hard it threatened to shake out of his hand. The fire opals in the scepter glowed white as the salamander inside expressed its fury.

Lazily, Evander pointed a finger at Will and the goblins before addressing his skeletons. "Slay them, my minions. Spare no one."

Chapter 4

Howling like madmen, the goblins charged Evander and his nightmarish army of skeletal animals. London and Brooklyn led the attack, backed up by Vial and Mr. Niff. Will ran straight for Evander Hollow, determined to take the wizard out of the fight before he could use his magic. The skeletons shrieked and met the charge with sharp claws and snapping jaws.

Normally goblins would start a fight by throwing things at their enemy, including rocks, loose bricks, fallen branches and small furry rodents. Barring that they would try to lure enemies into prepared traps that involved concealed pits, foul smelling liquids, pies or some revolting combination of the three. They'd do just about anything to even the lopsided odds goblins usually fought against.

The goblin horde threw nothing, and they didn't even try to maneuver the skeletal animals into the maze and its battery of traps. Frothing mad, they headed into the fight without a second's hesitation, too overcome with disgust and rage to even consider tactics. Will would be appalled if he wasn't seized by the same all consuming hatred.

Evander sneered and watched the two small armies slam into each other. His expression went from contempt to surprise, however, as the first rank of his skeletons was smashed apart. The trolls battered them to bits with their fists, while goblins double or triple teamed individual skeletons and tore them to pieces. Vial tossed bombs into Evander's troops and blew them up as Will used his scepter to burn a path through the skeletons on his way to the wizard.

"Unusual," Evander said. The four pixies danced around his head and giggled at the sight of so much violence.

Most of the goblins present were veterans of the war with King Kervol. They'd served under Will before, and the experience gave them confidence not often found in their kind. That confidence coupled with the revulsion they felt for their enemy kept them in the fight, and they pressed on where other goblins would have run.

The skeletons fought back. Shrieking, they plowed into the goblins. Here and there they knocked down individual goblins, but before they could strike their helpless opponents they were set upon by more goblins. Larger skeletons swatted their foes aside until they ran into the trolls. The troll brothers forced them back and wore them down with blow after blow, littering the ground with shattered bones.

More goblins poured into the fight, running out from the city gate and from a tunnel in front of the city. Goblins working on the maze scampered off their scaffolding and joined in. Together they hit the skeletal army from the side, and Evander's army buckled under their assault.

Will forced his way through the skeletons and found Evander serenely watching the battle. He pointed his scepter at the wizard and shouted, "Call them off or I shoot!"

Evander studied his fingernails, not even looking at Will. "Go ahead."

FOOM! The scepter belched out a cloud of white-hot flames. The fires swallowed up several skeletons and left nothing but ashes before reaching the wizard. Evander muttered arcane words and tapped his staff on the ground, and a wall of dirt and rocks three feet thick sprang up between him and the flames. The fire hit the wall and stopped, unable to burn through it. When the flames died back the wall sank into the ground to reveal Evander smiling and unharmed.

"Fool," the wizard sneered. "You are an ant trying to stop a lion. Do you think you're the first person to attack me with garbage magic like that?"

Will kept the scepter pointed at Evander. With bravado he didn't feel, he said, "If I'm not the first, I'll settle for being the last."

FOOM! Will fired the scepter at Evander a second time. Again Evander made the ground rise up to shield him, but this time he didn't let it fall back down. After it blocked Will's attack, the wall of dirt and rocks whirled together to make a giant fist ten feet across rising up from the ground it was made of. It swung down and Will had to run out of the way. The fist swung again, but Will dodged and fired at Evander. FOOM! The fist intercepted the jet of fire and crumbled under the attack.

"Is that all you have?" Evander asked snidely. "A defective fire scepter? Tell me you're not trying to defeat one of the fifty most powerful magic weapons with a cheap, mass produced toy."

"No, I'm keeping your attention on me," Will told him. "How's your army doing?"

Evander frowned as he studied the battlefield. His skeletons weren't just losing. They were being annihilated. Fewer than a quarter of them remained, and they faced goblins on all sides. In a few seconds the last of them was reduced to bone fragments. Evander was alone.

"I believe you were leaving," Will said.

"I believe you were dying," Evander replied. He pointed the staff at the goblin army and uttered a string of arcane words. More plants died around him, withered by the foul incantation he employed.

The four pixies following Evander flew out over the goblin army. Before anyone could knock them out of the air with rocks, Evander raised the Staff of Skulls above his head. Black lightning shot from it and arced to the pixies. The tiny winged creatures screamed as the black bolts hit them and then struck the ground. Broken bones rose up like whirlwinds around each pixie.

The whirlwinds died away and the pixies were gone, replaced by four horrifying creations. They looked like human skeletons made of bone fragments fused together, but of massive proportions, standing ten feet tall and weighing hundreds of pounds. A hateful red glow came from their empty eyes. The hideous things threw back their heads and howled unearthly screams before lumbering into the goblins.

"And there's another reason why we don't like pixies," Domo said.

Will ran back to help the goblins while Evander laughed. He reached the nearest bone monster as it began to wade through the goblins. Will aimed his scepter at it, only to have the ground rise up under his feet and knock him over. Under Evander's control the dirt rose up to form a fist and toss Will aside. The bone monster he'd been heading for saw him on the ground and marched toward him.

The other three bone monsters were busy throwing goblins around. Goblins struck the monsters with their clubs and threw rocks at the towering things, neither to much effect. The monsters were so large they shrugged off the attacks.

London and Brooklyn charged one of the monsters and hit it in the legs, knocking it over. The brothers pounded on it, but the monster got back to its feet and effortlessly sent the trolls sprawling with one swing. They landed next to a pile of construction supplies for the maze.

"Let's not tell mom about this," London said.

Brooklyn got up and spotted a wood pallet loaded with 500 pounds of bricks. He pointed at it and asked, "A little help, brother?"

"Sure thing," London said with a smile. He and Brooklyn picked up the pallet and ran back into the fight. They charged the skeletal monster that had hit them and reached it just as it was bending down to swing at a goblin. "Hey, ugly! Back at you!"

The monster looked up in time to see the trolls swing the pallet like a giant hammer. The pallet and bricks broke apart under the force of the impact and sent broken fragments of brick everywhere, but not before smashing the upper half of the monster to powder.

A second skeletal monster was trying to crush Mr. Niff underfoot. Mr. Niff ducked and dodged, staying too close for it to get a clean shot at him. He slashed at its ankles with his knife to no effect, but that didn't deter him in the slightest.

As the monster tried to grind Mr. Niff into paste, Vial joined the fight. He took off his lab coat and managed to snag it on the bottom of the monster's ribcage. Vial ran out of its reach and shouted, "Mr. Niff, if you would care to join me?"

Mr. Niff ran away, ducking under another swing. Vial pointed at his lab coat, drawing both Mr. Niff's and the giant skeleton's attention to it. The coat swung open and showed Vial's remaining explosives. He'd used a lot early in the fight, but there were still two complete rows of bombs.

"If you would kindly help me with an experiment and set those off?" Vial asked.

The red light in the monster's eyes flared brightly as Mr. Niff smiled and drew the dagger he'd taken from Christina Dredmore earlier that day.

With skills honed over many years, he threw the dagger into Vial's coat and hit a bomb. That bomb set off all the others and blew the skeletal monster apart.

Vial dusted bone shards off his shoulder. "Not real magic, of course, but still very nice."

The third monster fought against the unruly mob of goblins. They clung to it tenaciously, biting it and hammering away with whatever weapon they had. Nothing worked. It brushed them off and headed for Will.

It didn't reach him.

The air rippled as the collective stupidity and craziness of the goblins reached critical mass. There were too many goblins too close together, and their excitement made space warp more quickly. The monster looked around in confusion as expired high school ID cards fluttered down around it. Instead of warping the monster away, the goblins accidentally warped in an avocado green 1972 refrigerator thirty feet over the monster's head. After that gravity did the rest. The refrigerator came hurdling down on the monster and smashed it to pieces.

That left only the skeletal monster heading after Will, who already had enough problems. Evander laughed as he used magic to control the ground under Will. Every time Will got back up a giant fist made of dirt slapped him down. The skeletal monster stood over Will and raised both fists.

Will scrambled to his feet. Just as he saw the dirt fist and the skeleton swing at him, he fell over backwards. *Whoosh*. Will vanished, trading places with a goblin scarecrow thirty feet away by using one of the more predictable forms of goblin warp magic. The scarecrow wore a copy of Will's green and black uniform tacked to a post, and when he reappeared he was wearing that uniform and left his old clothes behind. Will pointed his scepter at his attackers as they tore apart the empty clothes he'd been wearing. FOOM! The skeletal monster and giant dirt fist both disappeared in the intense fire.

The battlefield fell silent. Will walked slowly toward Evander. The ground between them was littered with bone shards that crunched underfoot. The goblins caught their breath and regrouped, following Will closely. Will found his headache fading quickly with the last of the skeletons gone. Evander stood his ground, staring back at Will, seemingly unconcerned that a hundred of his creations were destroyed and he was horribly outnumbered.

Bruised and out of breath, Will kept walking toward Evander. The wizard looked him in the eye and said, matter-of-factly, "You taught the vermin how to fight."

"I've had it," Will said in disgust. "You waltz in here, mess things up, disrespect my followers, and that includes the scepter. We beat those…things you brought, and you still talk about us like we're bugs. I've had it. You're leaving, you're doing it now, or so help me I'm going to see just how much damage I can do to you with an army of goblins, two trolls and one seriously ticked off scepter."

Evander chuckled. "Ah, the arrogance and stupidity of youth. Was that supposed to be intimidating? I haven't spent much time among you fools lately, so it's hard for me to tell."

The wizard walked over the battlefield, his boots crushing broken bits of bone. "I have torn down the walls of countless cities and watched people of all races flee before me. I have toppled the towers of lesser wizards and burned their libraries. Armies have fallen at my hands. Kings tremble at the mere mention of my name. You speak as if you have accomplished something today. You speak as if any of this mattered."

The goblins surrounded Evander, keeping some distance between them and the holder of the dreaded Staff of Skulls. The trolls joined Will. They all looked grim, but not one of them backed down.

Evander tapped his staff against the ground. The dirt around him rose up ten feet in the air and spread out in a wave. It raced across the field in front of the city, plowing into the army surrounding Evander. Goblins screamed as they were knocked off their feet and thrown in the air. Will and the trolls were tossed to the ground.

"This doesn't matter," Evander said. He formed another wave of dirt that threw the goblin army around like corks on an angry sea. "*You* don't matter. You said I spoke of you like you were bugs? Bugs are higher than you are. You're nothing."

Evander raised the staff and pointed it at Will. The staff sparked with black lightning. As a bolt of pure destructive power built up on the tip of the staff, Evander stopped and let it dissipate. He looked at the staff as it spoke in countless conflicting voices. "You're sure?" he asked. "Silly question, of course you are. If the bottle isn't here, then where?"

Will climbed back to his feet. He'd managed to keep hold of his scepter even when he'd been knocked down like a bowling pin. If the wizard was busy talking to himself then now was the time to strike. Will staggered toward Evander and raised his scepter.

Evander's attention was wholly on the staff as he continued his one sided conversation with it. "It was too much to expect it would come to the only city in this filthy excuse for a kingdom. Can you locate it? That's unfortunate. If our quarry is absent then there's no point staying here. Even a second wasted risks everything."

Without so much as a backward glance, Evander caused the ground under Will to buck like a steer. Will hit the ground hard. The wizard waved the staff in a circle and a black cloud formed over him. It rose into the air and carried him away, leaving behind Evander's haunting words.

"If you were half the threat you pretend to be, I would extinguish your life here and now."

The goblins got back to their feet, dusting themselves off and helping each other up. One of them opened the refrigerator and checked inside. "Hey, there's cold fried chicken in here. Anyone want chicken?"

Still flat on his back, Will raised a hand. "I'd like some chicken. An aspirin would be nice, too."

"Sorry, we don't have painkillers in the kingdom," Domo told him. The little goblin waved for his fellows to come over and said, "Somebody help me scrape the King off the ground and get him inside."

The goblins limped back into the city over the next hour and the troll brothers carried Will into the tunnels below. His followers went in with him, battered but not broken.

"This hasn't been the worst day of my life, but it's in the top five," Will said as they descended into the tunnels beneath the city. He rubbed his bruised shoulders and winced in pain.

"Yeah, it could have gone better," Mr. Niff replied. He smiled and said, "Blame it on the booze!"

"I don't drink!" Will protested.

Mr. Niff leaned in close to Domo and said, "It's never good when they can't remember how much they've had."

Will's friends helped him back into his throne room and gently lowered him onto a crate he used in place of a throne. Gladys the magic mirror waddled in front of him and shook her head in dismay. "What were you thinking? You don't attack the holder of the Staff of Skulls. You run for your life and hope he doesn't follow you!"

"How was I supposed to know that?" Will asked. "It's not like the kingdom came with an instruction manual. I don't know anything about magic super weapons or wizards."

"He wasn't a wizard, not anymore," Domo said as he limped into the throne room. "He's a necromancer, a magician who animates dead bones and turns them into those monsters we fought."

Will rubbed his head. "Good God, my head still hurts."

"That's not just from the hits you took," Domo told him. "Necromancy does that to you. Just being around it is like getting an itch you can't scratch. Getting close enough to see those abominations gives migraine headaches to everything alive."

Domo sat down and grimaced in pain. "Some of those abominations wandered into Kervol's kingdom back when I was a youngster. Their presence made everyone hurt like they had a toothache. The humans formed a mob to hunt them down and everybody joined, even goblins and a passing ogre. It wasn't until we got rid of them that we felt better."

"Pixie trash!" London snarled.

"Yeah, how did he make those four monsters from pixies?" Will asked.

Gladys frowned. "Necromancy is a perversion of dwarf magic. Dwarfs blend two things together to make a whole stronger than its parts. So does necromancy. You take a pixie and merge it with the bones of a dead animal or person. The pixie provides magic and hate while the bones provide strength. Every so often a wizard gets it in his head that there's got to be an easy way to be more powerful. Some of them find banned books of necromancy, and from there it just gets ugly. Every kingdom on Other Place offers a bounty on necromancers."

"Even elves don't tolerate them," Domo added.

Worried, Will asked, "It's that bad?"

Mr. Niff nodded. "I know it sounds weird coming from us. Nobody likes us, either, but that's different. Sure we make trouble. We've tied cats together by their tails, glued knights to their horses and filled buildings with road gravel. One time we even moved an entire town a mile down the road while everyone slept. But doing *that*, digging up dead stuff and turning them into those *things*? That's not how we play."

"And making things a whole lot worse, our new pal the necromancer has the Staff of Skulls," Gladys said. "I saw the fight through a scarecrow and heard what he said. He wasn't bluffing. His magic is ten times stronger with the staff in his hands. That staff is responsible for kingdoms falling."

Will's jaw dropped. "It's taken out whole kingdoms?"

"Near enough," Gladys answered. A bookcase appeared behind her in the surface of the mirror and she took out a book. Flipping through it, she said, "The first wizard to find the Staff of Skulls went on a rampage lasting months. The Grand Conclave of Wizards finally cornered him with their entire membership of 59 battle-hardened sorcerers. They won the fight after nineteen hours and managed to stop him for good, but it took them five years to recover, and the staff survived the fight."

"Yikes," Will said.

"The second wizard to get his hands on the staff ravaged the capital of the Kingdom of Tristavol, home to 100,000 people. He attacked the city with no provocation and there was nothing they could do to stop him. The wizard and staff left after two hours to attack another city. It took the people of Tristavol a generation to rebuild their capital. I know another dozen stories just as bad, but you get the picture."

"The staff is also called The Corrupter," Domo added. "It's alive and completely evil. For hundreds of years the staff has gone from person to person, spreading fear and misery. It taints the mind of whoever holds it. People don't use it; it uses them. Doesn't matter if you're a saint or a madman, once you pick up the staff it takes control of you to do unspeakably evil acts."

Surprised, Will asked, "You mean it makes them go into politics?"

Domo frowned. "Well, no."

Horrified, Mr. Niff asked, "It turns them into lawyers?"

"No!" Domo yelled. He grumbled and said, "A person can be really evil without being a politician or a lawyer. It's rare, but it happens."

Will stretched out his arms and ran his fingers over them. He was sore, but no bones seemed broken or dislocated. "So why is the staff looking for the Bottle of Hope?"

"To destroy it," Gladys answered. "There's some kind of feud between those two going down through the centuries. The Staff of Skulls would devastate a kingdom, and afterwards someone would turn up with the Bottle of Hope and use it to heal the injured. After that happened a few times the staff took it personally, and now it uses its owners to hunt down the bottle."

"Great, we're in the middle of a magical grudge match," Will said. "I'm going to go out on a limb here and guess that the other clouds had more skeletons on them."

"It is a logical assumption," Vial said.

"Let me check," Gladys said. Gladys disappeared from the surface of the magic mirror and she looked through scarecrows scattered over the kingdom. Some scenes were peaceful and showed no treasure hunters or skeletons. Others showed skeletons rampaging through the kingdom, tearing up the landscape in their search for the Bottle of Hope. Goblins and treasure hunters both fled before the onslaught.

Will's heart sank as he watched the pictures. There were about a hundred skeletons in each group and fourteen groups fanning out through the kingdom. Somewhere out there Evander Hollow the necromancer was directing them and adding to the damage. Will and his friends had thrown everything they had at that madman and failed.

"This is bad," Mr. Niff said as he watched the carnage on the mirror. "I almost wish the elves would come back with an army. At least they'd stand a chance against him."

Brooklyn rubbed his chin. "We can take out a few groups of those skeletons, no question, but if the necromancer shows up with the staff then all bets are off."

Will rubbed his aching head. "Can we get help? If everyone hates these guys maybe they're willing to help us get rid of them."

"And risk drawing his attention?" Domo asked as he pointed to the mirror, which showed Evander float over the landscape on his personal cloud. Bolts of black lightning flashed from the Staff of Skulls and blasted gaping holes in the ground. "Nobody in their right mind wants to get in the way of that kind of firepower. The other kings are going to keep their heads down and thank their lucky stars it's us getting hammered instead of them. Even Barbecue the dragon wouldn't take on the staff."

Will watched the magic mirror in despair. What was he supposed to do? He was a business major for crying out loud! Here he was, no help at hand, a lunatic and an army of dead things rampaging across his kingdom. Making things worse (if that was possible), there were dozens or possibly even hundreds of greedy treasure hunters spreading out over the place. He'd beaten King Kervol by the skin of his teeth, and now he faced a threat far worse.

"Excuse me, but there may be someone we can turn to," Vial said.

Will looked up in surprise. "Who? Where? How much do they charge?"

"My Liege, we do have one resource available to us," Vial explained. "There is a witch named Esmeralda living in the kingdom. She stays to herself for the most part, but we may be able to persuade her to help. After all, she's in as much danger as the rest of us with those wretched skeletons in the kingdom."

"How's she supposed to help?" Domo asked.

Vial twiddled his thumbs. "Esmeralda offers a variety of services, but in this situation the most valuable of these is acting as a seer. Helena the blind fortuneteller and the Staff of Skulls both believe that the Bottle of Hope is here. I think they are correct. If Esmeralda can locate it for us we can either get it out of the kingdom, and thus relocate the threat, or we may use the bottle ourselves."

"You think that could work?" Will asked him.

"Not really, no, but all other options seem likely to result in grievous injuries and large medical bills."

Will leaned back. He watched the magic mirror and saw Evander blast open a hill. The necromancer howled in anger when he found nothing buried there. Enraged, he used his magic to tear apart a cliff. If Will didn't do something soon he wouldn't have a kingdom left to rule.

"Do you know where the witch lives?" he asked them.

"She advertises," Domo said. "Esmeralda leaves fliers all over Ket Kingdom, and they include a map showing where to find her. We eat the fliers people throw away. There should be a few left around here somewhere."

"Good," Will said. "Get me a copy. Tomorrow we're going to pay her a visit. I also need you to get some goblins for search parties. They'll need to be enough goblins in each group to fight off the skeletons. Gladys, look for places that Evander and his buddies haven't been to yet. We'll look there, and hopefully find the bottle without the witch's help and before Evander does. We'll have to tell the goblins to run for it if Evander shows up."

Will tried to stand, only to have his body cry out in protest. He lowered himself back down and asked, "Uh, can someone help me up?"

London picked Will up and set him on his feet. Will staggered a bit and headed for his bedroom. "First thing, ouch, first thing in the morning we head out. I know this is difficult for all of us, but we've got to keep trying. Evander seems like he's nuts enough to come back here and start blowing things up if he doesn't find what he's looking for. We have to, ouch, draw him off or find a way to beat him."

"We'll be ready," London said. "Trolls don't know the meaning of the word defeat."

"You don't know the meaning of lots of words," Domo said.

Brooklyn nodded. "Troll education puts more time on smashing than on fancy words. We get good school attendance that way."

Will limped off and his followers dispersed. As he headed to his room, Mr. Niff caught up with him.

"Are you going to need a cane?" Mr. Niff asked.

"No, just let me get a good night's sleep and I'll be better in the morning." Will leaned up against a tunnel wall. "A little better, anyway. Sorry about today. If I'd known Evander was that tough I would have told everyone to run instead of attacking him. Dumb move, huh?"

"Oh yeah, it was dumb," Mr. Niff agreed. "If it makes you feel any better, most of the guys would have gone after him anyhow, what with him breaking the laws of God and man by making those monsters. But they would have run sooner if you weren't there."

Surprised, Will asked, "No kidding?"

"Sure! You charging him like that was an inspirational act of stupidity. I mean, you'd have to look in a history book to find a mismatch in strength that big!"

"You made your point," Will said sourly.

Smiling, Mr. Niff continued. "We've had dumb kings before, but nothing like that! King Allen the Doubter once tried to fight an ogre, and King Sidney the Odd attacked a tree for reasons no one's quite clear on, but you went head to head with one of the most dangerous weapons on the planet! That's the kind of stupidity that usually happens in early childhood. You know, when you're still in diapers."

"You can stop any time."

Mr. Niff was too excited to stop babbling. "I mean, survival instincts alone should have told you to run for your life. The only creature in the animal kingdom that would have faced odds like that is the wolverine, which is pathologically insane, as any animal psychologist will tell you. A lemming might rough it out, but he'd jump off a cliff afterwards."

"Are you done?" Will demanded.

"No. Goblins respect stupidity. It's all we have. Everyone except the trolls and purple puppet people hates us. We're smaller and weaker than everybody except gnomes. We get kicked out of every nice place we live. Anyone else would have looked at the odds against us and given up long ago, but we're dumb enough that we hold on. Sure, run straight at the big scary monster and nine times out of ten you'll lose, but sometimes that pointless act of stupidity is what it takes to get you out of a mess. For goblins, one win in ten is enough."

Will stared at Mr. Niff. "That's not stupidity you're describing, Niff. It's hope."

"Six of one, half a dozen of the other. When you first came here you were dumb enough to think you could fight a human army and win. Anyone with an ounce of working brains would have run for his life. What happened? You won. Today you thought you could beat a necromancer armed with the Staff of Skulls. It was laughable. What happened? You didn't beat him, but you're still alive and you hurt the guy worse than he thought you would. That may not be a human's idea of winning, but it's a goblin victory. The way we see it you're two for two."

With that said, Mr. Niff scampered off. Will called after him, "You think we can beat Evander?"

"No, but I didn't think we could beat the last guy, either."

The next morning Will climbed off the rag pile he used in place of a bed. Before he left his bedroom he changed into a uniform that was clean and didn't have any pieces hacked off. His aching muscles protested yesterday's abuse with every step.

"Morning," Domo said as he met Will in the tunnels. "Doing any better?"

"Nothing a few days of bed rest won't fix. Too bad I won't get it anytime soon. You're looking well."

Domo smiled. "That's goblin health for you. If something doesn't kill us outright we heal up in a hurry."

"Do trolls heal fast, too?" Will asked.

"I don't know. A better question would be were they hurt at all in that fight, and the answer is no. Even young trolls like London and Brooklyn are tough as nails."

Will came to a junction in the tunnel network and took a passage that led to the courtyard of the Goblin City. "They're just kids?"

"They're about fifty years old, which means by troll standards they're rowdy teenagers. They won't be considered adults until they reach two hundred. They'll also be strong enough to toss fully loaded wagons. Of course once they get that big they'll calm down and go back to the Troll Kingdom."

"That's not my biggest concern right now," Will said with a frown.

"Why the long face?"

Will stopped walking and threw his hands up in the air. "We got beat by one man! I should have called everyone off until I knew what we were up against. As it stands I just led the guys into a rout. I'm going to need their help fixing this mess, and after what happened yesterday I'm not sure they'll follow me."

"That's what has you upset?" Domo asked. He chuckled and walked out into the courtyard. "I wouldn't worry about it."

Will stepped into the courtyard and froze. The place was smothered in goblins, and not just the ones involved in yesterday's battle. Those goblins were back alongside thousands more. They were armed with weapons they'd made themselves or scavenged from King Kervol's army months ago, plus a hodgepodge of ill-fitting armor and wood shields. Some of them carried goblin banners with a black spiral on a green background, and all of them looked angry. London and Brooklyn were holding them back so Will had enough room to stand.

"It's the King!" a goblin shouted.

"Come on, boss, let's get the jerk!"

"Second time's the charm!" a goblin yelled. "Or the third time! We'll settle for the tenth time to gets that pixie loving lunatic out of here!"

The goblins roared in approval. They stomped their feet in unison and banged their weapons on the ground. The air began to ripple as their stupidity and craziness warped space.

Domo shouted to Will over the noise. "Most of them just found out the kingdom was invaded by those abominations! You won't be able to hold them back!"

Will raised his hands and the goblins slowly quieted down. He took a deep breath and hoped he wasn't making a terrible mistake. Then he smiled and spoke.

"Some of you were here yesterday when we were attacked by a necromancer named Evander Hollow. He thinks the Bottle of Hope is here and he wants to destroy it. We fought back, and it didn't go well."

When none of the goblins laughed at that understatement, Will felt confident enough to continue. "But I think we can beat him. We can't do it by attacking him head on, yesterday proved that point in an extremely painful fashion, but we can beat him. If the Bottle of Hope is here, and we're not sure it is, that should give us the edge we need. What I need you to do is split up into teams and search for it. If you find it, bring it here. The teams will be big enough to defend themselves, but you have to run if you're outnumbered. I know you hate these things, and that even being close to them hurts, but you need to fall back if things look bad. Don't worry, I'm giving you help."

As if on cue, Vial and his lab rat goblins came out behind Will pushing carts filled with fizzing bottles of explosives. Will looked at the collection of moderately unstable bombs and asked, "You were up all last night making these, weren't you?"

Vial patted the stacks of bombs. "It was a labor of love."

Will plucked out a single bomb and held it up for the horde to see. "The teams will have lab rat goblins with as many bombs as they can carry. This should even the odds a bit. While you're doing that I'm going to find Esmeralda the witch and get her help. Are you guys ready?"

"Yeah!" they screamed.

"Good! Is Gilbert the goblin lobbyist here?"

A goblin in a business suit forced his way through the crowd and stopped in front of Will. Gilbert was responsible for spreading misinformation and outright lies, but today Will needed him for another reason. "You require my aid?"

Will put a hand on Gilbert's shoulder. "I need you to go into Ket Kingdom and spread the word that Evander is here with the Staff of Skulls. Make sure the treasure hunters and adventurers know what's going on."

"Hmm, yes, I can do that, but how will it help?"

Will smiled. "If we can scare some of them off then we won't have to worry about them attacking us. If they come in anyway, they'll know there's a bigger threat and focus on dealing with the skeletons. Who knows, maybe we can pit one side against the other."

Gilbert rubbed his hands together eagerly. "I believe I can provide that service, yes."

Will directed his attention back to the goblin horde. "Evander has one of the most powerful weapons on the planet. We're going to get a magic super weapon of our own and see how he likes a fair fight!"

Their cheers were deafening.

Chapter Five

The next few hours were a frenzy of activity. Will divided the goblins into search parties, armed them with Vial's bombs and sent them out across the kingdom in search of the Bottle of Hope. Hopefully most of them would follow his instructions. He also sent Gilbert the goblin lobbyist with a crowd of goblin warriors to spread the word that Evander and the Staff of Skulls had arrived. They would alert all the goblins they found, plus the treasure hunters scattered over the kingdom. With any luck the treasure hunters would decide to leave or fight the larger threat. Once that was sorted out, Will gathered up the troll brothers, Domo, Gladys, Mr. Niff and Vial to support him in dealing with the witch. They left the city with night fast approaching.

"What are you bringing me along for?" Gladys demanded. She walked too slowly on her bronze eagle feet to keep up, so London carried her on his back.

"I need you to keep me informed about what's happening in the kingdom," Will told her. "Where Evander and his skeletons are, how the goblins are doing and if anyone finds the Bottle of Hope. I'll have to adjust my plans if the situation changes."

As they walked into the woods outside the city, Will asked, "Speaking of plans, exactly where are we going? I've never visited the witch before."

Domo reached into his robes and took out a sheet of paper. "I found this while you were telling everyone what to do. It's the latest advertisement Esmeralda put out."

Will took it from him and studied it. The ad was printed on cheap paper and said: *Sleepy? Exhausted? Run out of energy halfway through the day? We can help, with reasonably priced potions and elixirs to soothe your pain and strengthen your body. Come to the Kingdom of the Goblins, just north of the border with Ket by Route 9, get off at the lightning damaged tree and ask for Esmerelda. All sales are final. The seller is not liable for injury, illness or spontaneous transformation into newts. In case of an emergency contact someone else.*

"Has anyone ever met this witch?" Will asked.

"Witches, plural," Vial corrected him. "Esmeralda picked up two other witches a while back and they work together."

"You know them?" he asked.

Vial shrugged. "Not really. I trade with them for alchemy supplies I can't buy or make myself. We haggle a bit, both parties make threats and I leave after we're finished. I once saw them acting as seers for a farmer missing a horse. They charge a fee, but you may be able to negotiate with them."

"Those witches are crazy," Domo said. "They live in a filthy little hut so small even I'd be cramped inside. Then there's the whole issue of smell."

"They are a tad pungent," Vial agreed, "and coming from us that's saying something."

"I don't care where they live or what they smell like if they can help us," Will told them. "When we get there I do the talking. London and Brooklyn keep guard in case skeletons show up."

"If the witches get uppity, can we rough them up?" London pleaded.

Will considered that. "Depends how uppity. If they live in the kingdom with us I'd like it if we could get along."

"He's being reasonable again," London complained.

Brooklyn nodded. "He's an optimist. One day they'll find a cure for that."

Will shook his head and kept walking, frustrated with his situation if not his friends. He always made an effort to be reasonable and get along with people. It never got him anywhere. Time and again he would try to be helpful, or at least mind his own business, and it always backfired. He'd tried very hard to make peace with King Kervol Ket, the idiot king who fought a war with him months ago. No amount of pleading or common sense worked. The man was dead set on needless violence. Will won that war, and Kervol had spent the last five months telling everyone what a villain Will was.

If anything, winning the war had made things worse! People were used to looking down on goblins, or at least ignoring them. They didn't like the idea that goblins could be a threat. All the neighboring kings hated Will since he might lead an army of goblins against them like he did against Kervol, or that the goblins in their own kingdoms might rise up against them. Merchants hated Will since he didn't buy anything (what with him having no money), and because Will and his goblins could do a lot to disrupt their business. So far the neighboring powers were just snubbing him or sending hate mail.

That hadn't mattered until now. Will had tried to mend fences with them, but every attempt ended in failure. At the time it hadn't seemed important, but now the entire kingdom was in mortal peril and there was no help to be had. King Kervol was probably laughing himself silly at the thought of how much danger Will was in. The other kings would be equally glad to see the goblins get taken down a peg. Will was reduced to looking for witches who sounded like snake oil salesmen. Yet again life proved it could get worse.

Will and his companions walked out of the woods to a rolling prairie, and they saw a small group of goblins on top of a nearby hill. That wasn't unusual, but they were gathered around what looked like a piñata built to look like a large blue donkey. Odder still was the fact that a man's boot was sticking out of its mouth. The goblins were adding a few finishing touches on the piñata when they saw Will and his party approach.

"Hey, it's the King," a goblin with shaggy hair said. "What's up?"

"Ruin, invasion, the usual," Will said as he climbed to the top of the hill. He saw the boot sticking out of the piñata wiggle. "I'm going to regret asking, but what's the story behind this?"

The boot wiggled again as the shaggy goblin spoke. "Oh, him? It's a funny story. Me and the guys were just walking around and squashing pixies, when all of a sudden a man with a sword comes up to us. He says the Bottle of Hope is here and we're gonna tell him where it is or else. So my pal Earl here—"

"Hello," a squat, dirty goblin said cheerfully.

"Yeah, Earl asks, or else what? Which struck us as a reasonable question, I might add. Anyway, the guy with sword says 'or else I'll cut you down like wheat at harvest time.' Not very sociable."

The boot wiggled again, and from inside the piñata a man's muffled voice said, "I would like to take this opportunity to say how very sorry I am."

Will looked at the goblins. There were only ten of them, and none were armed. "Let me guess, he didn't take 'I don't know' for an answer."

The shaggy goblin smiled. "Yeah, but all the noise he was making brought in more goblins. They tripped him and the rest of us jumped him and tied him up. So we're wondering what to do with him, and Earl—"

"That's me," the squat goblin said helpfully.

"Yeah, Earl says he's an artist, which I didn't know at the time."

Will walked around the piñata and tapped it. "So you made a piñata and stuffed him inside."

The shaggy goblin smiled. "We figure we'll drop him off in a human village and hope someone's having a birthday party."

Will bent down next to the piñata and asked, "And did you threaten to kill these goblins?"

There was a pause before the man trapped inside replied. "I...may have said something of that nature."

"Take his weapons and let him go," Will told the goblins. "We've got bigger problems than this goof, and I need your help."

Disappointment in his voice, the shaggy goblin asked, "You mean we did all this for nothing?"

Will put both hands on top of the piñata and ran his fingers over it. "Well, I suppose we should teach him a lesson."

Will shoved the piñata and sent it rolling down the hill. The goblins cheered and the man trapped inside screamed. Bits of the piñata broke off when he hit the bottom of the hill. The man wasn't entirely trapped anymore, but his arms were still pinned to his side and he had to look out of a hole in the piñata donkey's butt. He staggered out of the kingdom, moaning as he went.

"You guys head to the city and see if you can help out," Will told them. The goblins left, laughing as they did.

"That was surprising," Domo said.

Will looked at him and asked, "What was?"

"Ten goblins took down a human. It sounds like he was an adventurer or a treasure hunter, which means he wasn't a total loser."

"He's right," London said. "One farmer is equal to ten goblins in a fight, and a soldier or adventurer is worth fifteen or twenty. The little runts shouldn't have been able to pull that off."

Exasperated, Will said, "Come on, guys! We won a war a little while back, and we trashed all those skeletons yesterday. Yeah, the trolls and I did our part, but a lot of that was you guys fighting tooth and nail."

Mr. Niff smiled. "Tooth, nail, club, piano leg, plucked chicken, we're inventive when it comes to weapons."

"That's not what I mean," Will said. "I've seen you guys do some impressive things in the last five months. You have to stop being surprised when you win."

"We're surprised because it doesn't happen often, at least not until now," Domo said. "Remember our record of failures?"

"It's a broken record," Will told them. "You've won before and you'll win again. Have a little faith."

The sun had set by the time they finally reached Esmeralda's place of business. Vial pointed to a dense grove of pine trees next to a large oak scarred by lightning. Inside the grove was a clearing lit by a fire that sent black, oily smoke up through the trees. They heard women talking and laughing by the fire. Somewhere nearby an owl hooted.

"There they are, My Liege," Vial announced. "I recommend using nose plugs."

Will walked into the grove of trees with his followers. The full moon overhead cast a pale light over the grove, while the witches' flickering fire made the shadows dance. Inside the grove they saw a small hut made of branches and mud, capped with a moldy thatched roof. Plants, some of them quite large, grew from the thatch. Next to the hut was a fire with a black iron pot suspended over it. Three women stood around the pot, stirring it and gossiping.

The witches were hunched over and wore dirty blouses and skirts. Soot stained cloaks covered their backs. They weren't old, but they were ugly, with warts, missing teeth and other blemishes. They were dirty and had greasy hair, and smelled of rotting meat so strong it stopped Will in his tracks.

"We three greet you, man from another world," one of the witches said in an irritating, high-pitched voice. The other two witches cackled and stirred their pot. "Allow me to introduce myself and my fellow practitioners. I am Esmeralda and these are Witch One and Witch Ever. Come, sit by our fire and warm yourself."

Will took one look at the crude hut and glared at the witches. "Oh come on, you can't expect me to believe the three of you live in that. You'd be lucky to fit one person in that fire hazard."

Esmeralda scowled and leaned against the hut. In a more normal but still irritable voice she said, "Look, I'm trying to do this right and you go and poke holes in my act. Cut me some slack!"

"What act?" Domo asked.

"This act," Esmeralda said sourly. "It's all fine and dandy for you to come in here and judge me. You have a working brain. Well, most of our clients don't! They're uneducated, illiterate, superstitious clods. They go to a witch, they expect to see someone who fits the stereotype, and they'll take their business somewhere else if they don't get it. So we threw together a hut, put on dirty clothes and use some makeup to look the part."

Witch One smiled and pulled off a wart. "They come right off."

"The smell is fake, too." Esmeralda pointed to the east and said, "We've got a townhouse a mile over that way. Cost a bundle to build, but it's warm in the wintertime and we don't get many salesmen."

Will kept his distance from the witches, more from the smell than the fear that they might hurt him. "I heard from my followers you live inside my kingdom."

"Your kingdom?" Esmeralda snickered. "You're here against your will, as were all the other Kings of the Goblins before you. Does the prisoner own his cell?"

"Hey, it's my kingdom!" Will retorted. He held up his king contract and said, "I've got the paperwork to prove it. I don't want it, but until I can find a way to get rid of it, it's mine. Back on topic, exactly what is it you do here?"

Esmeralda smiled as she stirred her pot. "We brew potions to enhance a man's strength and endurance, and sell them for a surprisingly high markup. We find living here offers protection. We're close enough to towns that clients can get to us, but far enough away the authorities don't usually come here. As a bonus, disgruntled clients have to fight their way through a lot of goblins before they reach our camp. The noise from the fighting gives us time to escape and lay low until they leave."

Witch Ever leaned toward Will and said, "We find most of our ingredients here, which keeps expenses down. As a bonus there are no anti-dumping laws."

Esmeralda bumped Witch Ever out of the way. "I came here after being burned out of my last home for patent violations... and accidentally turning the mayor into a newt. That was blown *way* out of proportion, and I'm told he's feeling much better now. Over time my companions joined me. We three have thrived in your lands. I should thank you."

Will smiled "Well, there's a quick way to do that."

Witch One cackled. "We know. Long have we anticipated your arrival."

"Really? I just decided to come visit you yesterday," he replied.

Esmeralda sighed. "They always hire the stupid ones. What's it been, five months since you got here? You came because of your king contract, stupid! You want to find a way out of it. All the Kings of the Goblins come to us."

"You can get me out of my contract?" he asked excitedly. Will had spent months trying to defeat the cursed document and he always came out second best. He held it up for the witches to see what he was up against. *Article 53, subsection 9, paragraph 11, line 41*: *The King cannot escape his contract by creating, summoning or otherwise bringing about a natural disaster to destroy the kingdom, as it sets a bad example to fellow monarchs.*

"No, we can't." Esmeralda took a legal contract from inside the hut and showed it to Will. "King Flynn the Exaggerator came to me ten years ago, back when I was a solo act. He showed me his king contract and I helped him out of it in return for him dealing with some angry clients I had hanging around. Cickam, Wender and Downe found out I freed one of their kings and sent a pack of rabid law school graduates after me. Let me tell you, that was one ugly fight. Anyway, long story short, I agreed to never do it again, so buy something or get out."

"I'm not here about my contract," Will said. "I wish to God that was my biggest problem."

Witch Ever frowned. "Didn't see that coming."

"This isn't about your contract?" Esmeralda asked skeptically.

"No." Will pointed his scepter to the north and asked, "You know about the necromancer invading the kingdom with an army of skeletal animals?"

Esmeralda nodded and waved her ladle around. "Oh yeah, magic cloud carrying all sorts of fiendish abominations, violations of the laws of nature, blah blah blah. We saw it."

"They're here for the Bottle of Hope," Domo told them.

The three witches laughed. Once she managed to catch her breath, Esmeralda asked, "People are here looking for that again?"

"Yeah, they are," Will told them. "There are treasure hunters all over the place, and hundreds or even thousands of skeletons tearing the kingdom apart. The person controlling the skeletons is a necromancer named Evander Hollow, and he's got the Staff of Skulls."

"Oh, bad business, that is," Witch One said, and clucked her tongue.

"Explains why we haven't had many clients lately," Witch Ever agreed. "We may have to relocate for a while."

"I'm glad you appreciate how serious this is," Will said. "If the Bottle of Hope is here I haven't found it yet and neither has anyone else. I'm told you three can act as seers. I need you to locate the bottle so I can use it to fight off Evander."

Esmeralda stroked her chin. "Hmm, that's not the worst plan you could come up with. The rivalry between the bottle and staff is great. One could be used to destroy the other, but you'd be in great danger."

Will pointed to the Goblin City. "We're already in great danger! Evander dropped by yesterday and beat the snot out of us. The skeletons he's let loose are spreading out over the entire kingdom and wrecking everything they come across. If he comes back and we don't have the bottle, we're toast."

"What you say is true." Esmeralda leaned over the pot and whispered to the other witches. They looked at Will with calculated glances, and he heard them use words like 'net worth' and 'liquid assets'. Esmeralda finally broke away from the other two and approached Will. "We *could* help you, for the right price."

"Right price?" Domo demanded. The troll brothers balled up their fists and Mr. Niff drew his knife.

"You have to know I don't have any money!" Will protested.

"Then get some," Witch Ever replied calmly.

Will ground his teeth together in anger. "Of all the short sighted, ignorant...do you have any idea how much danger we're in, all of us? If you delay even for an hour, that lunatic with the staff can blow up even more of the kingdom. He said he's done terrible things, and I believe him. You can't possibly be willing to let him go on wrecking one part of the world after another!"

"This look like a charity to you?" Esmeralda demanded. "It costs a lot of money to brew potions, plus advertising, travel expenses, insurance, lawsuits, bribes and incidentals. This girl is out to make a profit."

"You won't make a profit if the necromancer comes for you!" Will shouted at them.

Hesitantly, Esmeralda asked, "Why would he do that?"

Will started to shout, but managed to get his voice under control. "I came to you to find the Bottle of Hope. If the necromancer can't find it on his own there's a good chance he'll come here, too. Do you think he's going to pay you, or is he going to attack and force you to help him?"

Esmeralda reeled back as if struck. "He, uh, he'd…"

"We could run away," Witch One said.

"And leave behind your nice house?" Will asked. "How much of your supplies will you have to abandon? I'm guessing you don't have a cart and horse to carry your stuff."

Esmeralda winced. "We'd only be able to take what we could carry."

"That's assuming he doesn't come after you while you're leaving. You'd have to dump your bags to run fast enough to escape," Will continued. The witches moaned in agony at the thought of so much lost profits. Will let them carry on for a while before he said, "Or you can help me. If I find the bottle, I can get rid of the necromancer."

"But, but you have a magic mirror!" Witch Ever said. "Use that to find the bottle."

"Can't," Gladys said. "An old owner blinded me. I can only see out of scarecrows the goblins put up."

Esmeralda considered Will's suggestion for a second before she nodded. "We'll deal. But first you must answer our riddles three!"

"What!" Will gripped his scepter tightly and the trolls advanced on the witches. "I'm trying to save the kingdom *and* the three of you!"

"We know, but anyone who needs us to act as seers must answer three riddles as proof they are deserving. No exceptions."

Will looked at Vial and said, "You didn't say anything about riddles."

"They didn't do this last time!" Vial protested.

Esmeralda nodded as Witch One and Ever cackled. "It's true. To be honest, the seer act was getting kind of stale. We kept getting morons who wanted us to find missing house keys. We figured this would spice up the act and keep the losers away. Ever, what's the first riddle?"

Witch Ever picked up a book from the hut and read from it. "A train leaves from Boston Massachusetts at 8:15 AM Monday headed for Phoenix Arizona, traveling at 70 miles an hour. At 11:00 AM the same day a trains leaves from Phoenix to Boston, traveling at 55 miles per hour. If the distance between the two cities is 2500 miles, at what time and what distance from Boston do the trains meet?"

Will stared at the witches for a few seconds. He turned to his followers and said, "London, I'm going to need some rope."

Fifteen minutes later the three witches were tied to stakes. London and Brooklyn piled dry brush around them while Vial and Mr. Niff poured lamp oil on the brush. Domo went through the witches' camp while Will used his scepter to send bursts of fire into the air.

"We'll do it!" Esmeralda screamed.

"What did she say?" Will asked Domo. He shot off another jet of fire. FOOM!

Domo looked up from a pile of junk he'd taken from the witches' pockets. "I don't know. A lot of people were saying things."

"We'll do it!" Esmeralda screamed again.

Will walked up to her. "No more riddles?"

Sweating profusely, Esmeralda said, "No riddles, I promise. No tricks of any kind. I swear we'll do everything in our power to find the bottle and keep our agreement."

The trolls untied Esmeralda and her cohorts. Will stood in front of the witches as they gave him evil stares.

Will clapped his hands together and smiled. "Okay, ladies, here's how it's going to work. You're going to help me find the Bottle of Hope. If I need your help with anything else in the future, you're going to do that, too, and all of it free of charge."

"Mercy!" Witch Ever cried. "You'll bankrupt us."

"I'll only call on you if it's an emergency," Will told them. "You also agree to do nothing illegal or immoral. In return, I agree not to demand taxes."

"Taxes!" the witches screamed.

"Whose kingdom are you living in?" he asked them.

The witches backed away from Will. Panicking, Witch One asked, "You, you'd tax us?"

Will smiled. This was one of those rare and happy times in his life where it was helpful to be a business major. "Oh yeah. There could be property taxes, income taxes, a business license, plus I bet you never paid taxes to the other kings before me, which brings up the whole issue of back taxes."

Witch Ever trembled and grabbed onto Esmeralda's arm. "Oh, I'm feeling faint!"

Will tapped his scepter on his palm. "If you agree to my terms I won't ask for money now or in the future, and if you're ever in danger my followers and I promise to protect you. You can take my offer or take your chances with the necromancer."

The witches looked at each other and whispered. They glanced at Will, but now with respect instead of contempt. The three nodded to one another. Esmeralda shook Will's hand and said, "It's agreed."

"I'm glad to hear it," Will replied.

The witches stirred their pot and peered into it. They dropped in all manner of arcane ingredients and made a concoction that resembled goblin stew. As Domo, Vial and Mr. Niff drooled, Esmeralda cast a final handful of mushrooms into the pot.

"I warn you, this may not work," she cautioned. "Many magic items include security features to prevent seers spying on them with crystal balls and the like."

Witch Ever nodded. "We have little chance against something as mighty as the Bottle of Hope. If finding it was this easy it would be in someone's treasury by now."

Witch One stirred the pot and added, "Our success depends greatly on whether the bottle wants to be found."

"Is it alive like my scepter?" Will asked.

"Yes, but vastly more powerful." Esmeralda took the ladle out of the pot and whispered a spell. The goop in the pot turned crystal clear and showed the three witches. The view changed, rising high into the night sky and then flying out over the woods and canyons in the kingdom. "So far, so good."

The image in the pot whirled by, sweeping over vast sections of the kingdom. They saw goblin search parties and skeletons, treasure hunters and wildlife. Witch Ever looked deep into the pot and said, "Hold on, I'm getting something."

The image froze over Evander Hollow, scowling as he surveyed the landscape from atop his black magic cloud. Suddenly he looked directly at the witches and demanded, "Who dares spy upon me?"

"End the spell!" Esmeralda screamed. The witches chanted and backed away from the pot. The image blurred, but not before they saw Evander point the Staff of Skulls at them. "Get down!"

"You would meddle in my affairs?" Evander yelled. "Burn for this invasion of my privacy!"

Bolts of black lightning burst from the pot as everyone threw themselves to the ground. The bolts hit the surrounding trees and blasted them to ashes. One bolt barely missed Will and vaporized the king contract tucked in his belt. The pot exploded, throwing shards of iron like shrapnel, but the magic attack stopped.

For a few seconds everyone stayed down in case another attack was coming. Witch One was the first to get to her feet. Coughing, she waved away the smoke around her. "That could have gone a tad better."

London got up and looked at a charred tree behind him. "He almost took my head off!"

"Might be an improvement," Domo said.

Will's king contract reappeared in front of him and drifted to the ground. He tucked it back into his belt and said, "Black magic can't destroy it, either. This thing is tougher than a cockroach."

"We got the wrong target," Witch Ever said. "With two magic items that powerful so close together we mistook one for the other."

Esmeralda shook her head and straightened out her skirt. "No, it didn't feel like that. The necromancer must have cast an interceptor spell to detect seers before we started. The spell allows him to detect attempts at remote viewing and to retaliate. I've seen it done before, but never so strong."

"Sorry about the pot," Will said. "Can you try again without it?"

"No pot, no seeing" Witch One replied.

Esmeralda stroked her chin and looked at Gladys. "There is another option. We can use the mirror."

"I told you I was blinded!" Gladys snapped. "You deaf as well as ugly?"

"Ugly!" Witch Ever cried. She put her hands on her hips and said, "Look who's talking."

Will got between the mirror and the witches. "No name calling. Gladys already looked for the bottle and came up with nothing."

Esmeralda walked up to Gladys and ran her fingers down the mirror's ornate bronze frame. "Your mirror is blind because key spells were removed. If the three of us work together with the mirror, we may be able to replace the missing spells."

Gladys' jaw dropped. "You can make me see again?"

"For a short time," Esmeralda cautioned. The other two witches joined her and studied the mirror. "It will be more of a patch than an overhaul. Installing the patch won't be dangerous, but you saw what happened when the necromancer detected us. If he discovers us again he'll retaliate the same way, or worse. Your mirror could die."

"Do it!" Gladys shouted.

"Are you sure about this?" Will asked Gladys. "I don't want you to get hurt."

Gladys' face was no longer pouting and irritable. Her expression softened as she spoke. "Will, I'm a magic mirror who can't see anything. If it weren't for those stupid scarecrows I'd be totally blind. I don't care if this only lasts a few minutes or if it's dangerous. I'll be able to see again. Please, let them try."

Will reluctantly waved the witches on to Gladys. The witches placed their hands on the mirror frame. They closed their eyes and Esmerelda said, "Try to view the Goblin City."

The mirror made a crackling sound and glazed over as if covered by a thick layer of ice. Esmeralda frowned and said, "Anyone who would do so much damage to a treasure this valuable is a fool."

"Fool, cheater, liar, he was a lot of things," Gladys said. "This happens every time I try viewing the world without looking through a scarecrow. Make with the magic and let me see again."

The witches chanted and made strange gestures. Glowing words appeared in the air and sank into the mirror. The icy film began to shake. Cracks appeared in the film and the crackling noise died away. With a final shout from the witches and a flash of light, the film shattered to reveal the Goblin City in the mirror's surface.

"It worked!" Gladys cried out in joy.

"I need you to find the bottle as fast as you can," Will said. "You'll be in danger if Evander figures out what's happening."

"Don't worry, I know what I'm doing," Gladys told him. The mirror showed the city and then backed away. Gladys scanned the kingdom far faster than the witches had, and checked many places they'd missed. "I'm picking up hundreds of strong magic sources. A few of them belong to magic weapons the treasure hunters brought with them, but I'm not sure about the rest. Hold on, I got a weak fix on it!"

"Vermin." The word came through the magic mirror and chilled everyone to the bone. It was Evander. He'd detected them again and was interrupting Gladys' efforts. "Was one warning not enough?"

"Gladys, shut down now!" Will ordered. The mirror's surface turned black and the witches backed away. The mirror began to rattle, and sparks shot from it. "Gladys!"

"I can handle this," she grunted. The sparks grew into a fountain of fire and the mirror shook wildly. There was a flash as the sparks died away and the shaking stopped.

"Gladys, are you okay?" Will asked.

All was silent for a moment before Gladys reappeared in the mirror's surface. She looked exhausted and mopped sweat off her brow with a handkerchief, and the mirror's bronze eagle feet wobbled. "Whew, he's a determined little cuss, isn't he? Don't worry about me. I held off the worst of what he was throwing at us."

"Did you find the bottle?" Will asked her.

Gladys nodded. "Evander stepped in before I could get a strong fix on it, but I have a general location for you. The bottle is in the wastelands in the north of the kingdom, near the old dwarf refinery."

Shocked, Mr. Niff said, "There's nothing there, not even grass!"

"I know what I saw!" Gladys snapped.

"Does Evander know it's there?" Will asked.

Gladys shook her head. "He didn't find out through me. If we hurry we can get there before he does."

Esmeralda looked at Will and put her hands on her hips. "We've lived up to our end of the bargain. Dare you say otherwise?"

"You did good," Will told her. "I couldn't have done this without you. You'd better hide in case Evander comes looking for you."

Witch One nodded. "He might trace the spell back to us."

"He might at that," Esmeralda said. "The staff has been a pox on this world for far too long. Destroy it if you can, Oh King. If you succeed you shall win the thanks of an entire world. If you fail, I look forward to dealing with your replacement. Hopefully he won't be as shrewd as you are."

Domo tugged on Will's sleeve. "Come on, let's get out of here. We can make camp away from the witches' hut and head back to the city in the morning."

Puzzled, Will asked, " Shouldn't we go straight to the bottle?"

"We need food and water for the trip," Domo explained. "It'll take a couple days to get there, and all of us are going to need supplies."

That surprised Will. "Why would you need supplies? I thought goblins could eat almost anything."

"We can," Mr. Niff replied, "but we can't eat nothing. There's no food, no water, no shelter, not even dirt in the wastelands."

Domo nodded. "Better pack everything, because we're going where even goblins can't survive."

Chapter Six

It wasn't until noon the next day that Will and his followers got back to the Goblin City. The city was nearly deserted with the goblin residents off searching for the Bottle of Hope, and Will found the silence eerie. Once they arrived, they searched houses for supplies they'd need for their trip to the wastelands.

"How bad is this place?" Will asked them.

Mr. Niff filled a hollow gourd with water from a well as he replied. "Think of the nicest place you've ever been. Somewhere with pretty trees, good food, nice places to live and lots of friends. The wastelands are as far away from that as you can get. It's not dangerous, since there are no monsters there or angry knights, but there's no food, either, or water or wood or even garbage. If it wasn't for birds flying over it there'd never be anything alive there."

Domo nodded. "It didn't used to be so bad. Once upon a time it was a forest before the dwarfs came here to mine and refine iron ore. The refineries turned out pure iron and tons of slag, useless molten rock with all the iron taken out. They dumped the slag on the ground and let it cool decade after decade until they created the wastelands."

London filled a leather bag with salted fish and dried apples. "It's rock as far as the eye can see. Not boulders or sand, just flat rock covering the ground from one horizon to the other."

Will loaded another bag and accidentally knocked over a pile of supplies onto Domo. "Sounds like a giant parking lot. And the Bottle of Hope is there?"

"Definitely," Gladys said. "I can't say exactly where, but it's there."

Will pulled a bag off Domo. "How did the bottle get there? And if this place is so empty why didn't someone find it by now?"

"Who knows how it got there," Domo said from underneath the bags. "The bottle's been stolen hundreds of times. You'd think someone would have chained it down. Whoever had it last may have hidden it there for safekeeping and wasn't able to come back for it."

Vial put on a new lab coat with a fresh supply of explosives inside. "It is a good hiding place when you think about it. No one can survive in the wastelands for long, and there's no reason for people to visit. Anyone looking for the Bottle of Hope wouldn't think to go there and couldn't stay long if they did."

After an hour's work they had a pile of supplies for their journey. There were hollowed out gourds filled with water and buckets of food, or at least what goblins considered food. London carried a folded up tent and more food that he and his brother could digest. Will had his bag of food from the inn, which would have to last a while. It was quite a stack of bags and bundles.

"I don't suppose we have a horse and cart to carry this with?" Will asked hopefully.

"We used to, but we ate the cart," Mr. Niff replied.

Will stared at him. "You ate a cart?"

Mr. Niff shrugged. "It was late, nobody wanted to go out for dinner, the cart was there, problem solved."

"And the horse?" Will asked.

Brooklyn said, "It ran off after it saw what happened to the cart."

"No help there," Will said. "The animated skeletons don't need food or water, do they?"

"Nope," Domo told him.

That worried Will. "Then they can stay in the wastelands to look as long as they want and we can't. We're going to have to load up so we can stay on site as long as possible. The sooner we get the bottle, the sooner we can do something about getting rid of Evander."

"That's assuming we get there carrying all this stuff," Domo said.

Will put on a backpack and grabbed two gourds. Still bruised from the fight with Evander, he almost fell over from the weight. "Yeah, assuming."

Mr. Niff snapped his fingers and ran into an empty house. He came back smiling and triumphantly presented Will with a paperback book. "I knew I'd seen a copy of this around here somewhere. Don't worry about going through the wastelands, boss. Last year the guys and me wrote a book on how to get through tough times. We won't have any problems now!"

Will took the book from him and read the title, *Surviving Wars, Plagues, IRS Audits and Other Life Threatening Events.* That seemed to cover the peril they were facing, but he doubted how useful a book written by goblins could be. Will opened it to the first page, and the brief hope he'd felt melted away when he saw what was written inside. He gave Mr. Niff a disapproving look as he read aloud the first line in the book. *"Chapter 1: So You're Considering Cannibalism."*

Vial looked down and shook his head sadly. "Sales were disappointing."

Many miles away, Evander Hollow stood before a limestone cliff. He could feel power radiating through the rock. The Bottle of Hope was hidden inside the cliff, he was sure of it, but he hesitated to blast it open. He finally pointed the Staff of Skulls at the cliff and fired. Bolts of black lightning sent shards of limestone flying through the air as he tore the cliff apart. But there was nothing inside, and the feeling of power disappeared.

"This is impossible," he told the staff. "The bottle hides itself, pretending to be in a hundred places at once. Every time we eliminate one false lead it makes a dozen more."

The staff spoke to him in dozens of voices. Evander waved at the sundered cliff in response. "We've been doing this the entire day, and we're no closer to finding the bottle. Our great mission can't begin with that threat hanging over us."

Evander gazed over the landscape. His skeleton followers were searching through the kingdom, digging up prairies and tearing through woods. For all their work they were as empty-handed as he was. This wasn't supposed to be so hard!

The staff spoke again to Evander. He nodded in agreement and replied, "I won't fail you. Others did before me, too weak and too fainthearted to see the mission through, but I remain strong. This world needs you, needs your determination and strength, your guidance. If we are ever to be strong again it must be through you."

Satisfied its puppet wasn't going to give up, the staff issued more commands. Evander listened attentively before answering. "We can't afford to stay long. Already the bottle draws fools to defend itself. I can feel their presence. So weak, so insignificant, but if there are enough of them we may lose this opportunity."

A skeletal bear approached Evander and interrupted his discussion with the staff. Its voice was rasping and defiant. "Creator, we have found nothing."

"I know. You will receive new instructions shortly."

The skeletal bear scratched the ground. "We were not made for digging in the dirt. There are villages to the south. We want to attack them."

Evander turned slowly to face his creation. This was hardly the first time one of his skeletons had proved disobedient. While they were brutally effective in battle and always spoiling for a fight, animated skeletons were notoriously hard to control. "I don't *care* what you want. You exist only to serve me. Resume your work or I shall I destroy you myself."

"You used to take us places and blow them up," the skeleton complained. "Towers, bridges, castles. You used to be cool."

"Get back to work!" Evander yelled at it. The skeletal bear's red eyes flashed in anger, but it lowered its head and rejoined the rest of its kind. "Ungrateful creature, I made you and I can take you apart!"

The staff's discordant voices spoke to Evander again and got his attention. It went on at some length until he understood its plans. "That's dangerous," Evander counseled. "The risk to you is great."

For a second the staff was silent before it spoke back to him. He said, "No I don't have any better ideas. Your plan is risky, but we'll follow it. I'll keep our servants working so no one notices what we're doing. It's still possible they might find the bottle."

Evander summoned another magic cloud and flew up to the top of the battered cliff. He landed and touched the end of the staff to the rock.

Power flowed through the staff and the skull on top glowed brightly. Nearby plants blackened and died as Evander and the staff poisoned the land with their foul magic. The staff's voices grew louder. People couldn't hear it, but pixies could and would be drawn to it from many miles away. It would take time, but Evander and the staff were patient.

"We'll be ready when we find the bottle," he promised the staff. "I shall replace the servants we lost while we wait. Our mission shall not be long delayed."

Will and his followers left the Goblin City and headed north. They stopped twice along the way for Gladys to see what was happening across the kingdom. Gladys showed that the search parties hadn't turned up anything and neither had the treasure hunters. Both goblins and hunters ran into animated skeletons also searching for the bottle, and more often than not fights broke out. Will watched as a man with a whip and a woman with two small crossbows destroyed a lone skeleton, only to see the pair be chased off by fifty more skeletons.

"The necromancer is losing guys fast," London said. Gladys showed another animated skeleton get destroyed, this time by a lab rat goblin backed up by diggers.

"He had a lot to begin with," Domo reminded them.

Will nodded. "Yeah, he did. You think we should call off the search parties? We already know where the bottle is. The longer our guys are in the field, the better the chance someone's going to get hurt."

"How do we tell them to stop looking?" Mr. Niff asked. "They're scattered all over the kingdom, and the nearest bunch is miles away."

"We need them out there," Brooklyn said. He pointed at the magic mirror, where Gladys showed a mob of goblins ambush two skeletons and destroy them. "The little runts aren't doing too bad. In a couple days Evander won't have an army left to fight with."

"He's right," Domo said. "Evander can gather his skeletons in a hurry with those magic clouds. When we get the bottle we still have to do something about him. If he gets his whole army together and sends them after us, we're in trouble."

Will frowned. "I'm putting them in a lot of danger."

"They're goblins," Domo said. "They've been in danger since the day they were born, from men, elves, dwarfs, monsters and usually from each other. Don't worry about the guys. They know when to cut their losses and run."

They continued on their journey to the wastelands. The land north of the city was light forests and grassland, with the occasional hut built by goblins. There were signs of damage by Evander's army, torn up ground and holes blasted into hillsides. They found a few scarecrows torn apart, but most of them were still up. Either Evander didn't know what they were for, or he knew and didn't care.

"There's one thing I don't understand," Will said as they walked.

Domo chuckled. "*One* thing?"

"Okay, there are lots of things I don't understand, like quantum physics or why the light goes off when you close the refrigerator door," Will admitted. "But in this situation there's one thing I don't understand. The Bottle of Hope got its power from the holy man Nathaniel Lightwell. How did the Staff of Skulls get its power?"

"Elves made it," Gladys said. The bookcase reappeared in the surface of her mirror and she took out a book. "A long, long time ago elves ruled almost all of Other Place. All the races except one followed their orders."

London puffed out his chest in pride. "And that was the trolls! Our ancestors never bowed to them."

"Who's telling this story, you or me?" Gladys snapped. She grumbled and went on. "The trolls had the only independent kingdom left. Elves ruled everything and everyone else. They were powerful and controlled magic much greater than we have today…more unpredictable, too. A man couldn't walk three blocks down the street without being turned into a frog. The elves were condescending and treated other races like children. They even created all new races like the harpies and sylphs, and a lot of the monsters we have nowadays, too. There wasn't an outside force that could threaten them."

"So what happened?" Will asked.

Gladys opened her book and pressed it against the mirror's surface. Will saw a picture of a magnificent city filled with tall elegant towers and buildings that were architectural masterpieces. All the buildings in this marvelous picture were engulfed in flames, and crowds of screaming people fled the city.

"The elf emperor went nuts, and I don't mean your garden variety nuts," Gladys told him. "He did incredibly stupid things, like declaring war on the moon, ordering all cats to be renamed Clyde and he charged a moose with treason."

"The moose was framed!" Mr. Niff shouted.

"Stop interrupting!" Gladys snapped. "His own followers finally pulled him from the throne when he ordered his musicians to play polka at an imperial ball. Once he was gone they fought each other over who would be the next emperor. A civil war broke out that lasted decades. The contenders for the throne pulled out all the stops, using powerful magic weapons nobody in their right mind would even touch. When that didn't work they created new and more powerful weapons, ones that were nearly as dangerous to their owners as to their victims. One of those weapons was the Staff of Skulls."

Gladys shuddered and put the book away. "All the new weapons did was increase the damage. When the fighting ended the empire was gone. Countless cities were destroyed and never rebuilt. An entire mountain got taken off the maps. The elves lost too many of their people to rule anymore and the other races gradually took over. It took a long time to fix the damage that war caused, and in some cases the land never healed. There are old battlefields where it's still not safe to go because of curses and old magic still active even after so many years. Bad as it was, everybody was grateful that at least the fighting was over. Then one day some poor fool explored the ruins of an elf city and found the Staff of Skulls. It was built to capture the throne of the elf emperor and it's still trying to do that today, taking control of its owners and using them like tools."

"It's fighting to control an empire that doesn't exist?" Will asked.

"Best as anyone can tell, it doesn't care," Gladys replied. "Maybe it thinks it can rebuild the empire. Maybe it's nuts and thinks there's still an empire to rule. Maybe it just likes blowing stuff up. In the end it doesn't matter. Whenever the Staff of Skulls shows up, trouble is sure to follow."

"So the weapon we're fighting is deranged, evil or both," Will said.

Mr. Niff smiled. "Deranged is something we can deal with, even appreciate. Now evil, that's a problem."

Vial cleared his throat and asked, "If you can buy me time to gather ingredients, might one of my larger bombs deal with the staff?"

"Not a chance," Gladys said. "I'm not slighting your work, Vial, but there's nothing you could make that would hurt it. Not much of anything can stop it."

Domo waved his walking stick. "Not true. The hero Julius Craton defeated the last necromancer who held the staff."

"I didn't say you couldn't beat the guy holding it, I said you can't hurt it," Gladys said. "The staff has been beat plenty of times, usually by lots of powerful people teaming up and taking out the guy holding it. That you can do. But the staff can't be cut, crushed, burned, melted or vaporized. Each time it's been beaten, the winners were left with the staff intact and ready to cause trouble the next time someone picked it up. They usually hid it somewhere they thought no one could find it, or someplace no one could reach. It never worked. Some moron always came along who thought he could control the staff and dug it up, and then the whole mess started up again."

"The Guild of Heroes offers a 5000 gold coin reward for destroying the staff," Domo said. "Obviously no one's claimed it."

Will climbed over a tree knocked over by Evander Hollow's rampage. "That's just lovely. The staff isn't just nuts or evil: it's also immortal. What are we supposed to do with it if we beat Evander?"

"Bury it deep," Gladys said.

Brooklyn scratched his head. "Could we throw it down the bottomless pit?"

Brooklyn's suggestion had merit. Early on in Will's tenure as King he'd instructed the goblins to dig a bottomless pit. The project was intended only to keep his followers busy and out of his hair for a while, but after a few days Will had a fully functional bottomless pit and no idea what to do with it. Now he did.

"Hmm, no one's tried that before," Gladys said. "That could take it out of circulation for a while."

"Hold on," Will said. "The staff blows stuff up and the bottle heals people. Why does the staff want to destroy the Bottle of Hope? I mean, if the staff ever gets the empire it wants, it could use the bottle to help its followers, right?"

Domo crawled under the tree had Will climbed over. "You're being reasonable again. Really powerful magic devices like that have strong personalities. I've never heard of a person having more than one of the strong ones in their possession at a time. I don't think the bottle and staff would work together."

Will frowned. "This still seems like a lot of trouble to go to if you don't have to. I suppose if the staff is nuts then anything's possible, but while it's going after the bottle it can't do much about making an empire to rule."

"It's been after the bottle for a while, too," Domo said. "All the stories I've heard about the staff say it's been trying to destroy the bottle for hundreds of years."

Gladys shrugged. "Maybe when you live forever you don't mind wasting a few centuries on a grudge."

Will stopped the group as night fell, and they made camp in a grove of young maple trees. The goblins left to forage for food and the trolls set up the tent, while Gladys looked through nearby scarecrows. Will got a fire going and sat down to rest. He also took time to read his king contract. *Article 54, subsection 1, paragraph 4, line 12: The King can't escape his contract by pretending to be dead. If he is dead, he will be stuffed, mounted and hung over the fireplace.*

Will stretched out next to the fire and relaxed. The air was cool and moist, and smelled sweet from wildflowers and earthy from damp dirt and decaying leaves. It was quiet, too. All in all, this was far nicer than the Goblin City.

"You know, this reminds me of when I went camping back home," Will told the trolls. "I mean, there weren't homicidal wizards with cursed magic staffs running around, but otherwise it's the same."

"Sounds like a tough neighborhood," London said.

"Not really." Will took out a piece of beef jerky and ate it. "When I think about it, my world isn't much safer or more sane than this place. There were the same wars long ago and people today who can't seem to let them go, just like the staff can't. I could never understand that. If you've been hurt bad then stop the guy who did it to you. Throw him in jail or something. But fighting over events that happened hundreds or thousands of years ago? It boggles the mind."

Brooklyn and London finished setting up the tent and sat down next to him. Casually, London said, "We trolls settle our problems right away and that's the end of it. We're too practical to hold grudges."

Brooklyn opened a package of food and shared it with his brother. "That's one thing trolls respect about goblins. They don't hold grudges, either. They don't hate the elves for invading five years ago or Kervol for attacking a few months ago. They figure if something happened in the past you can't change it, so why worry about it? Doesn't matter what you do to them or they do to you, by morning they figure everything is forgiven."

"I wish more people were like that," Will said softly. He looked up at the night sky filled with stars. "Look at all those stars. It looks a lot more peaceful up there than it does here."

"I once said the same thing to my mom," London said. "She told me stars are giant balls of flaming hydrogen, and they're peaceful because nobody's stupid enough to bother them."

Brooklyn frowned. "I never knew when mom was telling a joke or not."

Will looked at the night sky and tried to find the Big Dipper or Orion. It took a second for him to realize those constellations were what the stars looked like from Earth. He wouldn't find them on another world. Then again, Other Place might have something similar. "Do you guys have constellations here? You know, patterns of stars in the sky."

"Sure!" London said eagerly. "Those stars up there make Jeremy the Hamster, a sign of good luck. And over there is the Puffin of Wrath. Now that one over there is Quentin the Wombat, symbol of bowel disorders."

Will spotted a light low in the sky, brighter than all the other stars. He pointed at it and asked, "What about that one?"

Brooklyn squinted at the twinkling light. "There isn't supposed to be a star there."

"Huh?" Will stood up and looked at the light carefully. "It's not a star. I don't know what it is, but it looks like it's coming from the top of a cliff."

"Long way away," Brooklyn grumbled. "Got to be pretty bright for us to see it from here."

"Wonder what it is?" London asked.

There was a rustling noise in the distance as something ran through the brush and tall grasses. The troll brothers got between Will and the sound, but they relaxed when they saw it was only Mr. Niff running back to camp.

"What's the hurry, Niff?" Will asked.

"Get behind the fire!" Mr. Niff shouted. Vial and Domo were right behind him, all three panting and sweating from running hard. When Will and the trolls only stared at him, Mr. Niff shouted, "Hurry!"

There was a rumbling noise in the distance, accompanied by the sound of panicked animal cries. Will and the trolls got behind the fire along with the goblins. Mr. Niff tossed more wood on the fire and Vial pulled two bombs from his lab coat.

"What's going on?" Will asked. The noise grew louder and more varied. Will heard hisses and snarls, growls and whines. Whatever it was, it was big, headed their way and moving fast. "What is that?"

"Stampede!" Domo shouted as he added fuel to the flames. "We saw it coming and got back just ahead of it. Maybe they'll avoid the trees, but they'll definitely stay out of the fire."

"They who?" Will asked. "What's stampeding?"

Domo looked at Will, fear showing in his eyes. "Everything!"

The noise grew to unbearable levels. Domo tried to say more, but Will couldn't hear him over the deafening rumble. The stampede was almost on them and Will couldn't even see it in the dark. Desperate, he pointed his scepter into the sky and turned it on. FOOM! The scepter blasted a column of fire into the sky and illuminated the land for a mile around.

Domo wasn't kidding. Every animal imaginable was running, crawling, slithering or hopping toward them. There were rabbits, bears, wolves, foxes, coyotes, snakes, frogs, skunks, raccoons, deer, mice and even more animals Will couldn't identify as they ran by. Covering the ground were ants, spiders, centipedes, termites and beetles. There were even a few monsters in the stampede, including a unicorn and a giant snail with a shell as tall as a wagon wheel. All the animals had two things in common. The first was that they were running straight at Will and his friends. The second was the terror in their eyes.

It wasn't just animals on the ground, either. The sky was filled with birds and bats, swarms of bees and clouds of gnats. Most of these animals were only active during the daytime, and many preyed on one another. But they weren't sleeping and they weren't fighting. To an animal they were leaving the kingdom as fast as possible.

The stampede parted in front of the tent and trees, doing everything they could to avoid the fire Will shot into the air. Vial tossed two bombs out to further discourage them. The animals thundered past without sparing them a moment's notice except to go around them. Will and his friends pulled together behind the fire for protection as thousands of animals ran by. Gradually the wave of fleeing animals began to lessen, and then shrank to a trickle. Their frightened cries died away and Will stepped out from behind the fire.

"What was that about?" Will asked. A turtle walked by him as fast as it could, eager to join the other escaping animals.

"I don't know," Domo said. "I've never seen that in all my years."

"Spooky," London said.

The light in the distance grew brighter. Will stared at it and felt an urge to run away.

Gladys walked up behind him on the bronze feet of her mirror and said, "This must be Evander's doing. You remember the headache you got being near his animated skeletons? Necromancy does that to everyone, even animals. It hurts just being around it."

Will stared at the light in the distance. "There were thousands of animals running for their lives. There were even bugs in the stampede! They didn't do that when he first showed up."

Gladys frowned. "It must not have been bad enough by the city to scare them away."

"What he did back at the city was more than we could handle. We're in big trouble if he's doing something even worse than that." Will looked again at the twinkling light on top of the cliff. He couldn't be sure, but whatever the animals were running from was in the same general direction as the light. He quickly assembled a scarecrow and pointed it at the light. "Gladys, can you get a picture of the light over there?

"Working on it," she said. Gladys disappeared from the surface of the mirror and was replaced by a blurry image of the light. She zoomed in and improved the picture until they could see a man standing on top of the cliff. The man wore a black robe and was holding a glowing staff.

"Ah nuts, it's Evander." Will kicked dirt onto the fire.

"Why are you putting out the fire?" Mr. Niff asked.

Will pointed at the distant light. "If we can see the light he's making, then he could have seen the fire I made with my scepter. If he comes after us and we don't have the bottle, we'll last as long as a candy bar in a room full of third graders! Take down the tent and pack up. We have to move to another camp site and fast."

Will woke up the next morning groggy and achy. He and his friends had moved their camp late last night and set it up again two miles away from the grove of trees. Will had stumbled a few times in the dark and tripped on a tree root. After wandering around in the dark for an hour, they'd made their camp in a patch of blueberry bushes that had been harvested long ago.

Will opened the tent flaps and walked outside. London and Brooklyn were already gone while the goblins remained asleep. He decided to let them rest and go have breakfast.

It was a nice morning, cool but sunny. The trees were beginning to change to autumn colors, with patches of red, yellow and orange in the foliage. But the land was deathly silent except for the sound of the wind blowing through the leaves. No birds sang or bees buzzed after last night's exodus of animal life.

"That's another thing I owe Evander for," Will grumbled. He dug through the mound of supplies and took out two hardtack biscuits for breakfast. "I like having birds around."

Back inside the tent, Domo woke up and roused Mr. Niff and Vial. They crawled out and sat down by the tent flaps. Domo yawned and said, "Morning, Will."

"Good morning, and welcome to another glorious day of trying not to die," he said with false cheer. In a more normal tone, he asked, "Do you know where London and Brooklyn went? They were gone when I woke up."

Vial wiped his glasses off on his lab coat. "Last night they said they were going to go foraging. I believe they are worried we might run out of food while exploring the wastelands. They hope to extend our rations with nuts and berries."

"Good thinking," Will said as he tried to take a bite out of the biscuit...tried and failed. His teeth barely scratched the tasteless biscuit that was, in theory, food. "Man these biscuits are hard."

"Hence the name hardtack," Domo said. "I've heard stories of hardtack staying edible thirty years after it was baked."

Will kept gnawing on the biscuit. "I can see why they don't spoil. Rocks are easier to chew."

"Probably taste better, too," Mr. Niff said. "I'm surprised people don't use hardtack for bricks or slingshot ammo."

The goblins also had their breakfast, eating what only they could consider food. They munched on worn out shoes and ripped couch cushions, deer antlers and bits of paper. Will had seen them eat many times before, but it never failed to amaze him what they could get nourishment out of. "I know you guys can eat that, but wouldn't you rather have something better?"

Vial held up the antler and said, "This is a good source of calcium."

Domo chuckled and added, “You’re one to talk. I’m not sure I’d call that stuff you’re eating food.”

“Don’t worry, we’re happy with what we have,” Mr. Niff said cheerfully. He paused and eyed Will’s baggage. “Unless you have cheese.”

“Sorry, no luck,” Will told them.

Mr. Niff leaned forward. “You’re sure? We’re not picky. Cheddar, Munster, Swiss, it’s all good.”

“He doesn’t have any cheese,” Domo said. “I checked his bags last night.”

“What about his pockets?” Vial asked.

“Guys, I’m very sure I don’t have any cheese,” Will told them. He was going to say more when he heard a soft rustling behind him. Before he could turn around, a shadow fell over him and he felt something long, hard and sharp press against the back of his neck. “I do, however, have a sword at my neck.”

Chapter Seven

"Oh joy, more treasure hunters," Will said sarcastically. He'd kick himself if there weren't a sword at his neck! He hadn't been worried about being attacked by skeletons during the night. Between the noise they made searching for the Bottle of Hope and the pain they caused just by being around, he'd have plenty of warning if they came and have a good chance to avoid them. Unfortunately people could be a lot sneakier. Will had assumed the skeleton invasion and last night's stampede drove off all the treasure hunters, but obviously a few were still around. Now one of them had got the drop on him. He should have posted guards during the night.

"Don't compare us to those thugs," a gruff voice behind Will said. He sounded like an older man. Will couldn't see him, but two other men wearing chain armor and armed with swords came into view. The two swordsmen held their swords high over the goblins. "Keep your hands where I can see them. Prince, the area is secured."

A boy no older than twelve walked into the camp. He wore chain armor and held a sword that was too big for him. The boy had dusty blond hair and looked worried. "S-state your name and position," he stuttered.

"You're in charge of this lot?" Will asked in disbelief. The boy blushed and looked down. "You're not even old enough to shave and you're threatening my life. I know people complain about kids these days, but come on!"

"Watch your tongue!" the man behind Will snapped. "The Prince is of royal blood. You'll show respect or you'll pay dearly."

"Oh, he's royalty, well that makes everything better," Will quipped. "I'd hate to have a commoner threaten to take my head off. What would people think?"

Will yelped as the sword scratched his skin. He wasn't bleeding, but the message was clear that his situation could get worse in a hurry. The gruff man behind Will said, "The Prince asked for your name."

"Put the swords away and we'll talk," Will replied.

"Not a chance," the man behind him said.

One of the swordsmen looked in the tent. "There's a magic mirror. They must be using it to find the Bottle of Hope."

The boy's eyes lit up. "Do you know where it is? Please, tell me!"

"Prince, we'll handle this," the man behind Will said. "You're traveling with three goblins, stranger. You'd only need one for a guide, and none of them are tied up. That means they don't want to escape. What power do you have over them?"

Will looked around for a scarecrow, but there weren't any. Barring a hasty escape, his best bet was to stall for time until the trolls returned. "There was a sale on goblins at the store, buy one get two free. They're cheap and easy to feed. You'd be surprised how useful they are."

"We're the perfect pet," Mr. Niff said cheerfully. "We can set traps, scout tunnels and distract enemies. And if you want your in-laws to leave, just give us five minutes alone with them and they'd rather chew off their own feet than visit you!"

The boy, the one they called a prince, ran his fingers over the mirror's frame. The surface of the magic mirror was blank, which meant Gladys was either sleeping or playing possum. "It's much fancier than the one we have at the castle. You saw the bottle with this?"

"Prince, please," the man behind Will said. "Your name, stranger. I won't ask again."

Will heard a birdcall in the distance. Since all the birds had left last night, the sound came from either the trolls trying to contact him or someone with these sword-wielding idiots. None of the men reacted to the sound, so Will figured it was the trolls coming to the rescue. He had to keep the men's attention focused on him.

"You want a name? I'm William Bradshaw, and I'm King of the Goblins. The last man to point a sword at me lived to regret it, and so did his people. You know what you're going to do? You're going to put that sword away, you're going to apologize for threatening me and then you're going to leave my kingdom."

The boy's face paled on hearing this news. The two swordsmen Will could see looked at him curiously, not in the least bit scared. Perhaps they didn't believe him or hadn't heard of him. More worrisome, they might believe him but be so confident of their skills that they weren't scared.

"You're not in a position to give orders," the man behind Will said.

There was another birdcall much closer than the last one. Will smiled. "Would you care to place a wager on that?"

"Got you!" London yelled. The man behind Will screamed as London picked him up and threw him into a tree. Brooklyn grabbed another swordsman and threw him into the first one, still on the ground. The last swordsman had only enough time to look shocked before Vial tossed a bomb at his feet. The explosion knocked him on his back. He tried to get up, but the goblins piled on him and held him down. The prince went for his sword, only to have Gladys kick him in the shin with the mirror's bronze eagle feet. The boy yelped and bent over to grab his shin. Gladys kicked him in the butt and tipped him over.

Will grabbed his scepter and pointed it at the men. They froze when they saw the weapon. The man who'd had his sword at Will's throat, an older fellow with scars across his face and armed like the other two, held up his hands. "Hold your fire!"

Will got to his feet and rubbed his neck where the sword had scratched his skin. "I'm trying to come up with reasons why I should, and you know what? I'm drawing a blank. How about you, Niff?"

Mr. Niff took the older man's sword. "I got nothing."

London threw the three swordsmen and boy together. "No good troublemakers coming in here and pushing people around. That's our job!"

Brooklyn slapped a swordsman in the back of the head. "Lousy scabs taking work from honest trolls."

The boy got up with tears running from his eyes. "Wait! I'm sorry."

"Prince!" the older man shouted. "If he is who he claims to be, then he's not a real king. He was given the position by lawyers."

The boy ignored him. "We, we should have approached your camp and asked for help. We're visitors in your kingdom and we haven't acted as we should. Please forgive us."

Will lowered his scepter but held onto it. "That's a good start. You're not the first person to attack me this week, and I'm getting sick of it. Pick up your things and leave the kingdom."

"We can't!" the boy cried. "Please, as one leader to another, I beg you to overlook our poor behavior and allow us to stay. We need the Bottle of Hope, badly! I, I fear in our desperation we did not act properly."

"You're royalty?" Will asked the boy.

"Prince Alexander Trecka at your service," the boy said. "I am no king, but if I fail in my mission I will be! My father, King Ethan, is gravely ill. The healers can do nothing but ease his pain. They say it is a matter of months until he passes. Most of his retainers offer condolences, but they whisper plans of what they will do when he dies."

"Politics," Will spat. "It's ugly wherever you go."

"Amen to that," the older swordsman said.

Will tapped the scepter against his palm. "That doesn't excuse you putting a sword to my neck."

Prince Alexander looked down. "I know. It's just that we've been looking for the bottle for days and haven't found a trace of it. We can't get a goblin to lead us to it. There are either none to be found or angry hordes of them too big to deal with. When we saw you camped with several goblins, we hoped they might know where the Bottle of Hope is hidden. I know we did wrong by threatening you, but there's so much at stake if my men and I fail."

"How did you even know to come here?" Domo asked.

"A fortuneteller told me the bottle was here," Alexander replied.

Will rubbed his eyes. "Let me guess, she was a young lady with a gray dress and wearing a blindfold."

The Prince took a step closer to Will. Excited, he asked, "You know of her?"

Will frowned. It looked like Helena had sold that bit of information to *a lot* of people. "We've met."

"She told me about the Bottle of Hope and where to find it," the boy continued. "One drop of its water can heal anyone. She charged a lot, but it's worth it if I can save my father. I told my father's retainers and noblemen about it, but they wouldn't even try to find it! They said it was too far away to reach in time, or that the fortuneteller was a fraud. In the end I found a few men who loved my father as I did and went to search for the bottle."

"Anybody know about this King and Prince?" Will asked his followers.

"King Ethan's not a bad sort," Domo said. "He doesn't start wars or tax his people into poverty. Compared to most of the clowns in charge these days he's okay."

"He doesn't have anti-goblin laws," Mr. Niff volunteered, "and given all the things we do he probably should."

"Do you have the Bottle of Hope?" Prince Alexander asked desperately. Now that Will had a chance to take a good look at him, he didn't look like a prince. He looked like a scared boy who was losing his dad. "This, it's the only chance my father has. I beg you, let me use it for just one day, just a drop, and by all that's holy I swear I'll return it to you or die trying."

Will put his scepter away. He kneeled down next to the boy. "I'm sorry, I don't have it. I'm looking for it myself. I don't know exactly where it is except it's somewhere north of here in the wastelands. That's where I'm going now."

"Then we must go there, too," the Prince said. "Thank you, sir."

"That's not a good idea," Will told him. "You saw the stampede last night?"

The Prince pointed south. "Our horses ran off when it happened. I sent a man to find them."

"The animals ran off because of a necromancer named Evander Hollow. He has an army of skeletons, and he's got the Staff of Skulls," Will explained. The men with Prince Alexander gasped in horror. "He's still in the kingdom looking for the bottle. I fought him once and I had a lot more people than you do. It wasn't even a close fight. He walked all over us. It's too dangerous for you to go after the bottle. Please, go to Ket Kingdom. There are towns near the border you can stay in. When I get the bottle I'll bring it to you. I swear, one leader to another."

The Prince looked into his eyes. "If it was your father on his sick bed, would you stop?"

"No," Will admitted.

"You've treated me better than I deserved after what happened," Prince Alexander said. "But this is my father's only chance. For his sake and for the kingdom, I have to find the bottle. With a necromancer out there armed with the Staff of Skulls, no one can say if either of us will survive. If I may ask a favor, should I fall in battle and you do not, will you bring the bottle to my father for me?"

"I can, but it's still not a good idea for you to stay," Will said.

"None of the choices left to me are good," Alexander replied. He saluted Will and left with his men.

Will watched them head north through the woods. "There goes one more reason why we have to find the bottle. Come on, guys, let's pack up and move on."

Dozens of skeletal animals milled around the base of the cliff while their creator Evander Hollow used the Staff of Skulls. The human skull on the end of the staff was brightly lit as power flowed through it. A cloud of pixies flew around Evander, giggling and squealing at the prospect of causing destruction. There was just over a thousand of the tiny winged creatures circling the necromancer, their faces twisted in evil smiles.

A skeletal wolf walked over to a skeletal bear. "He's been at it all yesterday and most of today, and that's all he's got to show for it?"

The bear nodded. "There should be a hundred times that many pixies. The stinking goblins must have cleared the place out."

"That'd be my guess," the wolf agreed. "At least he's been too busy to make us dig up the place. I hate doing that!"

"Tell me about it." The bear glanced at the pits they'd dug and trees they'd uprooted. "We dug everywhere he told us to and came up with nothing."

The wolf snorted. "I'm made from the bones of a wolf, not a gopher! When he said this was so important I thought we'd be ravaging the countryside, or at least pushing people around."

More skeletal animals wandered over, all of them grumbling. One of them said, "Nobody lives around here for us to attack. I haven't seen a single house we could set fire to all day. What's the point of being a force for pure evil when you never *do* anything?"

"Somebody should talk to him," the skeletal wolf said.

The bear shrugged. "I tried. He wouldn't listen. Then Larry tried."

"And?"

The bear pointed to a blackened patch of ground littered with bone fragments. The wolf shuddered. "Ouch. He's in one of *those* moods again."

"There better be a big payoff for all this work," a skeletal boar said. "I know he created us, but that only goes so far."

Evander finished his spell and the Staff of Skulls stopped glowing. He created another black magic cloud and floated down to the skeletons below. The pixies followed him and flew just over his head. "I have summoned more pixies to make good our losses. Gather bones so I can create more of your kind."

"Make good our losses?" the wolf asked. "What losses? How many guys did we lose?"

"Larry, for one," the bear grumbled.

Ignoring the bear, Evander said, "Some of you were lost at the Goblin City. Others were lost in subsequent battles. We have enough pixies to not only replace our losses but to enlarge our army until none can defeat it."

A skeletal mountain lion raised a paw. "Uh, excuse me? Hi, uh, I'm Bob. I've been with you for a while. Anyway, um, these losses you're talking about? I'm kind of worried about that. If there's somebody out there destroying us then shouldn't we hunt them down and take them out?"

Other skeletons chorused their agreement. Evander scowled. "The losses are negligible."

"Well, yeah, to you they are," the mountain lion said. "You're not one of them. All I'm saying is if we're losing guys then it's going to be harder for us to find the bottle. Am I right? So we should do something about the people destroying us."

"You dare question me?" Evander shouted. "I created you!"

"And we're grateful for that," the mountain lion said hastily. "We're just a bit worried. We're fighting goblins! We shouldn't be taking any losses."

Evander bared his teeth. "The staff has come up with a plan to destroy the Bottle of Hope. Once we've completed the plan we will forevermore be free of the bottle and can continue with our grand mission. That plan requires sacrifices."

"And we're the ones making them," the bear grumbled.

The skeletal mountain lion raised a paw again. "We're all excited to hear you've got a plan. Yes sir, very excited. And, um, we're keen on hearing this plan. Specifically, we'd like to hear the part that covers how many more of us are going to be sacrificed."

Evander raised the Staff of Skulls. Black bolts of lightning shot from it and struck the mountain lion, blasting it into powder and bone shards. The other skeletons backed away from Evander.

"Are there any more questions?" he asked. The crowd remained silent and Evander lowered the staff. "No? Good. You have your orders."

"Are we there yet?" Will asked as they marched through the woods.

"No," Domo told him.

"Are we there yet?"

"No."

"Are we—"

"I'll tell you when we're there!" Domo shouted. "Good gravy, my own kind is annoying enough, but I thought humans were made of sterner stuff. Honestly, one man threatens your life and you get all whiney."

Will rubbed his neck. "Easy for you to say. You weren't the one who was going to lose his head."

"We're still miles from the wastelands," Domo told him. "Be grateful, because you're going to regret leaving this place."

"Good food here," London said. He and his brother had found a rich supply of berries, nuts, mushrooms and edible roots. They'd also found a beehive and raided it for honey. The bees had fled in last night's stampede of animal life, so getting the honey was easy.

"Enjoy it, because once we reach the wastelands there isn't going to be anything to eat," Domo said. "I went there once to hide after the goblin accident insurance scam blew up in our faces. I had to come back when I didn't find any food, water or shelter."

"Accident insurance?" Will asked, not even trying to keep the disbelief from his voice. "What man in his right mind would buy insurance from goblins?"

"Quite a few people did, actually," Vial said. "An individual would buy a policy for someone they didn't like, and goblins would *ensure* the policy holder had lots of accidents, most of them pie related. Naturally there were complaints and the occasional torch-wielding mob, so the business venture was forced into bankruptcy. It's shameful how many roadblocks there are for the aspiring businessman."

Trying to steer the conversation back to something relevant, Will asked, "How big is the wastelands?"

Gladys filed her nails in the surface of the magic mirror. London was carrying her again since she couldn't walk fast enough to keep up with them. "It covers a quarter of the kingdom."

"That's a lot of ground to explore. Can you see anything in there?" Will asked.

Gladys snorted. "Not a chance. There are a couple scarecrows placed around the edges of the wastelands, but none inside. The goblins can't go far in without food, and there's no place to plant scarecrows since the ground is all rock."

"So we wander around aimlessly looking for the bottle until our food runs out? We need a better plan than that," Will said.

"Look, I've got a general idea where it is," Gladys said. "There's an old refinery in the middle of the wastelands. That's where I felt the bottle the strongest. It's within five miles of that spot, maybe closer."

Will swung his scepter like a golf club as he thought. "Are there any skeletons by the refinery?"

Gladys faded from the mirror and she checked the scarecrows near the wastelands. "It's clear as far as I can tell. The necromancer may have dumped some at the far edge or in the middle where I can't see them, so I can't guarantee anything."

Will stepped over a fallen tree and his foot came down on cobblestones. Surprised, he looked around and saw a road going north. Tree roots pushing the cobblestones up had broken parts of the road. Other sections were covered with a layer of dirt and rotting leaves deep enough to support a thick carpet of grass.

"I didn't know there were roads in the kingdom. Where does it lead?" Will asked.

Domo tapped the cobblestones with his walking stick. "This is the road from the refinery to the city. The dwarfs made it to carry iron to market."

Will scratched his head. "If it's supposed to go to the city then why does it stop here?"

Mr. Niff smiled. "We needed bricks back when King Horace the Confused asked us to build the maze. Builder goblins tore up the road and carried off the cobblestones for building materials. I'm surprised there's any of it left."

"But wasn't the road more useful as a road than as bricks?" Will asked.

Vial smiled. "My Liege, consider where the road leads."

"Ah," Will said. "Yeah, I guess there's no need for a road going nowhere. Well, today it's got a purpose again. Come on, guys, we've got a clear path where we're going."

Mr. Niff pried up a brick and smiled. "I've got to tell the builders about this when we get back. They'll be so happy there are more bricks to salvage."

They traveled on the road for hours, passing many signs of battle. There were uprooted trees and pits dug by the skeletons in their search for the Bottle of Hope. They also came across pieces of smashed bones where goblins or treasure hunters had clashed with the skeletons. It looked like Evander's army had already lost a lot of its strength.

Scattered across the landscape were ruins left by the dwarfs long ago. Along the road were abandoned inns, tollbooths and the occasional brick house. They'd either fallen into rubble or been occupied by goblins. The goblin owners were long gone, having either fled for their lives or joined the fight against the skeletons. The inhabitants had left their mark with graffiti, including the messages, *'A home just isn't a home without a small green frog (paid for by Small Green Frog Industries)'*, and *'Hunting is the world's oldest profession, and don't let anyone tell you otherwise!'*

"How many dwarfs used to live here?" Will asked.

"Thousands," Domo said. "They had thousands of human workers, too. I hear this place was as busy as a beehive back when the dwarfs were in charge. It was also dirty, smelly and dangerous."

"So not much has changed since you guys took over," Will said.

Domo pointed his walking stick at Will. "Hey, the dirty and smelly part is justified, but if things are dangerous around here it's because people come in and cause trouble. When the dwarfs were in charge, the mines and refinery were the threats. A lot of people never made it out of there."

"Dangerous work, mining," London said. "Not if you do it right, but dwarfs don't do it right."

Surprised, Will said, "I always heard dwarfs were good miners."

"A long time ago they were, before the dwarfs went corporate," Gladys told him. "Nowadays it's all about meeting monthly profit reports. They don't bother with anything that costs money, including safety equipment. They turn out good quality work at low prices, but it costs a lot more than money if you know what I mean."

"They aren't any easier on the land than they are on the people," Domo said. "They created the wastelands by pouring slag on the ground, and when there wasn't any more iron ore left they just walked away and left it. The dwarfs didn't care if they ruined the land forever, and no one was around to make them care."

Will frowned. "This sounds so much like home."

There was a crash ahead of them as a man with silver hair and dressed in black burst through a dense clump of bushes. He fell onto the road, and Will rushed over to help him up.

Sweaty and out of breath, the man gasped, "Thank you. You are a credit to the lesser races."

Will recognized the voice. "Thistle? Thistle the elf?"

It was the elf treasure hunter, all right. The elf was doubled over and gasping for air. Sweat dripped off his face and plastered his clothes to his body. Thistle held both his swords, and they had fresh scratches. The elf smiled at Will. "Yes, I think we met a few days earlier. Bradshaw, wasn't it?"

Will put his arms around the elf and helped him stand. "Yeah. What's wrong? You look like something the cat dragged in."

Thistle looked behind him before directing his attention back at Will and his friends. "An inelegant comparison, but sadly close to the truth. There are one, two, three, four, five, six of you. That should be enough."

"Seven," Gladys corrected him.

Thistle looked north again. "Sadly, in this circumstance you don't count."

"What did you mean we should be enough?" Will asked. Before the elf could answer, Will winced as a terrible headache hit him and the others. The sudden pain could only have one cause. "There are skeletons nearby. Ah, this hurts a lot!"

Thistle nodded. "You are correct, and I'm sorry to say there are quite a few of them. They are a determined lot and have been after me like a dwarf chasing gold."

"You led them to us!" Brooklyn accused him.

"Not intentionally, I assure you," Thistle said quickly. "However, since we've had the good fortune to meet like this, I would like to say how much I appreciate your help. When I have the Bottle of Hope and become a king, I shall reward you properly."

With that, Thistle ran south down the road as fast as he could. London shook his fist at the elf and shouted, "You no good, pointy eared, cowardly so and so!"

"Try to hold them for five minutes!" Thistle shouted back. "There's a good fellow!"

A chorus of roars and hisses came from the north as a band of skeletons tore through the bushes and ran onto the road. They were a mixed bunch, but the ones in the lead were made from the bones of mountain lions. The skeletons immediately spotted Will and his friends, and howled as they charged.

"Get behind me," Will said and he took out his scepter. The skeletons raced toward them and lunged for Will as he turned the scepter on. FOOM! The skeletons were burned to ashes and the road was cleared of brush.

"Well, that's a few less to deal with," Will said. But something was wrong. His head still hurt terribly and he rubbed his temples. "There are more around here somewhere, I can feel it."

"Boss, look out!" Mr. Niff shouted.

A skeletal bear broke through the brush much closer to Will than the mountain lions. It caught Will's scepter in its jaws and tore it from his hand, then tossed it into the bushes with a twist of its head. Worse, there were another twenty skeletons behind it. This second group ran onto the road and attacked.

London and Brooklyn slowed the charge down and battered the first few skeletons to bits, while Vial blew up another with a bomb. Mr.

Niff pulled a brick loose from the road and smashed a skeleton with it. Will and Domo struggled with a skeletal stag that was trying to trample them. The skeletons surrounded them, taking losses with each step but not giving up. The skeletal bear reared up and tried to maul Domo. Will grabbed Domo and pulled him back, only to have the bear rush into him and knock them back.

Still holding onto Domo, Will saw the bear rearing up again. There was a scarecrow just off the road, originally hidden by brush he'd burned with his scepter. Will focused on it and fell over backwards.

Whoosh. Will vanished and reappeared where the scarecrow had been. To his surprise, he saw that he'd brought Domo with him. Will set the goblin down and scrambled for his scepter. The bear tore through the empty clothes and king contract left behind when Will vanished. Angry, it looked around and spotted Will. It charged again, and both Will and Domo ran for their lives. The bear bowled them over and opened its jaws to attack just as Will's king contract reappeared intact and drifted to the ground.

And then the bear stopped. The bright red light in its eye sockets dimmed and the skeletal bear backed away and stood up. It either didn't notice or didn't care that the other skeletons were destroyed. Instead it looked at Will and began to speak in a rasping voice.

"You know, suddenly it occurs to me that this is rather pointless. I mean, me being here, fighting you, what's it all for? What am I really getting from it?"

Will stared at the skeleton in disbelief. He had both arms covering his face, prepared for a bite that could've killed him, and now the bear was just talking. Everyone stared at it.

Undeterred by the lack of response, the skeletal bear went on. "I thought I'd hit the big times when I was a pixie and Evander summoned me and merged me with these bones. Look at these teeth! No more being a little annoyance, I was able to do real damage! Then what happens? He orders me and the other skeletons to bury ourselves in a swamp and wait for orders. We wait and wait until finally he told us to come out for a grand final battle."

Will got up and helped Domo to his feet. They dusted themselves off and Will straightened his cape.

"But here we are, and look at it," the bear continued. "You call this a grand final battle? Good grief, we're digging holes in the ground! I should be terrorizing villages or destroying castles. Here I am, a force for pure evil in the world, and what am I doing? Digging holes! What's the point? It's not like I'm getting paid for this, or stealing loot or earning the respect of other dastardly evil beings. Chasing that elf was the highpoint of my life, and if that's not sad I don't know what is."

Will and Domo searched the ground for Will's fire scepter as the bear continued its lament. "I just don't feel I'm being properly utilized. I'm not reaching my full potential as an evil being. Does my creator care? No! He won't even listen to us. It's all 'obey my will', 'I created you', and 'I hold the Staff of Skulls'. The man is totally inflexible. What's the point of making an army of unspeakable abominations that are a blight on all creation if you never *do* anything with it?"

Domo found the scepter and handed it back to Will. The scepter hummed, glad to be back with its master. Will turned it over in his hands and looked for signs of damage. It seemed to be okay.

The bear looked at Will and said. "Bottom line, I just don't feel Evander respects me as an individual. Maybe the other skeletons and I should form a union, or a cooperative. You know, organize so he has to let us devastate villages and spread fear and chaos across the land. What do you think?"

Will pointed his scepter at the bear. "You know, you had me right up to devastate."

FOOM!

"Does someone want to tell me what that was about?" Will asked as the ashes settled. With the last skeleton destroyed his headache quickly faded and he could think clearly. The others looked relieved as well. "That thing went from rampaging monster to needing therapy in the blink of an eye."

Domo stared at the ash pile. "Something's very wrong here. It should have torn us apart. I'm not complaining, mind you, but they don't do that. Ever."

"And how did you take Domo with you when you warped to the scarecrow?" Mr. Niff asked.

Will shrugged. "I don't know."

"None of our other kings could do that," Domo said.

"None of them tried," Brooklyn pointed out.

Will held up his scepter. "Well, I bring the scepter with me when I switch places with a scarecrow. Why can't I take someone along for the ride?"

"No one has ever performed experiments on the King's abilities before," Vial pointed out. "You could have other abilities we are unaware of. We shall have to run tests when we get back. Oh this will be a learning experience!"

Will picked up his contract and tucked it in his belt. "We can ask questions when things quiet down. Come on, let's go find the bottle."

Chapter Eight

With the battle over, Will led his friends through the wilderness of the Kingdom of the Goblins. Signs of civilization (or what passed for it around here) were few and far between. There were some poorly built huts scattered about and the occasional cave dug into a hillside, but they saw little else among the trees. Of course goblins were experts at hiding, and given time they could conceal something even as large as a building. They could easily be walking through communities of goblins hundreds strong without realizing it.

One thing Will *was* certain of was that the goblins had done an exceptional job hiding their traps, and those traps were proving as dangerous to Evander's forces as the goblins themselves. They'd already come across five skeletons that had disarmed traps the hard way, including a skeletal bull that had fallen into a deep pit and had five hundred pounds of canned pinto beans fall on it with bone crushing results. Will wondered briefly where the goblins had gotten canned beans, eventually deciding that he didn't want to know. They stopped briefly by a snare that had caught a skeletal wolf and swung it against a large oak tree. Will whistled as he studied the broken bones scattered across the ground.

"You know, before today I would have never thought so, but I'm getting to be a real fan of the traps you guys make," Will told the goblins. "I'd be a bigger fan if you only set them during wars."

"Be fair, boss, how often does that happen?" Mr. Niff asked. He frowned and said, "I mean, before you showed up, because since then we've had two invasions in five months."

"Kervol's invasion was my fault, sort of," Will admitted, "but I'm taking *no* responsibility for this one."

"The traps are doing the job, all right," London said as he inspected the shattered bones. "Roughed him up real good."

"Yeah, they've got to be taking a toll on those walking bone piles," Domo added. "I bet Evander is losing ten guys every day he's here."

Will spotted another pile of broken bones near the oak tree. Picking through them, he said, "Hold on, the snare didn't destroy these ones. These bones look like they were cut."

Brooklyn waved his hand at the top of the tree. "I bet that guy did it."

Startled, Will backed away from the tree and looked up. High above his head was a tall, irritable looking man dressed in chain armor and carrying a backpack. He was sitting on a thick branch and looking down at them.

"Thanks a lot!" the man snapped. "Here I go and find a place where those boneheads either can't find me or can't reach me, and you go and blow my cover."

"Who are you?" Will asked.

"What are you doing up a tree?" London demanded.

"Do you have any cheese?" Mr. Niff asked.

The man answered, "Toby Mulward, hiding and no. I'm a procurement specialist for the Vastan Institute of Magic and Technology."

Will scratched his head. "Procure as in you buy, find or steal things for them?"

"There's a little bit of a) and a little of b), and I'd rather not talk about c)," Toby admitted. He put a hand above his eyes to shield him from the sun and looked around. "My boss sent me to bring back the Bottle of Hope, but, ah, there were some complications. Nothing's gone right since I came here."

"That's the story of my life," Will said. "I take it the skeletons chased you up a tree, but you can come down now. The coast is clear."

"So the entire kingdom isn't overrun with nightmarish monsters made of bones?" Toby asked.

"Sorry, that's still going on," Will replied.

"Then if it's all the same to you, I'd kind of like to stay here for a while longer," he said. He held up a sword with a blade snapped off just above the handle.

"That's going to cost a bundle to fix," Mr. Niff said.

"I'm less worried about the repair bill than being caught by those monsters unarmed and in the open," Toby said. "The skeletons I've seen are four legged, so they're none too good at climbing. I've got food and water to last me a couple days, so I'm safe up here until they move on or someone drives them off. It would be a different story if there were skeletal gorillas or snakes."

"You could come with us," Will offered. "We're trying to get rid of the skeletons."

Toby stared at Will in disbelief. "Yeah, uh, no thanks. I think I'd be happier where I am. Good luck trying not to get killed."

"Suit yourself," Will said. He led his friends on their way, and asked Domo, "Skeletal gorillas?"

Domo shrugged. "It happens."

"So there are fifty super powerful magic weapons out there somewhere in the world?" Will asked as they continued through the woods.

"Yeah, more of less," Domo answered. "There are lots of minor magic items like your scepter and Gladys, but every so often a wizard or holy man makes one of the big ones like the Bottle of Hope or the Staff of Skulls. It's been a hundred years since someone did that, but not for a lack of trying."

"I don't suppose there's another one of them nearby we could borrow?" Will asked. "I'd like any advantage I can get my hands on in case we go toe to toe with Evander again."

"Ha!" Gladys laughed. "There isn't another one within five hundred miles, and even if there was the owner wouldn't let you get close enough to see it. Magic that strong is a prized possession of kings, wizards and holy men. So far no lawyers have gotten their hands on one, which everyone agrees is a good thing. Given how many people have tried to find the Bottle of Hope over the years, I'm surprised it's here. Be glad you have even one of the big fifty to work with."

"And be very glad it's the bottle and not one of the other ones," Domo added. "The Bottle of Hope is pretty easy going, but using one of the others could cost you a lot."

"What do you mean cost me?" Will asked. He thought back to what he'd learned about the Staff of Skulls. Worried, he asked, "You mean those things can mess with your head like the staff is doing to Evander?"

"Some of them do that," Gladys replied. "Others, like Obed's Drum, are choosy about their owners and only let one person use them. You couldn't use most of them even if you had them. Some of the big fifty are missing and haven't been seen in years."

Vial raised a hand and said, "The location of Sarcamusaad the Walking City has been unknown ever since he marched into the sea a century ago. That's likely for the best given how grumpy he is."

Mr. Niff nodded. "Yeah, if he showed up then everybody would run and hide. Of course when we run we're called cowards, but when men and elves do it, it's a tactical withdraw. Words are funny things."

Will scratched his head. "If some of these magic items are lost then why are they on the list? For all we know they could be broken, or maybe they're not even on this world anymore."

Domo chuckled. "Yeah, it's a flawed system. The list of the fifty most powerful magic items is drawn up by the Grand Conclave of Wizards and the Archivists, two powerful organizations with a lot of magic and even more clout." Domo leaned in close to Will and said, "There's a lot of political interference when they make the list."

"It's a fair list," Gladys retorted.

Mr. Niff smiled and said, "I don't know. I hear there are bribes involved."

Domo nodded to Mr. Niff. "Everybody wants the bragging rights of having one of the big fifty. The riffraff leaves you alone and the neighbors don't dump their trash in your yard if you have a magic super weapon, or what you *say* is a magic super weapon."

Will laughed. "There are fake super weapons?"

"You bet," Domo told him. "Oh sure, the Archivists have the Instant Doom of Kilmith, and it could blow up the world, but they're missing three parts and the instruction manual. That thing is a forty-ton paperweight."

London said, "The dwarfs are real proud that they have the magic hammer Mountain Shaker, but they can't use it."

"The last dwarf king won't let go of it, and he's been dead fifteen hundred years," Brooklyn added. "They've got the hammer, but it might as well be gone."

Confused, Will asked, "But if people know you have something that powerful, what's to keep them from stealing it from you?"

"Common sense," Domo replied.

Gladys offered a more complete answer. "A person armed with one of the fifty most powerful magic items is a force to be reckoned with. They'd make dog meat out of anyone weaker than an army who tried to rob them. And many of the big fifty are particular about their owners, which makes robbing them a bad bet. A king once tried to take Obed's Drum from its owner. He got one hand on it before it retaliated. I hear the king healed up, eventually."

"But the Bottle of Hope isn't going to do anything like that, right?" Will asked.

"The bottle is the most peaceful of the big fifty," Gladys told him. "It's had a lot of owners over the years, and never hurt them or messed with their heads. But it is picky about who gets to use it. I can't find an example when an evil person held the bottle for long. It was always empty the few times they got their hands on it, and someone else always took it from them inside of a day."

Will stepped around a large rock on the trail and asked, "So which of the fifty is the most powerful?"

"That depends on what you're trying to do and the cost you're willing to pay," Domo said. "If you want to blow stuff up and drop property values like a rock, then you'd need the Staff of Skulls, Obed's Drum, Sarcamusaad the Walking City or Mountain Shaker."

Will frowned. "That doesn't help much when two of them are unusable, one is lost and the last one is trying to kill us."

Domo tapped his walking stick against Will's leg. "I'm not done. If you're trying to help people then you can't go wrong with the Bottle of Hope. If you want to rule a kingdom you need the sword Ennobled Truth. Each one has a thing they're best at without much crossover. Most of the time it's easier and faster to do something yourself than to get one of the big fifty to do it for you, but this isn't one of those times."

Domo walked on quietly for a while before he spoke again. "The truth is, we're in dangerous territory. The big fifty are powerhouses capable of amazing things. You have to be careful how you use even the ones that play nice. You don't want two of them near each other, especially if they're feuding. The power they unleash could be disastrous. We might not have a kingdom when this is over."

Will considered Domo's advice before asking, "Have any of these super weapons ever been destroyed?"

"Once," Gladys replied. The bookcase reappeared in her mirror and she selected a book. "The Dominion Crown was one of the fifty most powerful items years ago. The crown could force people of all races to obey its wearer if they were close enough to hear his commands. A warlord found it and used it to raise an army of men and monsters to conquer Other Place. A young woman named Yvette sneaked into his army under the cover of darkness and stole the crown while he slept. She realized using the crown even for a good purpose was robbing people of their free will, so she destroyed it."

Will came in closer to Gladys, "How did she do it?"

Gladys held up her hands. "Nobody knows. The warlord cornered Yvette, but she destroyed the Dominion Crown before he could kill her. They were the only witnesses. She never said how she did it, and the warlord's army turned on him when they got their free will back, so he never said anything again."

Will stopped in his tracks. "That's messy, and not nearly as helpful as I was hoping for."

"You want to bump off the Staff of Skulls?" London asked eagerly.

"It was on my mind," he admitted.

Smiling, Brooklyn slapped Will on the back, nearly knocking him over. "Talk about thinking big! The boss wants to snuff out one of the big fifty!"

Domo rolled his eyes and asked Will, "What is it with you? You ought to be glad the staff didn't squash you like a bug! Instead you're plotting to kill something that's immortal. Just when I think goblins have cornered the market on stupidity, you go and prove me wrong."

"Hey, I'm trying to look at all the angles," Will retorted and rubbed his bruised back. "Evander and the staff have beaten us at every turn. If there's a way to destroy the staff without ending up as greasy stains on the ground then I want to know about it! Yvette took down one of these weapons, so we know it can be done."

"Even if we knew how she did it, I doubt it's a one size fits all situation," Gladys told him. "The big fifty were built using different materials and different forms of magic. You can't expect what destroys one to work on the others."

Gladys grumbled. "Will, it's not a bad idea, but people who know a lot more about magic than you do have been trying to destroy the Staff of Skulls, and they've been at it for a long time. The best and brightest have come up empty handed."

"That leaves Evander as the weak link," Domo said. "Kill him and the staff is powerless until someone else picks it up."

"That's not an option," Will said fiercely. When the trolls looked likely to argue, Will said, "I know Evander has done terrible things, largely because he boasted about it, and that's revolting. But I am not going to kill the guy if there's any way to avoid it."

"A pity he doesn't feel the same," Domo replied.

Will nodded grudgingly. "Yes, he's evil, and he'd kill us if he got the chance. But that's proof we're different from him. Taking a life is something you can't undo, and it's not the answer. Gladys, Domo, you told me the Staff has lost owners before and gone on to do more harm later on."

"True enough," Domo said.

"To be accurate, *all* the staff's other owners were killed," Gladys added.

"Then killing him won't really stop the staff," Will said. "At best we'd slow it down until some moron decides he can control the staff and gets a hold of it. The Staff of Skulls is the one who's done the harm going back centuries, and if the chance comes I'd love to put an end to that. If we can't destroy it, then at least we can bury it so deep nobody ever finds it. As for Evander, he was taken over by the staff. It takes the blame for what he's done. We're going to do everything we can to save him."

"Without dying," Domo added.

"Well, obviously," Will replied. "Short term we need to keep away from Evander and the staff until we have the Bottle of Hope. After that...I'm not really sure what we're going to do. I mean, having the bottle would be nice, but not with Evander chasing after us. Anyone have a suggestion?"

Mr. Niff smiled and jumped up and down. "Give it to King Kervol! Let Evander mess up his kingdom instead of ours."

"I don't like Kervol, but I don't want him dead," Will replied.

"Kervol's got good archers," London said. "I bet one of them could put an arrow in Evander, no problem at all."

"Then we wouldn't get to rough up that no good necromancer," Brooklyn countered. "And I want to rough him up!"

Vial frowned. "That could result in Kervol gaining possession of the Staff of Skulls. I must say I find that an unpleasant thought."

"We'd still have to get it to Kervol without Evander killing us," Domo said. "That's days of walking with the necromancer, Staff of Skulls and those skeletons after us."

"We're not dumping the bottle or the staff on Kervol's lap," Will said firmly. "Keep thinking about it. We'll figure out something."

They walked on in silence for the next hour. Will spent the time deep in thought. He didn't want to kill Evander. His father once told him that murder is the last choice of a wise man and the first choice of a fool. There were too many people on both Earth and Other Place who went for their guns (or wands) when they should sit down and talk. He didn't want to be like that.

But that decision could have terrible consequences. Evander and the Staff of Skulls were evil, and powerful enough to do a lot of harm.

They could hurt people in the Kingdom of the Goblins and those living far away if he failed to stop them. Was he putting innocent lives in jeopardy by refusing to kill Evander? The dilemma left Will feeling sick to his stomach.

Will and his friends walked through the woods as night began to fall. The woods were empty of goblins, skeletons and treasure hunters alike, but there were signs of their presence. Here and there the land was dug up, with uprooted trees, torn up grasses and shallow pits dug into the soft ground. Narrow tracks from clawed feet were everywhere, proof of who was responsible for the damage.

"This doesn't make any sense," Will said as he stepped around a pit. "Evander can't hope to find the bottle by digging up every inch of the kingdom. It would take him years, maybe decades."

"I think there's something else going on," Gladys replied. "I sensed hundreds of strong magic sources when the witches helped me see. I'm sure one of them was around here."

Mr. Niff hurried over to Gladys and tugged on her bronze frame. Eagerly, he asked, "So there's good stuff we can find?"

Gladys kicked the goblin away. "Watch the hands, buddy! I don't know if there's magic here. I don't feel it anymore. We passed a few other spots where I'd felt magic. They weren't dug up, but I didn't feel magic there, either."

"Maybe Evander's boys found whatever it was and carried it off?" London suggested.

"A daunting prospect if true," Vial said. "An army of rampaging skeletons armed with powerful magic would be nearly unstoppable."

"That makes even less sense," Will replied. "Finding the Bottle of Hope in the kingdom is unlikely enough, but hundreds of magic items just showing up out of the blue? There's no way that could happen. If they were here, the goblins would have stumbled across them long ago."

"I don't have any answers," Gladys told him. "Whatever was here, it's gone now."

Will spent a moment pondering the problem, and then snapped his fingers. "Oh, oh that's clever!"

"What?" Mr. Niff asked.

"Gladys said the bottle won't let just anyone use it," Will explained. He waved a hand at the churned up ground. "What better way to keep people it doesn't like at arm's length than to lay a false trail? If there are hundreds of places that look like they might have the bottle, people who don't deserve to hold it would have to search all of them to find the real one."

Vial raised his hand and asked, "If you're correct, how do we know we're heading for the real bottle and not a false source?"

"That's a disturbing question," Will replied.

Mr. Niff smiled. "Not nearly as disturbing as what happens when fifty goblins eat baked beans. Woo boy was that nasty!"

"I know where the bottle is!" Gladys said angrily. "And Niff, if you ever remind me of that day again I'm going to stomp you flat. You idiots left our kingdom and half of Kervol's kingdom uninhabitable for days. Even I smelled it, and that shouldn't be possible!"

London nudged Will and said, "Boss, take a look over there."

Will saw what worried the troll, and it worried him, too. Not far from the ravaged land was a patch of blackened ground thirty feet across.

The plant life was dead as if scorched by a great heat, and the ground was coated in black powder that looked like coal dust. A tree at the edge of the circle of dead land had escaped with half of its branches still alive, but the other half had bark peeling off in strips and bore black, shriveled leaves.

"More of Evander's handiwork," Will said in disgust.

"He's been here all right," Domo said. He walked up to the edge of the desolate land and frowned before he bent down and picked up a blackened blade of grass. It crumbled apart in his fingers, turning into more black dust. "Kind of rough on the landscape, isn't he?"

Will walked up alongside Domo and frowned. "This is terrible. The land is just beginning to recover from what the dwarfs did to it ninety years ago, and now it's being ruined all over again. The dwarfs needed decades to wreck the place. Evander did it a lot faster. Is it going to stay like this?"

"Not forever," Gladys told him. "Toxic magic like necromancy lingers in the ground, but it breaks down in a couple months. After that plants can grow back. But you're right about how little time Evander needs to do this much damage. He couldn't have been here more than a few minutes, likely less. The longer he stays in the kingdom, the more land he'll contaminate and the longer it will take to heal."

The sun dipped down behind a hill and darkened the land. That irritated Will, as it meant they had no choice but to stop for the night. He resented any time lost in the search for the Bottle of Hope. Every hour the bottle was in the kingdom was an hour that Evander and the Staff of Skulls were here as well, and he had plenty of evidence at hand of how damaging their presence was.

But the night brought something else with it.

Will cupped his hand to his ear. “Do you hear that?”

“Hear what?” Domo asked. The others gathered around Will.

“I thought I heard people talking,” he told them.

Brooklyn stared into the dark woods and squinted. “I don’t see any lights. They’d need torches or lanterns to move around this late at night.”

“Wait,” Gladys said. “I hear it, too.”

“Where’s it coming from?” Mr. Niff asked.

Will looked around. “I can’t tell.”

The noise grew in volume, but so slowly they didn’t recognize the danger until it was too late. Seconds passed until they all heard a noise like many people talking at once so it was impossible to tell what any one voice was saying.

“It’s the staff!” Will shouted. He spun around and looked at the night sky, trying to spot Evander’s magic cloud. “Where’s Evander? Does anyone see him?”

“I don’t get it,” London rumbled. “The sky is clear. That no-good necromancer and his magic cloud are nowhere around here. Where’s the sound coming from?”

Mr. Niff drew his knife. “It’s getting louder!”

Will was beginning to panic. He didn’t know if Evander’s magic allowed him to see at night. Even if he couldn’t, the necromancer was a terrifying threat. How could Will and his friends hope to face him if they couldn’t even see him?

As the noise grew louder still, Will finally located the source. He turned to face the blackened land, his face showing disgust and surprise in equal measures. “It’s not from the Staff of Skulls. My God, the noise is coming from the ground it ruined.”

Just then the blackened land erupted into an ebony nightmare as giant black skulls reared up from the contaminated ground. Will had experience with animals from his previous jobs on Earth at a petting zoo and cleaning up road kill, and he recognized the animals these were based on. There were wide mouthed frog skulls two feet across, raven skulls three feet long, and snake skulls with fangs a foot long. The skulls spoke words that Will couldn't quite make out and had no desire to understand. Central to this writhing obscenity was a giant skull of a man, five feet across and howling as it rose from the ground.

Domo grabbed Will's leg and shouted, "Burn it!"

The crowd of skulls attacked Will and his friends with snapping, predatory jaws. Mr. Niff lashed out with his knife and hit a rat skull. His knife cut easily through the shadowy stuff, but the damage healed quickly. London and Brooklyn punched a snake skull that tried to bite them. They cracked it in half and knocked it back, but this skull also recovered. Vial tossed bombs into the giant skulls crowded together and destroyed a raven skull. None of this damage held the abomination in check, and it swelled to even greater proportions, producing yet more skulls.

Will screamed at it, a cry of rage and revulsion. He pointed his scepter at the skulls and turned it on. FOOM! The scepter rattled in Will's grip as it poured out torrents of fire. For a moment even this didn't stop the spreading darkness. It grew back quickly, replacing what the fire consumed, but the scepter belched out still more fire until the nightmare sank into the flames. The last part of it to burn was the massive human skull. It glared at Will before the flames washed over it and destroyed it entirely.

Domo tugged at his collar. "Wow, that was—"

The blackened ground stirred again. More giant skulls began to rise up, but this time all of them stared hatefully at Will.

"You got to be kidding me," Brooklyn said.

FOOM! Will unleashed the fire scepter's power yet again, keeping the fire on even longer. The contaminated ground burned and sparked as magic fought magic. There was a thunderous explosion when the necromantic magic lost, and the skulls vanished in the blast.

Will breathed hard, staring at the ground in case the black skulls returned. He wiped sweat off his brow and looked at Gladys. "I kind of wish you'd told me it could do that."

"I didn't know," she said. Gladys' mouth gaped and her eyes darted between Will and where the skulls had emerged. "I swear to God, I didn't know that could happen! None of my books said the Staff of Skulls could do that. It looked like necromantic magic, but not any kind I'd heard of. I, I think I'm going to be sick."

Staying well back, Domo pointed at the charred ground ringed with fires started by Will's scepter. "Evander was just here a little while and he made *that* happen?"

"The staff did it somehow," Will said. He held onto his scepter, worried there might be some lingering trace of the Staff of Skulls still present. "It changed the land and made it as corrupt as the staff, or it made it so it could work its magic through the land. I think it had to wait until it got dark before it could attack."

Worried, Mr. Niff asked, "Boss, what about the Goblin City?" Will looked at him, not understanding the question. Mr. Niff explained, "We've got a dead spot in front of the Goblin City from when Evander first showed up. Is the ground going to turn into skulls at night there, too?"

"I don't know," Will said.

"What about the other places Evander has been?" Domo asked. "He must have been in other kingdoms before he came here. Is all the ground he did this to going to sprout monster skulls until the bad magic breaks down?"

"Anywhere the staff goes, it blights the land and then these things can appear," Will said in shock. "If Evander and the staff stay long enough, the entire kingdom will die and those skulls can come out at night. If the staff does take over the world, it would only be a matter of time until there's nothing left but dead, haunted land."

"Spooky," Brooklyn said.

"Not wishing to make light of our latest near demise, but the possibility of such monsters being everywhere is almost unimportant," Vial said.

"Unimportant?" Domo shouted.

"If Evander brings the staff onto cropland and pastures, he can despoil them in seconds," Vial explained. "Should he do this over a prolonged period, he could leave entire kingdoms without food. We goblins can eat almost anything and wouldn't be affected, but other races would be ruined. Famine could take more lives than the staff's black lightning."

Domo stared at the ground, destroyed first by the Staff of Skulls and then by Will's fire scepter to burn out the contamination. "Whole kingdoms could end up like that. Maybe continents."

"The staff needs to destroy the bottle first," Will said. He hooked his scepter back on his belt. "Somehow the bottle is stopping it, or scaring it into putting all its effort into killing the bottle instead of ruining the planet. We need the bottle, and we need to get it to someone who can use it to stop the staff for good. Any time we waste ruins even more of the kingdom, and I am not letting that happen."

Chapter Nine

The next morning, Will woke up and climbed out of the tent. They were under an ancient oak tree and far enough off the road that no one should find them. In spite of that, Mr. Niff was awake and keeping a close eye on their surroundings. After what happened the last time Will had woken up, he'd assigned a rotating shift of guards to keep a lookout during the night.

"Morning, Niff," Will said. He was sore from yesterday's fight and the ones before that. Will rubbed his aching muscles until they stopped complaining.

Mr. Niff smiled. "Morning, boss. Breakfast is ready."

"Breakfast?" Will saw a hollowed out gourd sitting in front of the tent.

"Yeah. We drank the water in there last night so we're using it as a bowl. Anyway, the guys and I thought you were having so much trouble with those hardtack biscuits, so we tried to make them a bit more edible. London took some biscuits and ground them into powder and I went out to get food to go along with it. He mixed the powder with boiling water and I brought some berries and stuff to mix in. Sort of made porridge out of it."

Will looked into the gourd. "There are just nuts and berries here."

"It was disgusting. I mean, yeah, Domo and I ate it, but we can eat boot leather. I figured you'd be happier with this."

Will ate his food while the others got up. London looked at Will's breakfast and then glanced at Mr. Niff. "It was for his own good," Mr. Niff said.

"I understand hardtack is supposed to be fried in some kind of fat before you eat it," Vial said.

"Anything is edible if you fry it first," Domo said.

Will shrugged. "Doesn't help much since we don't have any fat. Do we have much farther to go?"

Gladys touched up her makeup in the mirror. "We should reach the edge of the wastelands in a few hours. I've been checking and I can't see anyone else around there. We'll be the first to reach the Bottle of Hope unless something changes."

"Then we'll have a chance against Evander," Will said. "Is there someone around here we can take it to that could fight Evander for us, a king or someone who could face him and win? After what Evander did to us last time, I'd kind of like to let someone who knows what he's doing handle the fighting."

Domo frowned. "There are a few people who'd stand a chance, but we're hundreds of miles from them. And getting the bottle from here to there without being robbed along the way would be hard work. It wouldn't help that Evander would be after us the whole time."

More casually, Domo added, "Of course going to another king and groveling for help is one of those things that costs you your dignity."

Will waved a hand dismissively. "Oh, that boat sailed a *long* time ago."

Trying to answer the original question, London offered, "We're not that far from troll lands."

"If anyone could stand a chance against the necromancer, it's the trolls," Brooklyn agreed.

Gladys shrugged. "It's a long way to walk with Evander raining necromantic magic down on us."

"Keep working on ideas," Will told them. "Once we've got the Bottle of Hope I need a person to give it to and a route we can take."

Will took a deep breath and blew it out. "You know, I'm starting to feel like we got the short end of the stick when it comes to magic super weapons. The bottle heals people, and that's cool, but Evander's staff makes him a super wizard. He shoots bolts that can tear a hill apart. I kind of wish we were on our way to get something stronger."

"You play the cards you're dealt," Domo said. "That's what being a goblin is all about."

Evander was also eating his breakfast, a mix of dried meat, nuts, berries and edible plants. He was still camped by the base of a cliff where he waited none too patiently for his followers to return. A cloud of pixies flew overhead as he ate, ready to be bonded with bones and become living skeletons.

"This place will have to go," he told the staff. "Once the bottle is destroyed, we can reduce this kingdom to ashes and all the ones around it. They are the most degenerate and corrupt of the lot. When we're done with them we can go on to bigger challenges."

The Staff of Skulls' many voices gave its approval. It had waited a long time to get rid of the Bottle of Hope. Once it was gone the real destruction could begin.

"It's not as if anyone would care they're gone," Evander continued. "The people won't even notice if these worthless kingdoms disappeared in a wave of fire. If anyone reacts at all it will be to applaud us! The few morons who oppose us, they're the exception. Just a few fools clinging to outdated ideas that never worked anyway."

Evander stopped eating and looked off into the distance. "It was different long ago. Back when the elves ruled, there were real cities, statues and paintings so beautiful men wept at the mere sight of them. One day it will be like that again. We will make it happen. The empire shall rise again once we get rid of the degenerates."

Evander's meal was interrupted when thirty of his skeletal animals approached him. He set his food down and commanded, "Show me what you've brought."

The skeletons looked at one another, their eyes flashing nervously. "Get on with it," Evander ordered. "Show me the bones you brought me to make more of your kind."

They stepped forward and left a small pile of bones at his feet. Most of them were small bird bones, and no two from the same animal. Evander looked at the meager offering and kicked it aside.

"You dare come before me with this! I sent you out yesterday and this is what you have to show for your work? I can't make anything from this."

"We know," the skeletal bear said, "but this is all there was."

A skeletal bull nodded in agreement. "We're in goblin territory. They eat old bones, along with anything else they can cram in their mouths. We didn't find anything else, and if you send us out again we won't find more."

"Impossible." Evander poked the tiny bones scattered in front of him. "There were herds of deer when we came, and bears fattening themselves for winter. If you couldn't find the bones of dead animals then you should have killed living ones and brought me their bodies to animate."

"Gee, I wonder how that idea could have slipped by us?" a skeletal wolf asked sarcastically. "Of course we looked for live animals, you dummy! There aren't any. Everything faster than a worm has left the kingdom."

Evander stared at them, dumbstruck. "That can't be."

"It is," said the bear. "Your magic scared them off. You should have sent us out before you cast the pixie summoning spell."

The staff spoke to Evander, and he nodded. "It's the first time I used that spell. I didn't anticipate side effects. This may slow us down."

"Gee, you think?" the wolf asked.

Evander bared his teeth, but said nothing. The staff gave him new orders in its discordant voices as his followers watched. One of the skeletons nudged the bear.

"Come on, now's the time," it said.

The bear nodded. "Hey, we got something to say."

Evander scowled. "I have no time for your excuses. The staff and I are coming up with an alternate plan."

"We're not making excuses. We're making demands."

That got Evander's attention. "You're doing *what*?"

The bear stood up so it could look Evander in the eye. "We got to talking while you were too busy gossiping with the staff to help us. It seems we're taking all the risks and you're giving all the orders. That's got to stop."

"I created you," Evander snarled. "You exist to serve me!"

"You made us all right, and you keep getting us smashed apart," the wolf said.

The bear nodded. "It occurred to us that we should have a bigger say in how things are done around here. We want to elect our rulers."

"What?" Evander was too shocked to be angry.

"Yeah, seems fair," the bear said. "If one of us is in charge, someone who's been through what we have, then there should be better orders coming down from the top. And if the leader is elected for a limited duration, say four years, we'll all get a chance to become hopelessly corrupt and screw things up."

"We'll need a bicameral legislative branch to come up with rules," another skeleton said. "With the number of officials based off both population size and region, and easily swayed by lobbyists for special interest groups."

"And we should have a judiciary independent of the legislature and executive branches," the wolf said. "A corrupt one you can bribe so cases comes out your way."

The bear pointed at the wolf. "Hey, that's not bad! Of course there'll still be a place for our creator. Heck, we'll need you to make more skeletons. I figure we can make you a cabinet official or something, kind of an adviser."

"An adviser?" Evander asked, his voice just above a whisper. His body trembled with rage, and he gripped the staff so hard his knuckles turned white. "You dare!"

"He likes saying that," the wolf said smugly.

The bear leaned against the side of the cliff. "Face it, it's one of you against all of us, and you need us. You're not going to go out there and risk your precious skin. So you can either deal with the changes we're making or you can shove off."

"Traitors!" Evander swung the Staff of Skulls around and raised it high in the air. Black bolts of lightning shot from it and arced toward the skeletons. The skeletal bear dove out of the way, but the other skeletons were blasted to powder.

"You can stop us, but you can't stop the revolution!" the bear shouted.

Evander fired again and blasted the bear apart. Still angry, he blew up some trees and blasted another hole in the side of the cliff. Overhead the pixies watched the destruction and giggled.

Evander stopped his tantrum. Breathing hard, he leaned against the staff. He'd blown apart thirty of his own skeletons. That plus the losses he'd already taken reduced his army by a quarter, maybe more. But that wasn't what scared him.

"They've never done that before," he told the staff. "They've questioned me, tried to follow the letter of my orders and not the spirit, but nothing like this! What's happening?"

The staff's conflicting voices replied. Shocked, Evander asked, "The bottle? But how?" More garbled words followed. Evander nodded. "Yes, it makes sense. But if it can affect the minds of our servants, and from such a great distance, what can we do? Our army may desert us."

The staff spoke again. Evander shook his head. "The plan isn't working. We can't stay here if it's subverting our soldiers. We have to pull back and try something else. We—"

Angry, the staff glowed brightly. There was no point having a puppet that doesn't follow orders. Evander's voice trailed off as the staff changed his mind for him. His body went stiff. His eyes stared off into space and drool dripped from his mouth. The staff stopped glowing. Evander blinked and nodded.

"Yes, you're right. You're always right. We can't pass up an opportunity like this. We, we just need to be patient. Our chance will come."

He stared off into the distance. "The bottle is gathering defenders, too many of them and too quickly. It's scared of us and it's trying to use them as a shield. We need them as well, but only one or two."

The staff glowed malevolently and Evander smiled. "We'll leave one group alive to find the bottle for us. The rest have to go."

"Not much further," Mr. Niff said as he ran down the tree-lined road. "I bet we'll be able to see the wastelands once we get to the top of this hill."

"Not that there's much to see," Domo said. "Thousands and thousands of acres of rock covered ground."

Will patted Domo on the back. "It's where we need to be. Don't worry, once we have the Bottle of Hope we'll leave right away."

Domo kicked a rock off the road. "We'll have to."

So far today they hadn't run into any surprises. No more skeletons came crashing through the trees and the treasure hunters were nowhere to be found. Even better, Evander kept out of sight. They went even faster by staying on the road since they didn't have to force their way through the thick underbrush growing between the trees. In just three hours they'd traveled roughly eight miles closer to the wastelands.

Mr. Niff ran out ahead of the group until he reached the top of a hill covered in hazelnut trees. He cried out in triumph and pointed north. "Hey, guys, we're here, we made it!"

Will and the rest of the band walked up the hill and looked out onto the wastelands. Somehow the name didn't do it justice. It was the most empty, desolate place Will had ever seen. No desert or tundra could compare to such a lifeless and foreboding place.

There was no gradual transition from forest to wasteland. The difference was as stark as a line on a page. A young and vibrant forest covered the land to the south, while inches north of the forest was a sheet of porous yellow rock that stretched as far as the eye could see. There weren't even boulders or loose rocks. It was a flat plane of nothing that seemed to go on forever.

Shocked, Will asked, "This used to be a forest?"

"Once upon a time, yeah," Domo said, "before the dwarfs came. They cut down all the trees and sold the wood, then mined ore and refined it, dumping the waste on the ground. It took a long time and a lot of hard work to make it this bad."

"How could they do this?" Will asked. "I mean, how could they do so much damage and just walk away?"

Domo shrugged. "Cheaper to walk away than to fix it."

"But to leave it like this." Will struggled for the words to express his disgust. The contrast between the land the dwarfs had left alone and what they'd devastated was too great to ignore. "I know fixing this would've cost money, but if they got rid of the rock then maybe the trees would grow back. Then they could harvest them again. Doesn't that make sense?"

"There you go being logical again," Gladys chided him. "Will, there's an old saying: trolls plan for the next millennia, elves for the next century, men for the next year, dwarfs for the next month and goblins don't plan at all. You expect a profit minded dwarf to care about trees that *might* grow back in a few decades? They don't think that way."

Will stared at the vast, blank landscape. After a few seconds he said, "Before we go in there, we're going to gather food and water to top off our supplies. We're also going to take any scarecrows we find with us so I can trade places with them if I have to."

It took two hours for them to fill their bags with food and hollow gourds with water. They found four scarecrows and added them to their already impressive pile of baggage. Once they were ready, they stepped onto the rocky wastelands.

Not far in they saw holes in the rock, each one twenty or thirty feet across and five feet deep. At the bottom of the holes grew grasses and seedling trees.

"Some of the plants are breaking through the rock," Will said.

"Alas, no, My Liege," Vial said. "This is my doing. When I first became interested in alchemy, I was somewhat more accident-prone that I am today. After a few explosions and one cave-in, I moved my laboratory here to reduce the damage. I stayed at the edge of the wastelands for two years until I was skilled enough to prevent most, well, some of my accidents."

"So this is where you tested your bombs?" Will asked.

"No, this is where I built my labs. Strange how often they blew up back then." Vial walked up to the nearest hole and stared into it. "Ah, this brings back memories!"

Will climbed down into the hole and dug his fingers into the ground. It was plain dirt, a bit rocky, but definitely able to support life. "If plants can grow here then the land wasn't poisoned, just covered over. Once we get the rock off, the forest can grow back."

"There are hundreds of square miles of this stuff," Domo protested. "Do you have any idea how long it would take? A hundred goblins with hammers and picks would need a week to clear just an acre of land, assuming they'd do something that boring at all."

Vial nodded. "He's right, My Liege. My lab explosions may have cleared a few patches of ground, but to remove the entire wasteland would take hundreds of bombs going off over many years." Vial's eyes lit up and he smiled. Rubbing his hands together, he said, "Hundreds of bombs going off one after another, each one of unprecedented size and power! Think of what we could learn. I must write myself a note. I'll get started once we're done here. No, wait, I can start now. I just need a few supplies and five tons of bat droppings!"

Will climbed out of the hole and headed north. Vial tried to run off in search of materials for his land clearing project, but Brooklyn grabbed him by the collar and dragged him along. Desperate, Vial cried out, "No, wait, it's the King's idea! He wants me to do it!"

Will and his friends spent hours walking through the wastelands. During that time they saw nothing save one another and flat, rock covered ground.

The wastelands proved to be empty of more than just trees and grass. It was empty of scents and sounds as well. The forest was filled with the sweet smell of wild flowers blooming just off the road, and the earthy scent of wet dirt and rotting leaves on the forest floor. There were sounds, too, even with the animals gone. Wind rustled among the leaves, brooks babbled and their footsteps crunched dry leaves and dead branches.

But here there was nothing. There was no smell without plants or even dirt. The wind made little sound since it wasn't going over or through anything. Their footsteps were nearly silent with nothing on the ground. There was nothing but rock covered ground, Will's group and the long shadows they cast from the setting sun.

"So I'm wondering, where did they get the man's skull on the Staff of Skulls?" Will asked.

"You think about things like that?" Domo asked him.

Will shrugged. "It's been bothering me. Where did it come from? Whose skull is it?"

"Did they have the owner's permission to take it?" Mr. Niff asked.

Vial smiled and joined in. "Does the owner expect it to be returned, and will there be a late fee if it doesn't come back on schedule?"

"We're getting a little off topic," Will told them. "I was wondering who it was because I saw Evander listening to it."

Brooklyn nodded. "Yeah, like listening to a sea shell."

"Wouldn't that be a hoot," Mr. Niff said. "You pick up a sea shell, and instead of hearing waves you hear a dead guy."

"I wonder if the staff says anything useful, like stock tips or seafood recipes," Vial pondered.

Will shook his head and gave up. Sometimes the guys were like this and he couldn't get them to take things seriously. He might get a better response with a different line of questioning. "Did the elves search here when they came with their army?"

"For a little while," Domo said. "Elf magic is based off nature, and they used it a lot when they were here. They animated trees and sent them searching, and they asked birds and rodents if they'd seen it. The elves were stymied when they got to the wastelands. There were no plants and animals to work with. They sent search teams, but they came back empty handed after a few days."

"I wonder why they didn't find it," Will said. He swept his arms out over the vast plain of flat rock. "It's not like there are a lot of places here it could hide. I figure a couple hundred guys searching for a week could turn up anything out here."

Domo raised his walking stick. "You're assuming the bottle wanted to be found."

"He's right," Gladys said. "The Bottle of Hope is one of the most powerful magic items on the planet, and it's intelligent. If it didn't want the elves to find it, it had power to spare to make sure they failed."

Exasperated, Will asked, "So what happens if it doesn't want *us* to find it? We'll be in the middle of nowhere, no food, no shelter and no chance of fighting Evander. What do we do if it doesn't like us, either?"

"Go home and play poker?" London suggested.

"Break down and cry?" Domo offered.

"Take cover," Mr. Niff said.

Will shrugged. "Well, that's a given."

"No, take cover now!" Mr. Niff shouted. "Magic cloud coming in at six o'clock!"

Will whirled around and saw a black cloud sailing across the sky, seething and twisting as it shot through the air. The cloud began to lower and swerved to head directly for Will and his friends.

"Not now, not here!" Will shouted. He looked around for anything to hide behind, but the flat, featureless plain offered no protection. Desperate, he said, "Spread out so he can't take us all out at once. Dump the supplies you're carrying."

The top of the cloud dissipated to reveal Evander holding the Staff of Skulls in both hands, his black cloak whipping around him in the growing wind. He laughed as the cloud flew over their heads.

"In ancient days your followers were compared to rats," the necromancer told Will. "An accurate description, as both are insignificant, worthless and hard to get rid of. I should have destroyed you before, but I thought you'd learned your lesson. Foolish of me to think anything as mindless as a goblin could learn."

Evander raised the staff high over his head and rained down bolts of black lightning. Will shot back with his fire scepter and intercepted the nearest bolts. Black bolts met white-hot flames and exploded in a shower of sparks. More black lightning came down and tore through the ground. Will and his followers barely dodged them as Evander flew over them and came around for another pass.

"Oh, it's been years since I did this!" Evander exclaimed. "The sheer joy of running down a pest and crushing the life out of it. It's a pleasure I've been without for far too long!"

Evander sailed overhead unleashing more destruction. Will fired back and blocked a bolt that would have hit Domo. The rest of the attacks blasted deep trenches into the rocky wastelands.

"Thanks for the save," Domo said. "Not that I'm not grateful, but how much longer can you keep this up?"

"I don't know." Will looked at his scepter and shuddered. "If I use the scepter too many times I'll exhaust it."

Domo watched Evander come around for another strafing run. "I think he can keep shooting longer than you can."

Brooklyn ran to the edge of a trench and pulled up a fist-sized rock blasted loose by Evander's attacks. "I'm not going down easy! The next time he flies by I'll knock him off his cloud!"

"He's too high to hit!" Mr. Niff cried out. His knife was equally useless against a foe flying a hundred feet in the air.

Will looked around, frightened for himself and his friends. Evander was coming around again, laughing and supremely confident. He had good reason to be. He was high enough they couldn't throw anything at him and hope to hit. He could keep firing at them all day, while Will would be lucky to keep this up another two minutes. There was no one coming to help them and nowhere to hide. Adding insult to injury, the winds were picking up to gale force intensity. Will's cape whipped around him, and he had to hold onto his hat to keep it from flying off.

Domo looked down at the nearest trench Evander had blasted into the rock. It looked deep enough to hide in. But as he studied it his eyes opened wide in surprise. "Hey, there's some kind of cave or tunnel below us! Evander blasted a hole into it that's big enough for us to get in."

"Where does it lead?" Brooklyn asked.

"Does it matter? Anywhere is better than here," Domo countered.

Evander was closing fast, black bolts of lightning crackling over the staff in anticipation of his next attack. He'd be on them before they could escape.

Will pointed to the hole and said, "Grab the supplies and go in. I'll buy us some time."

The goblins and Brooklyn hurried to obey, but London stepped in front of Will. "No. You go in and I'll slow him down."

"I have a plan," Will said. "Leave a scarecrow by the hole and I can switch places when Evander gets too close."

"It's too risky," London said.

"We don't have time to argue." Will pointed at the hole and shouted, "Get in there now!"

Will ran toward Evander, leaving London yelling for him to come back. The troll was stronger than Will and could shrug off injuries that would send Will to the hospital, but London couldn't hope to resist the awesome power Evander was unleashing. Speed would be more helpful here, and Will was faster than the troll. In seconds he was too far away for London to reach him.

Evander saw Will approaching. He slowed the cloud down and hovered fifty feet over Will. Amused, he asked, "Is this some fool example of bravery, or have you decided to accept the inevitable?"

Will stood his ground and shouted back, "Bravery? What would I need bravery for when I'm facing a coward?"

"I'm a what?" Evander laughed. "Oh, this is going to be good. Go ahead, little man. Tell me why I'm a coward. It might give meaning to the last few seconds of your miserable life."

Will folded his arms across his chest. "You have to ask? Come on, look at yourself! There you are, flying above me, no chance for a fair fight, and you don't see how you're a coward? You're always hiding behind something. First it was a bunch of cannon fodder skeletons, then a wall of rocks and dirt, and now you're flying instead of facing me man to man. Do you always hide from your problems?"

Chuckling, Evander asked, "And you'd like me to come down and do what? Settle this by boxing? Maybe have a game of chess to decide if you live or die? That's rich."

The wind blew even harder, threatening to push Will over. "No games, no boxing, just you and me. I'll put away my scepter, you drop the staff and we settle this like men. You'll still have your magic and I've got some tricks up my sleeve."

Evander stared at Will. "Drop the Staff of Skulls? Exactly what have I said that makes you think I'm that stupid? As if I'd be foolish enough to give up the most powerful weapon on this world to satisfy some primitive urge to prove myself to a wretched gnat like you."

Will glanced behind him. The guys were lowering their supplies down the hole, but they needed time to finish. He had to keep Evander busy a while longer. "Yeah, I figured you wouldn't take me up on that. Of course you won't give up the staff. You're nothing without it."

"What was that?" Evander demanded.

"I said you're nothing without the staff. The goblins told me how it makes you more powerful. You put that staff down and you're a nobody."

Evander snarled and bared his teeth. "You dare! I mastered elemental magic when you were still drinking your mother's milk. Fire, earth, water, wind, they obey me as master!"

Will pointed his scepter to the south. "Mastering? Is that what you did back at the Goblin City? All I saw was a couple cheap parlor tricks. I was able to hold you in check with my scepter. I'm trying to imagine what you'd be like without the staff doing all the work for you, and you know what? It's not a pretty sight."

Evander cursed angrily and pointed at the ground below Will. He uttered dark and arcane words of power. The power flowed into the rock covered ground, but instead of forming a huge fist or wave of earth, it barely swelled up ten inches.

Will laughed at him. "That's the best you can do? There's only a little rock between you and the ground, and your magic can't reach it. Lame!"

Evander roared in anger. He cast another spell and formed ten huge javelins of ice in front of him. The ten-foot long projectiles hovered in the air for a few seconds before flying at Will like guided missiles. Will raised his scepter and shot a blast of fire. FOOM! He melted the icy javelins long before they reached him.

The scepter's last blast wasn't as big as the ones before. Will had been using it heavily for days, rarely giving it time to rest and regain its strength. He didn't think it could keep fighting for much longer. When Evander realized it, the necromancer would come in for the kill. Will's friends hadn't finished making their escape, either. He had to keep the necromancer busy, hopefully without shooting.

"Is that all you can do?" Will asked. "Come on! That wasn't good enough for you or you would have never become a necromancer. Well if it's not good enough for you then why should it impress me? This is junk magic. I thought you were...oh. Oh, I get it. You're one of *those* types of wizards."

Evander's eyes narrowed. "What are you implying?"

Will swung his scepter and sighed. "I should have guessed."

"Should have guessed what?" Evander demanded as his cloud descended closer to Will.

Will gave Evander a pitying look. "You're just a stage magician, doing tricks for children's birthday parties. Pulling rabbits out of your hat, finding coins behind people's ears, piddling little stuff like that is all you can do."

Evander staggered back as if he'd been hit. Mercilessly, Will continued. "Yeah, I can see it now. There you were, a nobody getting by on a little bit of talent, and then you find the Staff of Skulls. You hit the big times overnight, but only as long as you do what the staff says and follow its orders like a dog. Of course you're not going to put the staff down, because if you do, you go back to being a nobody."

"Lies!" Evander screamed. "Every word a lie! I was the mightiest wizard on this world before I found the staff. All feared me!"

Will glanced behind him. His friends were safely underground, and they'd left a scarecrow for him to escape with. He could get away easily enough.

But he didn't want to run, not yet. His friends had said the staff took control of its owners and used them. If he could trick Evander into setting down the staff, maybe he could reach the man and help him to see what he'd become. It was a risk, but it was also his best chance to stop Evander without being killed.

Will focused his attention back on Evander. "Oh yeah, you're *all powerful* and *everybody's* scared of you. Don't make me laugh. Who decided to hunt down the Bottle of Hope, you or it?"

"What does that matter?"

Will folded his arms across his chest. "It matters a lot. It's the staff's plan, isn't it? You can't even come up with your own ideas. The staff gives you your power. It comes up with the plans. It does everything. You're not a powerful wizard. You're a lackey. You're just the guy that holds the staff while it does what it wants. I'm scared of it, sure, but you? Never."

Evander screamed, and black bolts of lightning arced in every direction, shooting into the sky and blasting the ground. The land turned dark and the wind grew even stronger. Evander pointed the staff at Will and cried out, "I'll crush you like a bug!"

"No you won't. The staff is going to kill me, not you. You can't do anything without it."

Growling like an animal, Evander said, "I don't need anyone or anything. I'll show you! I don't need the staff, I can—"

He didn't finish. The staff glowed as a hateful red light poured from the eye sockets of the human skull. Evander's vengeful rant degenerated into a strangled cry, and then a gurgling noise. Even though the mask covered the top half of his face, Will could see Evander struggling for control of his own mind. His eyes rolled back into his head. His body shook as he tried so very hard to stay angry, to have a thought of his own. He failed. The battle between Evander and the Staff of Skulls lasted mere seconds, and when it was over he thought exactly what it wanted him to think.

Evander sounded calm when he spoke again. "Your opinions are meaningless, as are you. Your pitiful attempt to provoke me has failed. You think yourself clever? You're an annoyance, the latest in a long series of annoyances."

"And you're a slave," Will said sadly. "You poor fool. I was scared of you before. Now I just feel sorry for you."

"Words cannot express how little that means to me." Evander raised the Staff of Skulls as black lightning built up around the tip. "This place will be your tomb."

Will fell over backwards, and with a *whoosh* he traded places with the scarecrow. Black lightning vaporized his empty uniform. Evander studied the landscape and spotted Will climbing down the hole into the cave below. Dispassionately, Evander prepared to fire again, but a rumble of thunder interrupted his attack.

Will looked up at the sky before heading underground. The sky was pitch black, filled with menacing clouds so close to the ground it seemed like he could reach up and touch them. Lightning, normal as opposed to magical, crackled through the clouds, and thunder boomed like cannons. In the distance Will could see rain falling as the storm swept toward them. It was no mere drizzle or light sprinkle, but heavy sheets of rain poured down. This was going to be the kind of autumn storm that overflowed rivers and washed away houses, and it was coming right at them.

The Staff of Skulls spoke to Evander in its many voices, and the necromancer snarled in reply. He shouted at the approaching storm and shook the staff at it. "This is your doing! You're a fool if you think we can't tell. This won't stop us. Nothing can stop us!"

Evander shot bolts of black lightning into the clouds. The winds grew so strong he was forced to land his magic cloud and take cover in a trench. He was still firing into the clouds and screaming insults when Will crawled below ground.

Chapter Ten

Will dropped down the hole and London caught him before he hit the rocky floor. The troll set him down and both of them stepped away from the hole as rain poured down.

Will and his friends found themselves in what looked like a mining tunnel ten feet across and eight feet high, with rails on the floor for moving carts. Old and pitted wood beams held up the ceiling. The floor was gritty from a thin coating of sand and gravel, while the air was cool and musty. The sides of the tunnel were rough cut and bore scars from picks and hammers. With no other source of light except the flashes of lightning coming through the hole above, Will could only see twenty feet in either direction down the tunnel.

Mr. Niff pointed up at the hole and said, "I'm beginning to think he doesn't like us very much."

"Understatement of the year," Will said urgently. "We have to move. Evander saw me come down here, and he might try to blast us out or bring the ceiling down on us."

Domo pointed both directions down the tunnel. "Neither way goes where we're headed, and it's pitch black down here to boot."

"I believe I can be of some service in that matter," Vial said. He dug through a bag he'd packed for the trip and took out a long, slender tube filled with pale green liquid. He shook the tube as hard as he could, and smiled as the green liquid glowed and illuminated the tunnel for forty feet in all directions. "Chemically generated light. I have two more like it, each one good for a few hours."

"After that we're basically screwed," Domo said.

"Move," Will told them. He hurried them along the tunnel. "We'll put some distance between us and Evander, and then figure out what to do next."

They ran down the tunnel for an hour, carrying their supplies and Gladys. The sound of the storm outside quickly faded, and Will began to relax in their still and silent surroundings. They stopped to rest when they came to a chamber fifty feet across and supported by smooth stone pillars.

Will peered into the darkness. It was very quiet here. Curious, he asked, "Does anybody know where we are?"

Domo shook his head. "It looks like somebody dug it out a while ago, but I don't know who."

Mr. Niff explored the edges of the chamber. He came back and reported, "There are three other tunnels leading away from here. I found a map carved into the wall, and some funny looking marks. I think it's dwarf writing."

Mr. Niff led them to the map and writing. The map was carved into a flat piece of stone, showing a sprawling network of tunnels going deep into the earth. The writing was a collection of symbols cut into the rock, triangles with notches cut into one, two, or all three sides.

"That's dwarf writing all right," Gladys agreed. The bookcase appeared behind her in the mirror and she took out a thick, leather bound book. Consulting the book, she said, "Let's see, the top one says 'Workers will be fined if they cause an accident. If the accident is fatal their families will be fined'. Yeah, that's dwarfs for you."

Domo looked around the chamber and tunnels leading from it. He turned to the others and said, "I figured it out! We're in the mine tunnels under the wastelands. This is where most of the iron ore was, so this is where most of the mine shafts were dug."

"Do any of these tunnels connect to the ones under the Goblin City?" Will asked.

Domo studied the map. "No. The two tunnel networks are separated by a couple miles."

"Can you find a way to the surface?" London asked him.

Domo frowned. "There are lots of notes on the map, but I can't read dwarf writing. They could say tunnels are collapsed or don't go through. Gladys, lend a hand here."

"Put me in front of it," she said. Gladys looked down at her book and translated the writing. "Here we go. 'If you're here you shouldn't be', 'Rations will improve when profits increase', 'Tunnel A-14 is closed until the tentacled horror is evicted'. Here's something, 'Entrance S-6 is closed until further notice due to tunnel collapse, use entrance S-4'. S-4 is a few miles north of us."

"Can you lead us there?" Will asked.

Gladys frowned. "I can memorize the map easy enough, but these tunnels are old and the shoring timbers look like they were bought from the lowest bidder. There's no telling how many tunnels have caved in since the dwarfs left."

Brooklyn flexed his muscles. "If they caved in we can dig them out!"

"Yeah, digging out a tunnel with an unstable roof, *real smart*," Gladys said sarcastically. "You'd just make a bigger cave-in."

"So we're looking for exits that might already be closed, and we don't dare try to open them," Domo said.

"Do we have alternatives?" Will asked. The others shrugged, frowned or fidgeted. "Okay, Gladys, tell us where to go."

They walked through the mining tunnels, with London carrying Gladys as the magic mirror directed them through the twisting tunnels. Vial's chemical light cast a pale green light around them, making the tunnels look sickly green.

"Is Evander going to follow us down here?" Mr. Niff asked.

"I'm thinking not," Will said. "The last time I saw him, he was threatening a storm cloud and shooting at it. Okay, I know the guy is nuts and makes horrible monsters from dead bones, but that was a whole new level of crazy out there."

Vial nodded in agreement. "He does seem rather antisocial. Perhaps he'd be better adjusted if we replaced his brain with some kind of vegetable."

The tunnel split into three passages, and Gladys pointed to the left passage. "This one. Yeah, Evander is a few cards short of a deck. I don't know how long he's had the staff, but even one day is too long. There's no telling how many years it's been messing with his mind."

"I saw it take control of him," Will said softly, still haunted by the sight of the man's mind being overwhelmed by the staff. "I guess it's surprising he's not a gibbering wreck."

"He will be," Gladys said as they marched down the tunnel. "He must have been a strong man once, judging by the way he held out for a few seconds back there, but there's only so long he can survive being messed with like that before he snaps. If somebody doesn't stop him soon, the staff will ride him into the ground."

Brooklyn grumbled. "I don't like the jerk, but nobody should have to go out like that."

Will snapped his fingers. "Can we use the Bottle of Hope to make him better? Healing people is what it does."

The tunnel branched again, and Gladys pointed to the right passage. "That one. How do you plan on getting it to him? He flies and casts spells that can blow up houses. Anybody who tries to help him is going to get fried long before they could use the bottle."

Domo cleared his throat. "Kind of like the mice deciding who's going to put the bell on the cat."

Will took a deep breath and let it out. "I don't know what else we can do. I hate what he's done, but when I saw the staff take control of him I felt sorry for him. Maybe he was a good person before it got to him. Even if he wasn't, he deserves better than to be used like a puppet."

Will looked at the tunnel walls. It was clear at a glance that no goblins lived here. They would have filled the floor of the tunnels with garbage and scrawled graffiti on the walls. They would have also dug rooms into the tunnels, places to live and work. Judging by the crumbling walls and layer of dust, nobody called this place home.

"Problem," Gladys said, and pointed ahead of them. The tunnel had collapsed into a pile of broken rocks.

Will took the light generating tube from Vial and went ahead of the group. He studied the collapse and found it filled the tunnel floor to ceiling with rocks ranging in size from road gravel to boulders five feet across. It appeared that the support timbers had broken some time ago and the ceiling caved in. There was no opening through to the other side, and the ceiling looked so unstable that it could come down on them if they tried to dig through the rubble.

"Is there another tunnel we can take to get around this?" he asked Gladys.

Gladys frowned. "The map showed a few ways, but I can't promise they're in any better shape than this one."

Trying not to sound as worried as he felt, Will said, "Take us to the nearest one."

Back on the surface, the storm poured down its fury on Evander. Wet, cold and angry, he used his magic to form a wall of dirt to hide behind. He'd made enough breaks in the rock-covered surface during his battle with Will for him to draw out dirt for the wall. But he had to continually rebuild it with his magic as the fierce storm washed the wall away.

Snarling, Evander cast another spell and created a hot fire to warm him. The wind changed direction, pouring icy rain on the fire to put it out and soak the necromancer again.

"This is a new low for you!" Evander shouted at the storm. "First you try to stop me with goblins, and now this? A storm?"

He raised the Staff of Skulls and fired bolts of black lightning into the storm. He may as well have spit on it for all the good his attack did. The storm answered back with bolts of normal lightning that hit the ground in front of him.

"I know you're doing this!" Evander shouted. "Cheap, tawdry tricks like this won't stop me. Nothing can stop me! You can hide all you want.

You can throw idiots at me until the sun burns out. It won't make a difference. Do you hear me? I will destroy you!"

The winds howled and the rain turned freezing cold. Lightning shot down from the cloud, blasting around the necromancer, effectively holding him in place. Hiding behind his magic wall of earth and rock, he was safe but dared not leave.

Evander howled at the storm. For all his might and magic, he wasn't strong enough to dispel a storm this massive. He couldn't bring any of his skeletons here, for the winds were so strong they'd tear apart the magic clouds that could carry them. There was no target for his wrath, nothing he could kill to make this stop. How long could the storm keep him holed up here? Hours? Days? He was so close to his goal, but no matter what he did it always seemed just out of reach.

Evander raised the staff high over his head and screamed, "I won't be denied!"

Will and his followers walked through mile after mile of tunnels. They were turned back a second time by a cave-in and had to make yet another detour. Worse, one of Vial's chemical lights went out. He lit a second one, but Will was deeply concerned that they weren't going to escape the tunnels before the lights went out.

"This got old a while ago," Domo said.

"There's an angry necromancer on the surface if you'd rather take your chances with him," Will replied. "It definitely wouldn't be boring."

"Ha, very funny."

"Thank you, I'll be here all night," Will said in a poor imitation of a standup comedian. He peered down the dark tunnel ahead of them and added nervously, "Hopefully not any longer than that."

They spent hours traveling through the tunnels. Were they any closer to getting out of the mine? It was impossible to say. Will saw five side tunnels they didn't take, all closed off by cave-ins. There were only so many ways they could go, and not all of them led to the exit.

Will held up his scepter and studied it for a second. "Guys, I have a question. How long does it take for my scepter to fully recharge? It seems kind of important to know for the next time Evander shows up."

"No clue," Domo said. "You're the only one of our kings to use it until it was exhausted, so I have no idea how long it takes to get its strength back."

Mr. Niff piped in, "The other kings used it once and then put it away for good. I figure you've used it more often than all the other Kings of the Goblins put together."

"Best guess, then," Will said.

"Days," Gladys grunted. "The more work it does, the longer it needs to rest."

Domo kicked a rock on the tunnel floor. "I don't think we've got that much time."

Will hung the scepter back on his belt. The fire scepter was the only weapon they had that could stop Evander for even a little while. When, not if, it ran out of power, they'd be at Evander's mercy, and Will was pretty sure the necromancer didn't have any. More and more, he worried that he and his friends were headed for disaster. The problem was he couldn't come up with a plan to could save them.

London walked closer to Will. Quietly, he told the goblins, "Make some noise."

They looked at Will. Will didn't know what was going on, but nodded to the goblins anyway.

"You know, I think this could be prime real estate one day," Mr. Niff said cheerfully.

"How's that?" Domo asked.

Mr. Niff pointed at the walls. "Plenty of space down here. We just need to shore up the ceiling and it would be great."

London whispered to Will, "Somebody is behind us."

"You're sure?"

London nodded. "I heard nails scratching the tunnel floor. We picked him up a minute ago. He's staying thirty steps behind us. Don't look back or he'll know we're on to him."

The goblins kept up their distraction. "It's nice enough, but it's going to take a forever to fix the place up," Domo said.

"Not true," Vial replied. "There are plenty of loans available to the small businessman. With a little money and a lot of goblins, we'd have the place livable in no time."

"Nobody loans money to goblins," Domo said.

Vial smiled. "Ah, but for them to turn you down requires them to know that you're a goblin. You just need an intermediary to help the process along."

Will resisted the temptation to look back. "I don't think it's a skeleton. Evander didn't have any with him when he attacked us, and I don't think he could bring them in through the storm."

Brooklyn nodded before whispering, "We're not getting headaches, either, and a skeleton couldn't resist attacking for this long. But there's nobody else it could be."

"You've done this before?" Domo asked Vial, still keeping the phony conversation going.

Vial nodded. "Oh yes, many times. I have a man of questionable morals stand in for me. He says he's representing me and I, his employer, am too busy to come in person. I use the money to order lab equipment I can't make or barter for."

"And that works?" Mr. Niff asked skeptically.

Vial smiled back. "Always! In the past I have pretended to be a fishmonger, a used wagon salesman and a deranged basket weaver named Irving. I haven't been turned down for a loan once."

"Let me guess," Domo said, "they never see the money again."

"London, can you throw one of Vial's bombs that far?" Will whispered.

London nodded his head toward Vial. "Yeah, no problem. That'll shake him up enough that we can catch him."

Will nodded. "We grab him, question him and let him go if he's harmless."

London edged closer to Vial as the goblins cheerfully babbled away. "I can honestly say I have never defaulted once," Vial said proudly. He opened his coat and let London take a bomb. "The sales potential of my wares is enormous. You'd be amazed how many people want my exploding outhouses. They're the perfect gift for all occasions. My best selling model is for wedding anniversaries."

London set down Gladys, spun around and threw the bomb as fast as a major league pitcher, sending it right on target. The explosion briefly illuminated the tunnel, showing something as small as a goblin with more hair and four (or maybe six) legs shying away from the blast. Before Will and the trolls could run after it, Gladys shouted, "Hold it!"

"What's wrong?" Will asked.

"What is that?" London demanded as he pointed at the thing.

"What's nine times fifty-four?" Mr. Niff chimed in.

Gladys waddled over on the eagle feet of her mirror. "We're not in danger. That's an UMLIS."

"A what?" Will asked.

"Here?" Brooklyn asked, shocked.

"Who would I see about these loans?" Domo asked Vial.

With the explosion finished, the tunnel returned to inky darkness. They watched as the UMLIS scrambled across the tunnel floor until it was at the edge of the light. It was impossible to describe the creature, as it always stayed at the very edge of their vision. The best they could tell was that it was short and furry. Will couldn't say how many arms it had, what shape it was or whether it was walking on two legs or four.

"What's an UMLIS?" Will asked.

"Unidentified Monsters Lurking In Shadows," Gladys explained. "They always stay just out of sight no matter what you do. These guys wouldn't hurt a fly. They used to live in cities, scavenging for food and supplies the same as goblins. The problem was they kept showing up at the edge of your vision, and unnerved people so badly they were driven off. Nobody knew where they went."

"Sorry," the UMLIS said in a thin, wavering voice. "Oh dear, I made a bad impression again."

"Uh, hi, Will Bradshaw, King of the Goblins," Will said. "Sorry about that. It's just we've been attacked a few times this week, and we were worried when we heard someone behind us. Are you okay?"

"Not to worry, I've been in worse scraps than that," the UMLIS said. "Sorry for sneaking up on you. It's second nature for us. I heard voices and wanted to see who'd come for a visit. Oh, where are my manners? I'm George 'it's only the wind' UMLIS. Nice to meet you."

Will kept trying to make out what the creature looked like, but it backed away as he approached. "I didn't think anyone lived here."

"My wife and I have been here for some time," George explained. "We're not as rare as people think. We just do a better job of staying out of sight than we used to. We rather had to improve how we work. You wouldn't believe how poorly people react to lighting a candle at night and finding one of us making a cup of tea in their kitchen."

Will watched the UMLIS. Trying to get a good look at the shadowy creature strained his eyes. "How did you get down here?"

George waved a hand. "We're always down here during the day. My wife and I spoke to a gentleman named King Vickers the Cunning who was King for a while. We were looking for a place to settle down and start a family, and after being evicted from our last three homes we thought it was best to ask for permission to stay here. He agreed and we found a nice little place down here to live."

"How come we don't know about this?" Domo asked.

"We were very careful about visiting him," George said. "He did scream a bit when he woke up to find us sitting next to him, everyone does, but once we explained the situation he was most helpful."

"How could you live down here?" Will asked and took a step closer. "There's nothing to eat and the place is falling apart. It's even more of a dump than the rest of the kingdom."

The UMLIS backed up, staying tantalizingly close but too far away to really see. "We just sleep down here in the tunnels. We go into the rest of the kingdom at night to forage for food. I do hope my wife and I haven't been too disruptive."

Will scratched his head. "Seeing as this is the first anyone's heard of you, I'd have to say no. Say, we've got a bit of a problem and maybe you can help us."

"Oh, I'd like that very much," George said eagerly. "This would be an excellent opportunity to improve our image by helping the neighbors. Give me a second to fetch my wife."

The UMLIS scurried back into the darkness. Once George was gone, Will said, "So, we kind of broke into this guy's house and threw a bomb at him. I wonder if I should have the word 'fool' or 'jerk' tattooed on my forehead."

"How about 'decisive'?" Brooklyn offered.

"I'd go with 'cautious'," Domo said.

Mr. Niff smiled. "I think 'asparagus' would be better."

"Perhaps 'space for rent'," Vial suggested.

George quickly scurried back with a second shadowy form beside him, this one also staying at the edge of Will's vision. The second UMLIS had a higher pitched voice and sounded cheerful. “You’re right, George, we do have guests.”

“I told you, dear. Everyone, this is my wife, Harriet ‘you’re imagining things’ UMLIS. Dear, these nice people are visiting and asked for our help.”

“That’s lovely,” Harriet said enthusiastically. “Would you like some tea?”

Will smiled and twirled his scepter. “No, but if you can help us find the way to the surface before our light goes out, that would be great. Or if you’ve got a copper water bottle with the word ‘hope’ stamped on it, that would be nice, too.”

Harriet looked at George. “I’m afraid we can’t help with the bottle, but the rest is no trouble at all. George and I have been exploring these tunnels for some time. We know where all of them go and which ones don’t go anywhere. We’d be delighted to help out, wouldn’t we, George?”

“It would be a pleasure.”

Will sighed in relief. “Thank you very much. We’re looking for an exit to the surface labeled S-4.”

George and Harriet looked at each other. “Oh dear,” George said nervously.

Will rubbed his forehead. “Let me guess, it collapsed.”

“I’m afraid so,” George admitted. “There were ten tunnels leading to the surface, but S-4 caved in years ago. So did S-1, S-2, S-3… it goes on like that for a while. I’m afraid we’re down to two exits, S-7 and S-9. The first one is right next to the edge of the wastelands.”

“We take that one to go out for food,” Harriet explained.

George nodded. "Yes, dear. The second is a not far from the ruins of the old refinery."

"That's where we want to go!" Will said excitedly. "How far is it from here?"

"Oh, no more than a day's walk north."

Vial checked his tube of chemical light. It was starting to dim. "We may have a bit of a problem there."

"How long can you keep that going?" Domo asked.

"Perhaps an hour, and another three hours for the last tube." Vial glanced at George and Harriet. "I hate to impose, but would you happen to have a fully stocked alchemist's lab down here?"

George shook his head. "Sorry. Afraid I'm not much of a host."

"Then we're on a time limit," Will said. "George, Harriet, I need you guys to get us to the exit by the refinery as fast as you can."

"Fast may not be safe," George cautioned. "Many tunnels are partially collapsed. It's no danger if you go slowly, but rushing could get you hurt."

Harriet added, "It's not just the ceiling coming down that you have to worry about. There are mine tunnels underneath us, and some of them have collapsed or been badly weakened. The resulting pits aren't bottomless, but close enough not to make much difference."

"Can we get through groping in the dark?" Domo demanded.

George fidgeted as he spoke. "I wouldn't recommend that, either. We can see just fine in the dark, but I think you'd have a few more moderately fatal accidents without light than with it."

"Then we'll have to rush," Will said.

The next few hours were nerve-wracking. Everyone ran as fast as they could through the tunnels, with George and Harriet leading the way. They hurried down the safer tunnels, slowing down to crawl through partially collapsed tunnels or edging around gaping holes in the floor. Vial's second chemical light tube went out and he used the third and final one. Worse, it was well past midnight and they were tired from a day of marching and running for their lives. The combination of exhaustion and going without sleep made accidents more likely.

"I'm curious about something," Will asked George as they ran. "Why didn't we see any footprints in the dust? I'd think the place would be covered in them with you two living down here."

"Trade secret," George said pleasantly. "We developed it over the years. You can't imagine how annoyed people were to wake up and see footprints in their kitchen. I tried explaining to them we just needed to use the stove to cook dinner, but they never understood."

Dreading the answer, Will asked, "And, uh, what qualifies as dinner for you guys?"

They came upon a deep pit that took up most of the tunnel floor. George went around it and said, "Mind the edge, it's crumbling. Dinner? I always fancied a bit of garlic and mice with a side of rotten eggs. I can't have that anymore on account of my weak stomach. Now it's skunks and mushrooms for me."

"I think the homeowners objected to the smell we left more than the footprints," Harriet suggested. "I did offer to buy air fresheners, but no one took me up on it."

"Some people," Will said as he tiptoed around the hole. Quietly, he repeated to himself, "Don't look down, don't look down."

"It was their house, I suppose," George said. He saw Mr. Niff look down the pit, pick up a rock and pull back for a throw. "I wouldn't do that if I were you. There's a tentacled horror hibernating down there."

Mr. Niff reluctantly put the rock down. "Bad idea to wake him up?"

"Oh, is it ever!" Harriet said. "We'd never hear the end of it at the tenants association."

Will looked up from the pit. "Tenants association? How many people live down here?"

"A few dozen," George said casually. "Most are UMLIS like us. The rest are monsters hibernating until better times come. They only wake up if something important happens."

Will had to think about that for a second. "You mean there are people, or creatures, or whatever they are waiting down here until the rocks covering the wastelands are gone?"

"Got it in one," Harriet said cheerfully.

Dumbfounded, Domo said, "That could take centuries!"

"Or longer," Gladys said as London carried her around the pit.

George nodded. "It's a bit of a wait, but it's quiet down here and nobody has tried driving us away. Besides, once the rocks on the surface are gone these tunnels are going to be prime real estate again, and we'd like to be in on it from the start."

"That's a long time to wait for things to get better," Will said.

George shrugged. "When you've been chased out of everywhere else, you learn to make do with what you can get."

Mr. Niff walked around the pit without the caution the others showed. Whistling, he said, "Amen, brother."

Once the pit was behind them, they picked up speed and headed for the exit. "I must say I'm surprised how fast we're going," Harriet said as she slipped under a boulder blocking half the tunnel. "It usually takes George and I hours longer to get this far."

"Have you ever done this while running for your lives?" Gladys asked.

"Hey, you aren't the one doing the running," London said as he slid her under the boulder.

"Complain, complain, complain," Gladys retorted. "I thought you were a troll, not an elf."

George looked at Harriet. "Now that you mention it, we haven't. It's more of a casual stroll when we go alone. It does seem to make a difference."

Exhausted, Will leaned against the rough tunnel wall. They'd been going for three hours. Will was in fairly good shape, but he simply wasn't up to this. The goblins were tiring, too. He looked down the tunnel to the limits of Vial's chemical light, but he didn't see an exit. Instead there was only twenty feet more of dusty, rocky tunnels.

"Wait a minute," Will said. The others gathered around him. The chemical light was only illuminating twenty feet. "Uh oh, the light is starting to go out. George, how much farther is it to the exit?"

"Half a day the way my wife and I travel," he said. "At this pace I'd say two more hours."

Vial shook the tube as hard as he could, but the light remained weak. "We have an hour's worth of light, and it will weaken with time."

"Are there more dangerous places ahead?" Will asked George.

"Five," George said, "and two of them are particularly nasty spots to have an accident. Oh dear, we finally have visitors and I'm going to get them killed. This won't help our reputation at all."

Will and his friends were in great danger without a source of light. There was an option, but it was risky. Reluctantly, he unhooked his scepter from his belt. Domo saw him and shouted, "Will, no!" He threw himself to the ground and covered his head, with Mr. Niff and the trolls following suit.

"I know it's dangerous, but we need light," he told them.

Vial looked at the scepter with interest instead of fear. "There is a very limited area for the flames to spread into, so the possibility of it coming back on us is high. I should also mention it will use up a lot of breathable air, and we don't have much of that to begin with."

Will looked at them and then at the scepter. "I don't think we can get through without it. You guys stand back just in case."

Will held out the scepter and was about to turn it on when Mr. Niff said, "If you're horribly burned to a cinder, we'll bury you someplace nice." Annoyed, Will glanced back at Mr. Niff, who added, "You know, with flowers and trees…good flowers too, not ones that wilt the day after you pick them."

"Don't jinx him," Brooklyn said.

Will looked into the largest fire opal on the scepter and saw the tiny salamander inside, burning so hot he was white. "I need you to understand something. We're in a real pickle here and it could get worse. If we have a light we can get through this, but only if it's a small fire. I need you to make as small a fire as possible, just enough to use as a torch. It's very important you do this right for everyone's sake."

Will took a deep breath, aimed the scepter down the tunnel and turned it on. There was no explosive FOOM. Instead the end of the scepter burst into fire, creating a yellow flame as big as a baseball that provided all the light they needed.

"All right, boss!" London cheered.

Mr. Niff jumped up and down. "You did it!"

Domo got up off the floor and watched in amazement. "Nobody's ever been able to get the scepter to work properly before. It's always too much fire or none at all. How did you do that?"

Will smiled at the scepter, but his smile faded quickly. He saw the salamander bent over, huffing and puffing. "You're not holding back. It's taking everything you've got to make this, isn't it?" The tiny salamander nodded weakly. "I'm sorry. I've asked so much of you over the last few days, and you're as tired as I am. Please, keep going for a bit longer."

"Can he keep this up for two hours?" Domo asked.

"He can do it," Will said. "Come on, let's get going."

It took the whole two hours to reach the exit to the surface. It was a large circular chamber, a hundred feet across and twenty feet high. The chamber was open to the sky, which was much more peaceful than the last time they'd been on the surface. Broken rocks and rusted scraps of iron littered the floor, and there were pools of water left from the storm. Ruined stone buildings stood at the chamber's edge with more dwarf writing on them. Gladys identified them as storage rooms for tools the workers weren't allowed to leave the mine with. Crumbling stairs at the north end of the chamber lead to the surface.

Dominating the circular chamber was a huge iron crane that had fallen in. It was three feet thick and badly rusted. Attached to the crane was a length of chain, each link two feet long. At the end of the chain was a hook that must have weighed half a ton attached to an even heavier iron basket. The crane had fallen in at an angle, the end with the basket leaning against one end of the bottom of the chamber and the other end leaning against the top edge of the opposite wall.

Will looked up and saw twinkling stars overhead. The storm was gone, leaving the air clean, cool and moist. It was early in the morning and dawn was still hours away.

As they walked out under the open sky, the fire scepter sputtered and went out. Will hung it on his belt and said, "Thank you. We couldn't have made it without your help."

"He's not the only one who needs some shut eye," Brooklyn said. "London and I are strong, but we need a couple hours of rest before we can tangle with Evander again."

Will pointed at one of the more intact buildings. "We'll make camp here and look around in the morning."

"Works for me," Domo said, and walked to the building.

"Here we are," George said from the tunnel. He and Harriet were staying back to remain out of sight. "Go up these stairs and you'll be at the old refinery. I hope you'll forgive us for not staying, but dawn's coming soon and we have sensitive eyes."

Will stifled a yawn. "That's fine, George. You two were a big help today, and we really appreciate it."

"Be sure to tell people about us," Harriet said as she and her husband drifted back into the tunnel. From the darkness, she added, "Good things!"

"Only the best," Will told her. He yawned and stumbled across the floor covered in debris. He was almost there, he told himself. A day or two more and he'd have the Bottle of Hope. He just didn't know what to do with it once he got it.

Chapter Eleven

Will woke up to the sight of ruin and wreckage surrounding him, which to be perfectly honest was typical of most mornings. But this time he was in the entrance of a long closed dwarf mine instead of the Goblin City. He'd made camp last night in a dilapidated stone toolshed, its walls crumbling and the floor covered in rubble and rusted bits of metal. Alongside him were his three most trusted goblins, still sleeping off last night's desperate march through the tunnels under the wastelands. Gladys the magic mirror leaned up against a wall, equally exhausted.

All of them were at the bottom of a cylindrical pit dug deep into the ground. High above they could see blue skies and a few clouds floating lazily by. Outside the pit was the dwarf refinery, abandoned for ninety years, and with any luck the resting place of the Bottle of Hope.

Will got up and looked outside, his muscles still aching from last night. The troll brothers were up and moving, busy sifting through the debris that covered the bottom of the pit. He left the shed and joined them.

"Morning," he said. "What are you looking for?"

"Coins, jewelry, that sort of stuff," London explained. "You wouldn't believe how many valuables get lost and end up in the trash."

Brooklyn showed off three silver coins so tarnished they were black. "When we first came to the Kingdom of the Goblins, we found all sorts of cool stuff lost in the trash piles. We sent everything back to mom and dad."

"Any trouble last night?" he asked them.

London shook his head. "Not while we were on guard duty. This place is as quiet as a tomb."

Will looked at the crumbling stone stairs leading out of the pit. "That's a really poor choice of words given our situation."

Vial, Domo and Mr. Niff staggered out of the shed, yawning and stretching. The goblins joined them and Gladys followed awkwardly.

"Gladys, how close are we to the Bottle of Hope?" Will asked.

"Within five miles," she said while applying her makeup in the mirror's surface. "I should be able to narrow it down in the next couple hours."

They climbed up the stairs, with Brooklyn carrying Gladys and Will leading the group. Smiling, Will said, "It shouldn't take long to find the bottle."

"How do you figure that?" Domo asked.

"We're in the middle of the wastelands," he explained. "There are no trees or bushes that could hide it, and it can't be underground or else George and Harriet would have found it themselves."

Climbing the stairs carefully, Domo said, "There is the refinery itself. I figure it's in pretty sad shape after all this time, but there's got to be lots of nooks and crannies the bottle could be hiding in."

Coming to the top of the stairs, Will asked, "How big is this place?"

"You're familiar with the Goblin City, the maze and the tunnels underneath them, right?" Domo asked.

"Yeah. So?"

They came out onto the surface and saw the dwarf refinery. Will looked at it, his jaw dropping as his eyes traveled higher and higher up the towering, rusting structures.

"It's about that big," Domo finished.

The refinery was the size of a city. There were gigantic ore silos, a collapsing foundry containing blast furnaces big enough to hold tons of ore, and forges for hundreds of workers to turn iron into tools and trade goods. They saw dormitories for thousands of people, plus kitchens, a bathhouse and a hospital. Huge loading docks sat next to warehouses the size of football stadiums. Administrative buildings stood by themselves surrounded by fences and watchtowers. Between the buildings ran streets wide enough for ten men to walk down side by side.

The refinery was huge, but it was more wretched than the Goblin City could ever hope to be. Parts of the refinery were made of cheap steel that was rusted through. The metal had a pebbly surface like a lizard's skin, except where the steel had broken apart entirely to produce edges as sharp as shark teeth. The stonework was also coming apart. On closer inspection, Will discovered it was actually concrete, but of such poor quality it was cracked and worn down. There were piles of broken concrete on the empty streets, and it looked like the remaining walls were holding together only because they were so thick.

It didn't help that last night's storm had dropped several inches of rain. Every depression and low spot was filled with pools of water, some of them supporting algae and tiny swimming insects. Larger and more intact buildings had pools of rainwater collected on their roofs, trickling down through holes like miniature waterfalls. The rising sun began to evaporate the water and made the air so hazy and sticky that it was impossible to walk through the city without being soaked through and through.

"Oh boy," Will said softly. He tried to guess how long it would take to search such a large place, and none of his estimates were encouraging. "So, it's somewhere in here."

"Wow, this place is huge," Mr. Niff said enthusiastically. "An army, a circus, a merchant caravan and a herd of elephants could fit in here with room to spare. Of course that's assuming the elephants aren't too chunky, cause if they were you'd only have room for half a herd."

Vial picked a piece of broken concrete off the ground and tossed it away. "This is shameful. What's the point in me offering to blow the place up when it's already coming down on its own? It's shoddy workmanship like this that puts dedicated explosives experts out of work."

Will gulped nervously. "Gladys, any suggestions where we should start?"

"I can't pinpoint the bottle. It's so strong that everything around us feels like magic. I may be able to get a better fix on it later, but for now you're going to have to do this the hard way."

"Don't we always?" Will asked. "Okay, we pick a building and search it top to bottom, and then move on to the next one. We'll mark buildings we've searched so we don't check them twice by accident."

They started at a rundown dormitory and found the work agonizingly slow. The situation was the same in each room they entered. The ceilings were caved in, the walls were flaking away and the floors were covered with the resulting debris. They sifted through the mess one square foot at a time, checking every place big enough to hide the Bottle of Hope. Even with Will, the trolls and three goblins, it took hours to go over the first building.

It didn't help that the ravages of time had left the dormitory a veritable deathtrap. Will's foot went through the floor twice, and he had to be careful getting out so the rest of him didn't follow. London leaned against a wall only to have that entire side of the building peel off and come crashing to the ground. The others looked at him, and he defiantly said, "He started it!"

Vial opened a cabinet and the doors came off in his hands. He set them down and asked, "The answer is likely no, but I would like to offer my services to blow the whole place up. Digging through the rubble can't be as dangerous as waiting for the refinery to collapse on us."

"Don't think I'm not tempted," Will said as he tested a staircase going up to the next floor of the dormitory. It seemed sturdy enough to hold his weight. "I'd take you up on that, but I don't know if you'd blow up the bottle along with the city. It might not be as indestructible as the Staff of Skulls."

Vial smiled. "What a fascinating question! I know most magic devices can be destroyed with enough force, but I wonder how much it takes to destroy one of the fifty most powerful magic items. It's an interesting topic of research."

"I'd prefer it if you spent your time and energy trying to blow up the staff," Will said.

Domo picked his way between holes in the floor. "The whole place is liable to come down on our heads without Vial's help. This reminds me of when I used to be with the builder goblins making their rattletrap houses. In case you were wondering, I didn't miss it."

They climbed up to the second floor of the dormitory, which if anything was in worse shape. The windows were sealed with rusty iron bars, and the beds were rusted wrought iron cots with the sheets and bedding reduced to nothing more than tatters. Large sections of the roof were gone, letting in sunlight and anything else that fell in. At the foot of each cot were wood storage lockers, empty and rotting.

"Lovely," Will said. "The place looks like a prison."

London brought Gladys upstairs and set her down. She surveyed the mess with obvious distaste. "And I thought your throne room was lousy."

Mr. Niff checked under the cots while the others searched the rubble piles and lockers. Domo called everyone over and pointed to writing on the wall. The messages were scratched into the stone in both human words and the notched triangles of dwarf writing. It included messages such as *'Cafeteria food doubles as glue'*, *'Fenton Pennyweather wears women's underwear'*, and *'For black market socks, contact Victor'*.

"Lots of gossip, but nothing about the bottle," Will said.

"Do you think Victor is still offering socks?" Mr. Niff asked. "I got a real taste for sock casserole."

"I have a good recipe for that," Vial offered.

Will went back to searching. "Save the cooking tips for later. Keep an eye out for messages in case someone who worked here saw it."

"Someone saw the Bottle of Hope, wrote about it and left it here?" Domo asked incredulously.

Annoyed, Will said, "Hey, if I could come up with good ideas I wouldn't be in this mess to start with."

They finished searching the dormitory and left. Will scratched the door with a loose nail to mark that they'd searched it. They walked to the next building, but only got twenty feet before they heard a noise behind them. The sound of ancient timbers breaking, rusty sheet metal tearing and cheap concrete shattering heralded the collapse of the dorm they'd just left. They turned around, silently watching the rubble settle and a dust cloud rise up.

Brooklyn raised his hand. "Can we go back to fighting Evander? At least we know what to expect from him."

The next few buildings offered nothing better. They found a few coins, keys for locks that either no longer worked or no longer existed, and a pinup calendar featuring attractive women from the field of undertaking. No other buildings came down, but it was clear that good intentions and little else were holding up the refinery.

They checked an administration building next in the mistaken belief it wouldn't be falling apart. After all, the people running this operation doubtless would have demanded better accommodations. This wasn't the case. If anything the administration building was even more barren than the rest of the refinery. The rooms had been stripped of anything even remotely valuable, and there was no graffiti.

"Kind of Spartan, isn't it?" Will asked as he searched the rubble on the top floor of the building. He turned up a silver coin and an accounting book, but no bottle.

"Dwarfs don't do pretty," Gladys said. "They don't do luxury, or even comfortable. If they could get away with it, they wouldn't even do livable. They're all about how much money you can squeeze out of a place and how fast you can do it."

This building had the same iron bars over the windows as the dormitory. Will figured they were intended to keep the miners from breaking in and going after their employers, which he would have done in a heartbeat if he'd worked here. He glanced out the window and saw a patch of open ground just outside the city, totally maybe sixty acres. It was the only place not covered in rock and was instead overgrown with weeds. It took Will a second to pick out the forest of headstones hidden by the plants. It was a graveyard.

Gladys waddled up beside him and frowned. "Dwarfs don't do safety, either. A lot of people never made it out of here."

Still looking at the graveyard, Will asked, "And why weren't the owners hunted down and beaten with sticks for what happened here?"

Domo looked up from a rubble pile he was digging through. "They sold cheap goods and lots of them. If a king or merchant can get what he wants without paying a lot, what does he care what happened to the people who made it?"

With the administration building finished, they moved on to the bathhouse. The building was holding up better than most, but it was infested with mold and mushrooms. One of the mushrooms was the giant variety that made goblins. Only seven feet tall, it would be years before it was big enough to open and release a cloud of spores and a newborn goblin. The water tanks that fed the showers were full courtesy of rainwater coming through the roof and pouring into them. Rotted towels provided the mold something to grow on.

It was almost nightfall by the time they finished searching the bathhouse. Exhausted and dirty, Will and his friends settled down in a corner of the building not totally overrun by fungus. Will asked Gladys, "Any luck finding the bottle?"

"Some. It's definitely inside the refinery complex."

"Maybe the next generation of goblins can find it," Domo said.

Angry, Gladys retorted, "Hey, I narrowed it down from a five mile radius to two."

"Can you get it down any further?" Will asked her.

"Maybe," she said. "I'll need some time."

Will yawned and covered himself with his cape. "We've got enough food to stay four more days, then we have to head home for supplies. Anything you can do between then and now is good."

The next morning, Will and his friends prepared for a second day of exploring the refinery. After they finished breakfast, Will checked their food supply and frowned. There was less left than he'd like. Fortunately the goblins found some foodstuffs in the form of decaying wood footlockers. Will watched in astonishment as the goblins gobbled down the rotting wood with a relish he couldn't imagine.

Trying to get his mind off that disturbing scene, he asked Gladys, "Anything new?"

"No," she said sullenly. "The whole place radiates magic. I'm trying to feel for stronger sources, but it's all strong."

"Okay, onto a different topic," Will said. "How are the goblin search parties doing? I'm worried skeletons might attack them."

Gladys disappeared from the surface of the mirror and was replaced with images from across the kingdom. Some showed peaceful scenes, with trees and shrubs decked out in bright autumn colors, babbling brooks winding between canyon walls and finally the empty Goblin City. Seeing the city left Will feeling oddly homesick. Other scenes showed devastation, the land torn up and crude goblin huts pulled down or set ablaze. The last image showed a forest glen where skeletons and goblins fought one another in a brutal, no holds barred battle.

But the goblins weren't fighting alone. Mixed in with the warrior, builder and digger goblins were heavily armed treasure hunters and adventurers. Human farmers also joined the battle, swinging hammers, scythes and shovels. Towering over the other combatants was a minotaur, and farther back several other monsters joined the brawl. This bizarrely mixed force fought side by side and with a ferocity Will had rarely seen, hunting down the skeletons to the last one.

"This wasn't in the recruitment brochure!" a skeletal stag cried out as the minotaur charged in and smashed it. Another skeleton fell as a farmer pinned it to the ground with a pitchfork and four digger goblins battered it apart with hammers.

"Wow!" Will said. "Where'd we pick up the help from?"

"It's the bad vibes necromancy gives off," Domo said. "We're not going to get any help from outside, but all the people who live around us are going to join in just to make the headaches go away."

They watched the mirror as two goblins tripped a skeletal wolf and backed away. The moment they stepped aside, the minotaur brought his huge ax down on the skeleton and smashed it. The minotaur howled in triumph, throwing back its shaggy head and shaking it, then joined the goblins in pursuing another skeleton.

Brooklyn pointed at the minotaur. "Now there's someone with a real sense of job satisfaction."

"Good to see a guy enjoying his work," London agreed.

"Isn't that the last minotaur to ask if he could work in the maze?" Will asked as the minotaur stomped on a skeletal hound.

"I think so," Domo said as he watched the minotaur's rampage. "Kind of happy he didn't take the job."

The minotaur ground another skeleton into the dirt, prompting Will to say, "Yeah, I don't think he'd take criticism too well. Everyone's on our side for a change." He was happy that the goblins and treasure hunters weren't fighting each other anymore. But there was a bigger threat, one that would make dog meat out of his followers even with the help they were getting. "Gladys, can you find Evander?"

The image faded from the mirror's surface and dozens more flew by in rapid succession. After looking through over a hundred scarecrows, the mirror went dark and was replaced by Gladys's pouting face. "There's no sign of him, and I didn't see any recent damage."

Will scratched his head. "I'm surprised he'd stay quiet this long."

"He's not staying quiet, he's just out of sight," Domo said. "Gladys can only see through our scarecrows. We've put up hundreds of them over the last few months, but there's one place we didn't put any."

"Here," Will said. "He's still somewhere in the wastelands."

"You think he knows about the refinery?" London asked.

Brooklyn snarled. "I hope he does. There are places to hide here and buildings we can take cover in. He won't have it so easy the next time around."

"Find the bottle first, then we think about getting even," Will told them. He looked down the deserted streets and pointed at a row of massive warehouses. "Come on, guys, we'll start there."

Miles away, Evander Hollow remained in the wastelands with the Staff of Skulls clenched in his hands. He stood as still as a statue except for his breathing. He hadn't left the spot where he'd attacked Will. Once the storm was over, he'd found the tunnel Will and his friends used to escape. He didn't follow them or even moving except for the few times he had to eat or relieve himself. His eyes closed, Evander stood and waited.

The staff's discordant voices spoke to him again, instructing him what to do when the time was right. He nodded in agreement, his first move in hours. When he spoke, it was with a growing sense of derision and hatred.

"Those meddling fools have distracted me, humiliated me and destroyed our followers. Every second we don't find the Bottle of Hope brings them closer to it."

Again the staff spoke to him, its many voices the only thing he heard in the desolate wastelands. Like water wearing away a stone, its words gradually brought Evander's anger under control. He nodded in response to its orders. "I shall follow your plan to the letter. We just have to be patient and wait until it shows itself."

Evander looked out over the wastelands. "When the bottle is gone and you are safe, we shall sweep this filth away, the corrupt kingdoms and failed nations, and then rebuild what was lost. It will be just as it once was, one empire ruling the whole world and you above all others, as it was meant to be."

Searching the warehouses proved surprisingly easy, since all but one of the cavernous buildings were empty. There was only dust and more graffiti, including the message '*For a good time go somewhere else*'.

Only one warehouse contained anything of value. Off in a corner was a stack of forty wooden crates hidden under a section of roof that was still intact. There was an old note yellowed with age pinned to one of the crates. Will plucked off the note and read the faint message.

"It says, 'We didn't have room on the wagons for these crates. Please have someone else come get them'."

London ripped a crate open and pulled out a handful of four-inch long nails. "Must have left this behind when they abandoned the place."

Mr. Niff climbed up on the stack of crates and picked up a nail. "They're in pretty good shape. I bet the builder goblins could use these. Let's take them back with us."

Will pulled Mr. Niff off the crates and set him on the ground. "We're not carrying fifty pound crates back home through the wastelands. We're looking for the Bottle of Hope, and that's it."

"What if we find gold? Can we keep that?" Mr. Niff asked.

"Yes," Will replied.

"What if we find a gerbil?" Mr. Niff pressed.

"No."

Mr. Niff smiled. "What if we find a gold gerbil? You know, like those statues they give great actors."

Exasperated, Will said, "They're not gerbil statues! They're people." He grabbed Mr. Niff and dragged him out of the building. "Okay, back to searching. Come on, everyone, we've got work to do."

London nudged his brother. "I'd keep a gold gerbil."

"Shh, he'll hear you," Brooklyn whispered.

Hours later, Will was busy searching the top of the forge. It was late and the sun was setting on the horizon, creating a spectacular sunset against scattered clouds. Will would've enjoyed it if he weren't searching rows of brick chimneys stained black by decades of soot. One floor down his friends searched dozens of stone tubs made for cooling hot iron, broken iron working tools, anvils, bellows and empty coal bins.

Will looked down through a hole in the roof and spotted London searching a tub filled with stagnant water. "Find anything?"

"Nothing worth keeping," London called back.

Frustrated beyond belief, Will punched the nearest chimney. He yelped and backed away as the chimney came loose and fell off the building. The others ran outside when they heard it hit the ground.

"Sorry," he said sheepishly. "My fault."

"Leave property damage to the professionals," Vial said as they went back into the building.

Tired and disgusted, Will sat down next to the stairs he'd used to get to the roof. He looked at his hand and saw he'd cut himself punching the chimney. It wasn't a deep cut, but it hurt. He pulled his king contract from his belt and studied it for a moment. *Article 61, subsection 1, paragraph 3, line 2: The King cannot be impeached for committing a felony, because quite frankly all the other kings have done worse things than you* <u>*ever*</u> *could, and they're still in office.*

Domo waddled up the stairs. "Looking for a way home?"

"Always. Don't worry, if I find a way out of my contract, I'll stay long enough to deal with Evander and the Staff of Skulls. I owe you guys that much." Will picked up a loose pebble and flicked it off the building. "So, how much of the refinery do you think we've searched so far?"

Domo shrugged. "Twenty percent. Maybe twenty-five, but that's stretching it."

"And we only have three days worth of food left."

"You and the trolls have three days worth of food," Domo corrected him. "There's enough stuff here for us goblins to eat for weeks. You three can go back for more food when you have to and we'll keep looking."

"That would leave you defenseless," Will said.

"Will, be honest, if Evander and the Staff of Skulls show up again is there anything you and the trolls could do to stop him?"

"No," Will admitted. "But I still don't like the idea of leaving you here alone. If I'm in charge then I'm supposed to share the risks."

Domo laughed. "You've been King for five months and you still don't get it. Kings don't share their followers' risks. They stay in the back and let other people put their lives on the line."

"Well, that's not the way I do it. The Kingdom of the Goblins is my responsibility. As bad as things are around here, it's going to get worse if I sit back and do nothing. I'm not just doing this for us. If Evander wins he'll destroy this kingdom and who knows how many others. He has to be stopped, and it's our bad luck that we're the ones who have to do it."

They could see for some distance on top of the forge, with only a few of the larger buildings blocking their line of sight. Unfortunately there was nothing to see but miles of flat, featureless rock and buildings crumbling from neglect and the ravages of time. The sunset with its red and purple clouds was the only source of beauty.

Will looked down the nearest hole in the roof and watched his friends for a moment. He studied the floor below for the Bottle of Hope. He didn't see anything even remotely like it, but something didn't add up.

"Domo, why did the dwarfs leave those anvils behind? They had to be worth money."

"Yeah, each of them would've been worth a few gold coins before they rusted," Domo agreed. "But bringing them to someone who might buy them would have cost twice that. You'd need to hire wagons and teams of horses or oxen to carry them, plus hay for the animals."

"Why would they need hay?" Will asked. He figured out the answer before Domo could reply. "Oh yeah, there's no grass for them to eat."

Domo sat down against a chimney. "Yep. When you come down to it, most of the city was worth at least a little bit. They could have sold the scrap metal and wood before it rusted and rotted, but it would have cost more to bring it to market than they would have gotten for selling it. So, they left it to the elements."

"The refinery and the land around it was expendable," Will said. He caught sight of the graveyard again. "So were the people."

Domo chuckled and picked dirt out from between his toes. "It's funny. The other races don't like goblins because they say we're messy, loud and obnoxious. There's a lot of truth to that, but we didn't make this place or the ones even worse than here."

Will swept his arms out over the panorama of decay before them. "How could anyplace be worse than this?"

"You've never *been* to Serjania, you don't *want* to go to Serjania and you don't even want to *know* about Serjania," Domo said. "That's just one kingdom on Other Place that proves there are worse things than having goblins around. I can give you more examples if you want."

"Don't bother, you made your point." Will saw something moving out of the corner of his eye. Curious, he walked over to examine it. It was a small flower growing against one of the chimneys. It was only a few inches high and rooted in a crack between the chimney and roof. Its green leaves and white flower fluttered in the breeze. "Well what do you know?"

Domo came over to admire the flower. "Pretty."

"I guess enough dirt blew in there for it to grow." Will stroked the flower. "The seed probably blew in, or came in with bird droppings. It's good to see something growing. Things won't stay bad forever. It's going to take a long time, but one day there will be animals and plants here again."

Will looked at the sunset one last time. It was beautiful in a land with so little beauty. The dying light of the sun bathed the city in golden rays, for a few minutes making it less ugly.

There was a flash, a sparkle of light at the outskirts of the refinery. Will leaned over the edge of the building to get a better look. The last of the sun's rays were shining off a small object tucked away beneath a tangle of rusting metal that used to be a primitive crane.

Will pointed at the sparkle. "Domo, do you see that?"

Domo squinted against the sunlight and looked where Will was pointing. "Yeah, I see it."

"It's shiny. Everything here is rusted. There's nothing reflective left." Will pondered that for a second. He looked down a hole in the roof and shouted, "London, come quick, and bring Gladys!"

"Coming!" London shouted. The troll hurried up a flight of stairs to the roof with Gladys on his back and the rest of Will's friends following him. London set down the magic mirror and asked, "What's up?"

"There," Will said, and pointed to the speck of light. "Gladys, can you get me a close up of that?"

"Put up a scarecrow," she ordered. They took a scarecrow from their supplies and stood it up. Gladys' pouting features disappeared from the mirror as she looked through the scarecrow. The mirror showed the speck of light and zoomed in quickly. Under the rusted crane was a crack in the rock-covered wasteland, a crevasse fifty feet long and four feet wide. At the edge of the crevasse was the source of the light, a bottle made of copper sparkling in the sunlight.

"We found it!" Will shouted. He slapped London on the back and smiled from ear to ear. "Come on, let's get it while it's still light!"

Happier than they'd been in days, they left the forge and ran through the deserted streets. Their excited shouts and laughter echoed through buildings and streets that hadn't know such noise in ninety years, and even then not often. Splashing through puddles left over from the storm, crunching through piles of broken concrete, they ran through the ruins until they reached the crane and crevasse below it.

The sun was almost down when they arrived. They gathered around the bottle and stopped in breathless anticipation. The prize they'd nearly died for was surprisingly small, as big as a one-liter soda bottle, and made of copper so clean it shined like a new penny. Will bent down and picked it up. The bottle was smooth and cool to the touch. It was also heavy and sloshed as he handled it. He turned it over in his hands, wiping off specks of dirt, and he saw the word 'HOPE' stamped on it.

"Wow," Will said softly.

"To think such a priceless treasure was hidden among this filth," Vial said reverently.

"I wonder how long it's been here," Mr. Niff said. "I'd have put something this important in a safe, or stuffed it up my nose."

Domo rolled his eyes. "It wouldn't fit."

"We'll never know unless we try," Mr. Niff replied. He made a grab for the bottle, but Will lifted it out of his reach.

Domo cleared his throat. "Will, I don't mean to rain on your parade, but are we sure this is the Bottle of Hope? It could be a forgery."

"It looks the part," Brooklyn said.

"Try it out," London suggested.

Will smiled. "Why not?" He pulled the stopper out and handed it to Mr. Niff. The bottle was filled with water. Cautious, he sniffed it. The water smelled faintly of peppermint, and when he touched the lip of the bottle it felt sticky, like it was smeared with candy. Will dipped his finger in and rubbed a drop of water on his cut hand.

The effects were both miraculous and lightning fast. The cut healed up in seconds as his friends cried out in delight. It wasn't just that, the aches and bruises he'd acquired over the last few days disappeared as well. Will felt incredible, better than he had in years, strong and healthy enough to run a marathon and win.

"It's the real thing," Will said in awe. "We found it."

Miles away, Evander stood grumbling in the wastelands, barely able to contain his growing anger. The Staff of Skulls was having more and more trouble keeping Evander under control. Privately, it wondered if it was time to find a new 'owner'.

Suddenly Evander opened his eyes and he pointed the staff north. "There! I feel it. The bottle has been opened, its power tapped. It can't hide from us any longer!"

Evander created a black magic cloud and stepped on it. He flew into the sky as the staff's many voices issuing orders. He smiled like a hungry predator that had caught a victim's scent. The Staff of Skulls flashed with black lightning in eager anticipation of ending a fight that began centuries ago.

The Staff of Skulls marshaled its power to finally destroy the Bottle of Hope. This would be the most important battle in its existence, and there could be no mistakes. His mind weakened by years of abuse and domination, Evander would be the weakest link in its plan. It would have to take measures to ensure his continued obedience.

Evander created ten billowing black magic clouds and sent them to gather his skeletal army. He summoned the cloud of pixies that were waiting none too patiently for their chance to join Evander's chaos. Bolts of black lightning shot from the staff and blasted the ground below. Unaware of what the staff had in mind for him, Evander shouted, "The bottle cannot run and cannot hide from us! It is doomed, as are those who found it!"

Chapter Twelve

It was late at night, and the air was cold and damp as Will stood guard in the ruins of the bathhouse. It was too late to begin the trip home, assuming that was where they were going, so Will and his friends had made camp here. While their temporary home had plenty of mold growing in it, it had the virtue of being one of the few buildings in the refinery intact enough that it wouldn't collapse on them.

Will gazed at the Bottle of Hope while his friends slept. One of the fifty most powerful magic items on the planet was in his hands, an item of incredible power that could do immeasurable good for the world. People would fight to possess it, and in the case of Evander Hollow and possibly others, they'd do anything to destroy.

Will glanced at Gladys and said, "I have no idea what to do next."

"Then you're in good company."

"Where can I take it where Evander won't follow?" Will asked her. "How am I supposed to get it there with him and half the world trying to take it from me?"

Gladys shrugged. "No easy answers for you. Evander's got a real speed advantage over us with his magic clouds, so running isn't an option."

"Fighting him won't work, either," Will said. "He's knocked us around twice and didn't even break a sweat. I'm not looking forward to getting shot at again. And as powerful as the Bottle of Hope is, it won't help much in a fight. Healing injuries doesn't compare with raining down black magic on your enemies."

Will looked down at the bottle again. "Letting him take it from us isn't an option, either." He stood up and began to pace, staying well clear of his sleeping friends. "The bottle is too important to lose. Just think of what we could do with it."

Gladys watched Will as he paced across the rubble-strewn floor. "What *are* you planning on doing with it?"

"Well, heal people." Will stopped pacing and held the bottle up so she could see it. "All it takes is one drop to heal any disease or injury, and there's got to be thousands of drops of water in here. We could go around the neighboring towns and cure people. We'd have to make sure no one saw us so we don't attract treasure hunters and thieves, but we could do it. Imagine thousands of people healthy, not in pain anymore, people like Prince Alexander's father."

"You could make a lot of friends doing that," Gladys said shrewdly, "or a lot of money."

"That doesn't matter," Will said. "Money won't help me escape my king contract, and that's all I really want. The blasted contract won't let me get close enough to a lawyer to hire one. Money won't help the kingdom, either. We're pretty self-sufficient, and even if we did need something, who would sell it to us? The kings and merchants around here think we're scum."

"They don't think it, they know it," Gladys replied.

"Same goes for making friends. I suppose people would be grateful for a little while, but how long would it be until the goblins messed things up with practical jokes and pie traps? I figure it would take the neighbors a year or less to decide they don't like us anymore."

Pouting, Gladys demanded, "Why are you so dead set on saving the bottle if you can't get anything from it? It's a lot of work and danger if there's no reward at the end of the day."

Will pointed outside the bathhouse at the ruined refinery. The full moon cast a pale light over the decrepit buildings, providing just enough light to show how incredibly foul their surroundings were. "There are too many ugly things in the world to let one of the beautiful ones be destroyed. I'm not going to be the man responsible for letting the Staff of Skulls kill the Bottle of Hope when it can do so much good."

Gladys filed her nails in the surface of the mirror. "Good intentions are wonderful, but we still have to deal with the staff and Evander. The trolls may have been on to something when they suggested taking it to the Troll King. He's smart, and a tough customer even without the bottle. Even someone as crazy as Evander is will think twice before going up against a couple thousand trolls. The Troll King has a healthy dose of common sense and no interest in conquest, which means we're not giving the bottle to someone who would abuse its power."

"Then that's where we'll head in the morning," Will said. "I hate dropping this problem on his lap, but it's too big for me to deal with alone. Getting there won't be easy, but we'll manage somehow."

Will went back to pacing. Gladys watched him for a moment before asking, "Trying to keep warm?"

Will stopped and considered the question. "You know, I'm not cold at all. I'm not tired, either. I can't remember the last time I felt this good."

"Must be the bottle," Gladys said.

"Huh? How?"

"You used the bottle," she reminded him. "Maybe just one drop, but that's all it takes. The bottle is strong enough to heal a dying man. The only thing you had wrong with you was a cut on your hand and some bruises that were almost healed anyway. It didn't have to do so much work with you, so there was a lot of power left over. That's probably why you're feeling good."

"I like it," Will said. "How long do you figure it's going to last?"

"A couple days," Gladys told him. "Don't push your luck. The Bottle of Hope can do a lot of good, but it can't bring the dead back to life."

"Don't worry, I won't take up bear wrestling."

Gladys yawned. "I need to get some rest. You want me to kick one of the others awake?"

"No, I'll keep an eye on things. You go to sleep."

"Suit yourself."

Gladys' garish image disappeared as the surface of the mirror turned black. Will sat down and looked out the front door of the bathhouse. He glanced at his sleeping friends before turning his attention to the Bottle of Hope.

"Hi there. I'd like to make it clear I usually don't talk to inanimate objects. Well, there was that one time I bought a used car, but I was mostly swearing at it, and in my defense I feel I was justified."

Will took his hat off and set it down. "I'd have tried this sooner, but I wanted some privacy in case it didn't work. Everyone I've talked to says you're alive. You don't eat or drink or breathe, but there's a mind in there. I'm hoping you can talk, because I'm in way over my head."

He pointed at the others, still contentedly dozing. "These people are my friends. Well, technically they're employees, but I like them and I think they like me. They've almost been killed a couple times since this mess started. We got through it, but there were some close calls. If I'm right we're going to be in danger pretty much constantly until we find you a good home."

Will pointed outside where the horizon was lit by false dawn. "The Staff of Skulls is out there somewhere hunting you. I understand you two have been fighting for a while. That's okay. I mean, I figure if I had the power I'd try to stop the staff, too. But I don't have that kind of power, and fighting the staff could cost the lives of everyone here. I don't know how to stop it.

"The staff speaks to Evander. Okay, it orders him around and messes with his head when he tries to think for himself. That's really not what I'm looking for, but if you can help I really need it. Can you talk? Because I don't know where to start, and any mistakes I make could leave people dead. If you have any advice I'd appreciate it. I mean it, I'd be happy with something vague like a fortune cookie message."

"You're not going to get an answer," Gladys said.

"Gladys, you're supposed to be asleep," Will said angrily.

Gladys reappeared in the mirror. "Yeah, I'm supposed to do lots of stuff. If it helps any, trying to talk with the bottle was one of the smarter things you've done, but it's not going to answer. It hasn't spoken to any of its owners."

"It can't?" Will asked.

"It won't." The bookcase reappeared behind Gladys in the surface of the mirror, and she took out a book and opened it. "It's a philosophical thing. The Staff of Skulls knows what it wants and forces its owners to do its bidding. They're little more than puppets. The Bottle of Hope hates the staff and everything it stands for. If it dictates how it's used, then how is it different from the staff? Make no mistake, the bottle made a choice to let you use it, but now that it made that decision it isn't going to give orders. Everything it has is yours, no conditions, no demands."

"No advice, either, huh?" he asked.

"Nope." Gladys disappeared from the mirror's surface, saying, "Hey, nobody said owning one of the most powerful magic items on the planet was going to be easy."

The next morning was cool and clear. Will's friends ate a quick breakfast and he told them where they'd be heading next.

"Cool," London grinned. "We can visit mom and dad after we drop it off."

"Just as long as we're out of there before dinner," Brooklyn said. "I don't want to get caught in another debate."

Curious, Will asked, "That happens often at your house?"

"All the time," London grumbled. "We'd be sitting at the dinner table, eating our food, minding our own business, then wham! You're in the middle of a debate whether cubism is a reinterpretation of Neolithic cave art, no warning at all."

"A perfectly good meal ruined," Brooklyn lamented.

"Okay, we'll drop off the bottle and then find a restaurant," Will said. He put his hat back on before leaving the bathhouse. "I haven't left the kingdom often and never for long. From what I understand of my king contract I'm allowed to leave the kingdom briefly, a few weeks at most, and only if the kingdom or my life is in great danger. Can we get there before the contract forces me back here?"

"No sweat," London replied. "The Troll Kingdom isn't too far away. I bet we'll be there in five days of hard marching."

Domo went through their remaining supplies. "I hope so. We're running low on food and water."

"It's less weight to carry," Will said. He led his friends out of the bathhouse and onto the rubble filled streets that ran through the refinery. "We can go without food a day or two if we have to. We'll leave right away and top off our water supply the first chance we get."

There was a sharp whistling noise, and Will suddenly found himself hatless. He reached up and touched his head where the broad brimmed black hat had been a second ago.

"Look!" Mr. Niff cried out. Will's hat was now hanging off the outside wall of the bathhouse, pinned in place by a crossbow bolt stuck through the brim.

"Ambush!" Will shouted. "Everybody down!"

Another crossbow bolt flew over their heads as they dropped to the ground. The bolt hit the bathhouse and shattered against a wall. But the sniper wasn't alone, and they heard footsteps kicking through the rubble as three people came around a street corner.

"Oh lord no," Will said. He recognized all three of them.

"Ah ha!" Sam Jarvis cried out. The tall blond adventurer drew a sword and left his bow strapped to his back. Thumac the incontinent barbarian and Helena the blind seer were alongside him. Will spotted Christina Dredmore, the fourth and final member of Jarvis' team. She was a few blocks away and standing on top of a warehouse, reloading a crossbow.

"Told you they were here," Helena said smugly.

"Yes you did," Jarvis replied. "William Bradshaw, King of the Goblins, I call upon you to surrender. Dredmore can shoot you in the back if you run, and we three can beat you if you stand your ground. You don't have an army of goblins to fight for you this time. Hand over the bottle and nobody gets hurt!"

Trying to keep behind an old lamppost, Will shouted, "Not now, Jarvis! I've got real problems."

Shocked, Jarvis only managed to shout, "Hey!"

Another crossbow bolt whizzed over Will's head and buried itself in the ground. Will took out his fire scepter and hoped it had enough time to recharge. Vial pulled a bomb out of his coat and Mr. Niff drew his knife. The trolls just balled up their fists, confident they wouldn't need weapons to win this fight.

"Real problems?" Jarvis demanded. "I'll have you know the five of us have accomplished great deeds in our time."

"There are only four of you!" Will shouted back. "The other guy doesn't count if he's in jail. Jarvis, you lost last time, and that was when I didn't have the Bottle of Hope. Now that I've got it you don't stand a chance. Even if you took it from me you wouldn't keep it long."

"Truer words were never spoke," a voice announced. It took Will a second to locate the speaker. A black clad figure with silver hair and armed with two swords walked down the street toward them, coming in opposite from Jarvis and his followers.

Will needed a second to recognize the newcomer, then covered his face with one hand and shook his head in disgust. "Jarvis, meet Thistle the elf. Thistle, this is Sam Jarvis and his assorted losers."

"Charmed," Thistle said as he walked leisurely down the street. Christina Dredmore shot at him. With speed and reflexes an Olympic gymnast would have envied, Thistle drew one sword, leaped up and hacked the crossbow bolt out of the air. He landed a second after the broken bolt and continued walking toward Will as if nothing had happened.

Will and his friends watched the spectacle and clapped. Mr. Niff shouted, "Do it again!"

"Perhaps later," Thistle said. "Your Highness, I see you are well despite the grim situation I left you in the last time we met. That pleases me. You told me you didn't want the Bottle of Hope and would be glad to be rid of it. I am here to take you up on your offer."

"Oh no you don't!" Jarvis marched down the street with Thumac on his right and Helena on his left. Armed, experienced and dangerous, they would have made an impressive sight, except Thumac ran behind a dormitory to go to the bathroom. "We've sunk everything we had into this job. There's no way we're leaving empty handed."

Thistle smiled. "Actually, there are quite a few ways that could happen. Most of them involve you being dead."

Will peeked around the lamppost and saw Dredmore aiming her crossbow at Thistle. Will smiled nervously and jogged back to the bathhouse. He pulled his hat free of the crossbow bolt and put it back on. "Well, it looks like you guys have a lot to discuss, so I'll be on my way. Let me know how this ends."

"I don't think so," Jarvis growled. "The Bottle of Hope is worth a fortune in gold, and you're not leaving with it."

"No," a young man behind Will said. "I am."

Will didn't turn around to see who it was, although everyone else did. Will rubbed his forehead, wondering how things could get worse. He asked Domo, "It's Prince Alexander and his swordsmen, isn't it?"

"Yep." Domo pointed his walking stick at the approaching groups and said, "Five gets you ten we can get these idiots fighting each other inside of two minutes and scram while they're busy."

"I like your plan," Will said.

Prince Alexander and his followers came up behind Will, keeping an even distance from Thistle and Sam Jarvis. The Prince looked determined and had his hand on his sword hilt. He hadn't drawn it yet, but the three swordsmen with him had their weapons out and pointed at Will.

The three goblins huddled together as Will prepared to confront these enemies. Domo studied the newcomers and said, "Good lord, we just got the bottle yesterday and we're already surrounded by idiots and thieves. You'd need a score card to keep track of them all."

"Not really," Mr. Niff said cheerfully. "Everybody here except us either attacked the King or got him into a fight. The way I see it, it's us versus the world, same as always."

Vial counted their opponents. "There are only nine of them, and they lack the advantage of surprise. I view this less as a challenge than an opportunity to test my explosives. Besides, London and Brooklyn will no doubt appreciate the exercise."

Will studied the three opposing sides before asking, "Before this turns needlessly violent, can I ask how you people found me? It's not important, I know, but I'm curious. While I'm at it, I melted your sword, Jarvis. Where did you get another one?"

"We found you when Helena saw the bottle more clearly," Jarvis said. "Once you used the Bottle of Hope its power was like a beacon in the night. As for my sword and Christina Dredmore's crossbow, that was a spot of good luck. It turned out a local innkeeper had a used sword and crossbow he was willing to sell. It cost us the last of our money, but it was worth it."

Helena smiled and waved her hands in the air, preparing to deliver yet another spooky and thoroughly overdone performance. Before she could start, Will shouted, "Skip the act, all right? I don't need it. You, Thistle, how'd you find me?"

Thistle smiled. "I tracked Jarvis and his allies here through the wastelands. It was obvious they knew where they were going, especially since they had the blind seer I'd paid to tell me about the bottle."

Helena smiled sheepishly as Jarvis frowned at her. Angrily, he demanded, "What's he talking about, Helena? And how could the elf have tracked us through the wastelands? It's all rock!"

Helena answered first. "You said we needed money for supplies. You said you didn't care how I got it."

Thistle smiled as he told Jarvis, "Normally tracking across stony ground would be challenging, but your barbarian friend left frequent signs of your passing."

Thumac rejoined his friends after pulling up his trousers. Jarvis shot him a dirty look, and the barbarian cast down his eyes in shame.

"What about you?" Will asked Prince Alexander.

"You said the Bottle of Hope was in the wastelands," the Prince replied. "We searched for days until we saw these buildings. I thought if the bottle was hidden anywhere, it would be here."

Jarvis pointed at Prince Alexander and shouted, "You gave *him* directions?"

"Not very fair," Thistle agreed.

"Okay, enough of this," Will said. He stepped away from his friends and held up the Bottle of Hope. Ignoring the startled gasps from the three sides, he said, "Yes, I found the bottle. I was telling you the truth when I said I didn't want it. I still don't. That being said, I can't give it to any of you."

"Why not?" Thistle asked curiously.

"This I got to hear," Jarvis said sarcastically.

"But my father needs it!" the Prince cried out.

Alexander's swordsmen and Jarvis' followers also demanded answers. They surrounded Will, preventing him from leaving and began pushing one another. Will tried to speak, but the crowd around him either ignored him or couldn't hear him over the ruckus. Will motioned for London and Brooklyn to come closer and asked them, "Can you quiet them down for a second?"

London and Brooklyn grabbed a side of the nearest building and pulled, tearing off the front wall and bringing the rest of the structure crashing down. A cloud of dust rose up. The competitors for the Bottle of Hope watched the display in shock, silenced by the show of strength. Will saw no reason to tell them that an enthusiastic toddler with a plastic hammer could have brought down most of the buildings in the refinery.

"Blessed silence," Will began. "Now then, I can't give it to any of you because there is another person after it. Evander Hollow, necromancer, holder of the Staff of Skulls and all around very bad person is also looking for the Bottle of Hope. He plans on destroying it. I already told Prince Alexander about him."

Will pointed at Jarvis. "If I give you the bottle, Evander will hunt you down to get it. You won't last long enough to sell it to anyone, and I guarantee you Evander won't pay you for it."

He pointed at Thistle. "Evander is tougher than all of us put together. Between his army of skeletons and the staff he can walk all over us. You won't be able to keep the bottle long enough to establish a kingdom with it."

Lastly he pointed at Alexander. "Evander rides on magic clouds, so he's faster than you even if you got your horses back. You can't outrun him. You won't be able to get the bottle to your father before Evander catches up with you."

Will stepped back from the others. They were clearly worried, but they still watched Will and one another with suspicious eyes. Will tried again. "Come on, people, you know he's out there. You've seen his skeletons."

"I've seen them, fought them and was chased halfway across your kingdom by them," Thistle said. "I saw a black magic cloud as well, an impressive specimen at that. Presumably this is the work of the necromancer you speak of."

"Yeah, that was him," Will told them. "I need a show of hands. Who here thinks they can fight off an army of skeletons? Nobody? Who thinks they can keep hundreds of rival treasure hunters from robbing you? Put your hand down, Thistle. Who thinks they can go toe to toe with Evander and the Staff of Skulls? That's what it's going to come down to. Nobody? Yeah, I figured as much."

Will set the Bottle of Hope on the ground and stepped away from it. "I'm on my way to deliver it to the Troll King. We hope he can keep it safe from Evander, and maybe take the necromancer out. My friends and I have to move quickly and quietly so Evander doesn't find us. It's going to be dangerous, but safer than if we try to keep the bottle. If any of you think you can get out of here alive with the bottle, go ahead and try. I promise as King of the Goblins that I'll give you a proper funeral when I find whatever's left of you."

"Your plan doesn't allow any of us to get what we desire," Thistle observed.

"Not necessarily," Will replied. "Jarvis and his crew want money. We may be able to negotiate a finder's fee from the Troll King. Thistle, you want to use the bottle to make yourself a king. Well, I figure the Troll King will be plenty happy to have the Bottle of Hope, and having him owe you a favor couldn't hurt your ambitions."

"What about my father?" Prince Alexander demanded. "I have to get it to him now. I can't use the bottle if we give it to the trolls."

"His dad's dying," Will explained to the others. Hardened adventurer though he was, Jarvis' expression softened. Thistle patted the boy on the shoulder.

"He shows proper devotion, and his need is legitimate," Thistle admitted.

"We'll have to figure something out," Will said. He rubbed his chin for a moment and then snapped his fingers. "Does the water still work if it's put in another container?"

"It does." Gladys waddled closer to Will. Everyone stared at her as the bookcase appeared behind her in the mirror's surface. She took out a book and flipped through it. "There are a few cases where people found the bottle but couldn't hold it for long. When they took a few drops of water and put it in a container, it kept its potency no matter how long it was stored. In one case a man kept some of the water in his mouth, walked ten miles home and healed his sick wife when he gave her the water with a kiss."

"That is so romantic," Helena said.

"Problem solved," Will said. "Vial, I need a clean container."

Vial dug through his lab coat and handed Will a glass tests tube with a rubber stopper. Will took it and saw that, while the outside of the tube was so clean it sparkled, inside it contained a fizzing liquid bomb. Will handed the bomb back. "I need a clean, *empty* container."

That request took a bit longer. Once Will had a clean test tube he opened the Bottle of Hope and filled the tube. Prince Alexander watched with awe as Will put a stopper in the full tube and handed it to him.

Prince Alexander held the test tube reverently. "There has to be hundreds of drops of water in here! I just need one."

"Find some other sick people and help them, too," Will said. "You got what you came for, so head home and don't tell anyone you have it. As for the rest of you, if anybody tries to take the water from him they'll have to go through me. Got it?"

Jarvis put his hands on his hips. "Hey, I've done a lot of things I'm not proud of, like looting ancient temples, beating up guards, impersonating a clown and hitting a bishop with a potato. I've been chased out of more cities than I can count, occasionally for good reasons, but I don't rob children."

Prince Alexander put the test tube in a wood box packed with cotton. Once he had the box secured in a backpack, he saluted Will and said, "Thank you. I will tell all I meet that you are a good man and a just leader."

Jarvis watched Prince Alexander and his men leave the refinery and head south before he said, "The little prince got what he wanted. What about the rest of us?"

"Fair enough," Will said. "As long as I'm doling this stuff out, I'm willing to give a drop to Thumac so he won't go to the bathroom all the time."

Jarvis raised his eyebrows. "Really? I guess that would work. I was just planning on selling the whole thing."

"Real classy," Will said sarcastically. He handed the Bottle of Hope to Thumac, who carefully drank one drop before returning it.

"We're heading out now," Will told them. "I'll share our supplies with you, such as they are, so we won't have to stop to hunt and forage. I know this isn't exactly what you wanted, but I think I can get you at least some reward. Are you with me?"

Thistle nodded reluctantly. "I shall consent to working with lesser beings if it improves my chances of victory, even if the reward is reduced. I win nothing if I'm dead."

"We're in," Jarvis said. "But if you or pointy ears here tries to double cross us there's going to be trouble."

"Glad to have you onboard!" Will said with false enthusiasm. "Grab your things and somebody tell Dredmore we're not trying to kill each other anymore. We head out in ten minutes."

Will wasn't sure he could trust Thistle or Jarvis. While neither of them was evil, at least not the same way Evander was, they were only looking out for themselves. There was a good chance either one would try to rob him during the night. But for the time being they weren't trying to kill him or one another, so there was a chance this could work.

Will left Jarvis and Thistle to pick up his share of the supplies. The troll brothers watched their new allies with suspicion while Mr. Niff and Vial made idle chatter. Domo walked up to Will and whispered his concerns.

"I don't like this, Will."

"That makes two of us, but I like the idea of being involved in a four way fight even less. Look on the bright side. I got Alexander and his men to go home. Now it's five of them against seven of us if a fight breaks out. That's a lot better odds."

Domo nodded and shielded his eyes from the rising sun. "I'm impressed the way you talked your way out of that. If I had any money, I would've bet on that ending in a free for all, or at least a pie fight."

Will smiled. "Yeah, that did work out well. Don't know if it's going to last, but not having people attack me is a definite improvement."

Domo chuckled. "You have low expectations for your life."

"Low and dropping all the time."

Will picked up a bag of food and a hollow gourd half full of water. The rest of his friends gathered up their supplies and London carried Gladys. Will was concerned how little of their food and water was left. It would go fast if he had to share it out with their new and not particularly loyal allies. Oh well, it was one more reason to move quickly.

As he was walking over to talk to Thistle and Jarvis, Will saw Dredmore climb down off the warehouse where she'd been acting as a sniper not long ago. Smiling, he said, "It'll be good to have her on my side for a change."

"It's not as nice as you'd think," Jarvis said. "She snores."

Dredmore was only halfway down the warehouse when she let go and dropped to the ground. Landing with a roll, she ran toward Will and Jarvis, slipping occasionally on the rubble.

"We're not in that big of a rush," Will said. He looked around and noticed the entire group was still present. "Nobody went to tell her we're working together?"

"I was going to," Jarvis said tartly.

"She can see we're not fighting, she doesn't know we're leaving, so why is she in such a hurry to reach us?" Will asked him.

Dumbfounded, Jarvis looked at Dredmore. "Uh..."

Just then Will heard a soft noise carried on the wind. He strained to hear it as it was repeated. The third time Will could make out the noise and its source. Far to the south and well outside the refinery, he saw Prince Alexander and his men running back at full speed. The Prince was shouting as loud as he could. Behind the Prince, Will saw the sky darken to an inky black.

"Take cover!" Prince Alexander shouted as he ran back to the refinery. "The necromancer has found us! Take cover!"

"No!" Will cried out. "Not again!"

It was true. Dredmore has seen the black clouds gathering from her vantage point on top of the warehouse, as did the Prince and his followers once they were outside the refinery and its tall buildings that blocked out so much of the sky. Coming from the south, black as pitch and seething like boiling water, black magic clouds came soaring toward them in direct opposition to the wind. There were ten clouds, each of them hundreds of feet across, and as they approached they merged together into one horrible writhing mass.

Dredmore reached them in seconds with Prince Alexander and his men coming shortly after. Gasping for breath, the Prince said, "We saw the clouds a few minutes after we left."

The foul cloud barreled in toward the refinery. With every passing second it came closer and lower to the ground. A wave of pain washed over everyone, dispelling any chance this wasn't Evander and his skeletal army. As the malevolent cloud drew closer, they could hear the shrieks and cries of skeletons coming from within as they prepared for battle. The cloud blotted out the sun, covering the land in shadows.

"Everyone follow me!" Will ordered them. London picked up Gladys while Brooklyn took their supplies before they followed Will. He led them through the deserted streets of the refinery, with friends both old and new close behind. Will went through the crumbling streets and past dilapidated buildings while the cloud came ever closer.

"Where are we going?" Prince Alexander asked.

"I came to the refinery through a network of mine tunnels under the wastelands," Will told him. "We can escape through there, and it's too narrow for Evander to send more than a few skeletons at a time after us."

"How far away is it?" Jarvis asked.

The black cloud descended over the refinery, transforming first into a dense fog and then dissipating entirely. All across the refinery the cloud set down hordes of skeletal animals before it broke apart. The skeletons spread out through the streets, swarming over abandoned buildings and shrieking as they searched for the Bottle of Hope.

"Too far," Will replied as he skidded to a halt in front of a pack of skeletal hounds. They were a few hundred feet from the tunnel entrance.

Flying over the chaos was Evander, who maintained a portion of the magic cloud just big enough for him to ride. He floated high above the refinery and cast a pitiless gaze over the wreckage. A cloud of giggling pixies flew above him, and a hateful red light poured from the Staff of Skulls as it issued orders to Evander and the skeletons.

Evander raised up the Staff of Skulls and sent bolts of black lightning down onto the refinery and the tunnel entrance. The tunnel collapsed and the ground over it sunk down, collapsing two nearby buildings.

"Do you have another plan?" Domo asked Will nervously.

"No, but I'm working on it."

High above, Evander's voice rumbled like thunder. "After hundreds of years and countless hosts, after trials and tribulations too numerous to count, I have found you. You would not face me, would not come to me, so I have come to you. I have come to you, and death comes with me."

Chapter Thirteen

Evander Hollow floated overhead, riding a black seething cloud and gripping the Staff of Skulls. The necromancer sneered, his contempt visible even with half his face hidden by his black enamel mask.

"So this is how the war between us ends, I with a mighty wizard, my skeletal army and enough pixies to replace my fallen soldiers, and you with nothing. A scared little boy crying for his father, an elf who can't pronounce his own name, treasure hunters without a single coin and an idiot in charge of a kingdom of idiots. I have to say, I expected better from you."

Confused, Mr. Niff asked, "Who's he talking to?"

It was a valid question. Evander didn't seem to be addressing any of the people standing in front of him. It wasn't just that. He said he *had* a mighty wizard, not that he *was* a mighty wizard. Evander's movements seemed jerky, almost artificial. Hesitantly, Will said, "I don't think Evander is doing the talking anymore. If I'm right the staff's in charge, and it's talking to the Bottle of Hope."

Sam Jarvis leaned over. "He's pretty messed up then, huh."

"You have no idea," Will replied. He'd seen the staff force Evander to change his mind and do what it wanted. Now it had taken him over completely.

Evander smiled, but it was the staff speaking through his lips. "Ah, a blinding flash of the obvious from the king of fools. I was beginning to think all your champions could be written off as imbeciles. In our previous battles over the centuries you brought legions of heroes, wizards and holy men together to defend you. Once you had an entire kingdom fighting in your name. If this is all the forces you could raise against me then your powers are slipping."

"Back away from me, slowly," Will told the others. He waved his hands at Evander and asked, "Hey, any chance you'd like to talk to someone who can actually answer back?"

"Hmm? Oh, yes, the idiot." Evander spoke for the staff as his skeletons edged closer to Will. "You proved most useful. The Bottle of Hope was able to hide from me, but I knew it was only a matter of time before it sought out an owner. I just had to wait until you found it for me. Odd it should select someone as slow witted and feeble as you, but I'll gladly take advantage of its mistakes."

"Is this the part where you say my reward for finding the bottle is a painless death?" Will asked. His friends and allies were moving farther back until Will had a clear space around him. "That's the cliché for this situation, right? We've already had the insane rant and petty gloating, so now you say something that's supposed to sound intimidating but when you think about it really doesn't make sense."

Evander stared at Will, more surprised than anything else. The staff stopped its chorus of voices for a second before it spoke through Evander. "You mock me? You mock the most powerful weapon in existence?"

"Doesn't everybody? Your army is nothing but cannon fodder. My goblins beat them every time. Let's face it, if goblins can beat you, you're not intimidating. At least tell me these guys didn't cost you money! And your wizard is a joke. His face looks like a prune, he's got no self-control and let's not even get into the whole issue of fashion. Is there some kind of evil dress code he's following? He's not wearing armor, either. How long until he ends up worm food like all the other people who've held you?"

Evander's face twitched, and for a second he looked like he was going to say something. The staff spoke more quickly until Evander calmed down.

"And you? Laughable. I've seen better planning in peewee football games." Will had plenty of room around him, enough so no one else would get caught in the crossfire once the fight started.

"Uh, Will," Domo said nervously. "Let's not make the magic super weapon angry."

That was exactly what he wanted. He needed the staff too angry to think clearly. The only way he was going to win this fight was if it made mistakes and lots of them.

Will taunted the staff some more. "You've wasted hundred of years chasing the bottle. You could have made an empire to rule in that time, like the one you couldn't conquer. It's no wonder the only followers you have are dead animals and a zoned out wizard. Your track record makes the Chicago Cubs look like a good bet, and they haven't won a World Series in over a hundred years."

"Insect!" Evander hissed as he spoke for the staff. "Fool! You understand nothing. Once the threat of the bottle is gone I shall sweep all inferior beings aside and remake my empire."

"Threat?" Will asked, momentarily too surprised to keep up the insults. The Bottle of Hope healed people. How could it be a threat?

"It will be glorious," Evander said, relaying the staff's words in an intelligible form. "There shall be towering cities of white marble, lush gardens that span whole continents, sculptures and paintings and jewelry of such breathtaking beauty to surpasses anything you could imagine! It shall be a land of order, of tranquility, of sophistication, and the likes of you have no place there. Once you vermin have been cleared away I can make the empire. I *can* save it!"

"Sounds like a real pretty prison," Domo said softly.

Will stared at the staff in disgust. "Okay, you're trying to save an empire that's been gone for a thousand years? And you're going to do it by blowing stuff up until things get better? Am I the only one here who thinks that sounds loopy?"

Will's friends had the good sense to stay quiet, as did his new allies. The skeletons, however, had a few things to say.

"That's what we're doing?" a skeletal boar demanded. "Hey, I was promised a life of pointless violence. Nobody said anything about making a utopia!"

"I have a reputation to maintain!" a skeletal wolf added. "If this gets out I'll never hear the end of it."

A skeletal bear shook its head. "I feel so used."

"Excuse me," Will called over the complaints. "Question over here. If the staff is making an empire with paintings, marble cities and kingdom sized gardens, where does that leave all of you?"

The skeletons stared at Will. He shrugged and said, "Well, I could be wrong, but I don't think the staff is going to want you guys hanging around in his fancy empire. Sophistication, remember?"

As one, the skeletons turned and stared at Evander. Skeletons were rabidly aggressive and mildly disobedient, which worked out well in battle but was unlikely to be helpful at tea parties. For the first time they began to wonder what would happen to them if they won. One of them said, "About that."

Not in the least concerned, Evander conveyed the staff's answer. "You are tools to be used and discarded. The same shall be true of all the citizens of the empire."

"Wait just one minute, bucko!" the skeletal boar shouted.

Evander chuckled. "I give you credit for originality. This is the first time you've tried to subvert my followers. But you did it too soon, and over the last few days I've found a way around it."

The staff's confusing symphony of voices grew louder. Fifty skeletons stopped complaining and began to shake wildly. Their glowing red eyes flashed as the Staff of Skulls corrupted their minds the same way it had Evander's. All fifty stared at Will and growled.

"Attack!" Evander yelled. "Destroy the Bottle of Hope and live! Fail me and die!"

"Run!" Will shouted. He pointed his fire scepter at the charging skeletons and turned it on. FOOM! The scepter belched out a blast of white-hot fire that engulfed the skeletons and consumed them entirely. He ran for his life before Evander could send in another mass of skeletons. Evander fired a bolt of black lightning, which Will countered with another blast of fire. He got around a corner and ran as fast as he could.

"There's nowhere you can hide where I can't find you," Evander taunted him, his voice echoing throughout the refinery. "There's nothing you can do that can stop me. Burn up half my army, run for days or fight for hours. It just delays me. I'll win! I always win in the end!"

Evander and the staff glanced at the rest of the skeletal army. Most of the skeletons were scattered across the refinery, but a pack of skeletal hounds remained close by. They shied away from him when he smiled at them.

"Uh, hey," one began, "I was thinking, maybe we could do something else that's really evil but safer. You know, like a pyramid scheme, or a phony charity scam."

Another skeletal hound eyed the ashes in front of it. Skeletons that attacked Will had a bad habit of ending up like that. "What about a protection racket? That's evil and kind of violent. How about it, huh?"

Evander smiled. "No, I don't believe so. Hear me, minions both far and near. Centuries of battle end today. Whatever cost must be paid, you shall pay it. Find the bottle. Destroy it. Destroy all in your way. So commands the Staff of Skulls!"

With those words the Staff of Skull's chaotic babble grew louder still, it's hateful presence spreading across the refinery and infecting the skeletons like a plague. They shuddered and writhed, fighting the staff's influence, but in the end failing. When their struggles ended they ran out over the refinery determined to destroy the Bottle of Hope.

"I know Kings of the Goblins are morons by tradition, but I didn't know they were suicidal," Jarvis said as he followed Will through the refinery.

"Oh, right, like I was going to talk him out of killing us," Will replied. He led his friends and allies through the rubble strewn streets, putting as much distance and as many obstacles as possible between them and Evander.

The goblins were trying to keep up, but they were short and couldn't run as fast as the others. Without a word, Will grabbed Mr. Niff and carried him. London already carried Gladys while Brooklyn picked up Domo and Vial, making sure no one was left behind.

"So what's the plan, boss?" Mr. Niff asked.

"Pick off his army one at a time," Will replied. "Make him use the staff early and often. With any luck he'll use up all its power and then we go after him."

Thistle scoffed. "He wields the Staff of Skulls. There are no limits on its power. If he uses it once a minute for an entire day it still wouldn't be exhausted."

Will turned a corner and ran toward a warehouse. "He said the bottle was a threat. Does anyone know what that means?"

A skeletal bull ran out of the warehouse and charged them. Brooklyn ripped a concrete lamppost out of the ground, lifted it high overhead and brought it crashing down on the bull. The skeleton was crushed and the lamppost shattered like glass.

"You know, it didn't come up in conversation," Jarvis quipped.

"Where are you?" Evander's haunting voice asked, his words echoing through the ruins. His words were overlaid by the staff's many voices as it drove its skeletons into a frenzy. High above the violence on the streets, Evander floated on his cloud. "So many places you could be hiding. Are you here?"

Bolts of black lightning came down on a guard tower and demolished it. "No, that's not where you were hiding. Maybe here."

A workers' dormitory suffered the next attack. Black lightning arced down and blasted through the roof. Broken concrete flew through the air as the roof caved in and the walls shattered. Two more bolts struck the building and collapsed it down to the foundation.

Will skidded to a halt next to an empty warehouse. Gasping for air after his panicked run, he held up his scepter in one hand and the Bottle of Hope in another. "We've got one of the most powerful magic items on the planet and it heals people. We've got a fire scepter that's good for a few more minutes of use. What else can we throw at him?"

"Bombs," Vial said cheerfully as he opened his lab coat. He'd used a lot of his homemade explosives, but he still had two full rows of bombs inside his coat.

"Good!" Will looked at his allies. "What about you guys? Magic weapons, tricks, gag gifts, bits of string, I'll take anything you have."

Prince Alexander held out his empty hands. "We have our swords and nothing else."

"I thought kings had loads of magic weapons?" Jarvis asked.

"I had to sneak away in the dead of night with my men to get here. I couldn't get to the treasure vaults or armories without being stopped by my father's retainers."

Will pointed at Jarvis. "What about you?"

"I have my bow and Christina Dredmore has her crossbow. As for magic, the only magic item we ever found was an enchanted sword that insulted us every hour on the hour. We sold it to buy shoes."

"They were nice shoes," Helena added.

"Thistle, what about you?" Will asked.

The elf shook his head. "I fear you mistake me for a more influential person than I am. Magic is for the rich and powerful."

Another blast of black lightning descended on the refinery. An administration building took a hit that caved in the roof, followed by five more bolts that reduced it to rubble.

"Why are you even bothering with this?" the staff asked through Evander. His magic cloud drifted over the refinery as he sent one bolt after another down into the buildings. The refinery was a wreck to begin with, and his hammering away at it was finishing what poor construction and decades of neglect had started. "I seek to create a perfect world. It is the reason I was made. When I am finished the worthy people shall live in splendor. You insects are delaying paradise!"

"We have to lure him into range," Will said. "Once he's down near street level we can hit him with arrows and bombs."

"And how do we get him down here?" Domo asked.

Will looked up as the cloud sailing over them. "Spread out and take cover. London, set up the scarecrows so I can make a quick exit."

Will walked out to the middle of the street while the others hid. Once they were in cover, he aimed his scepter at the cloud. While the odds against it were high, with any luck he could end this fight right now. He turned the scepter on.

FOOM! The scepter's stream of white-hot fire hit the belly of Evander's magic cloud. Half the cloud evaporated and Evander screamed as he nearly fell off. The magic cloud raced across the sky before landing on top of the bathhouse. Startled, Evander stepped off it and looked out over the city.

"I'm sorry, did that hurt? Looks like the insects are biting today!" Will shouted. His voice echoed through the empty streets. More seriously, he shouted, "If you want the bottle, you're going to have to come down and get it, because your skeletons aren't going to be enough!"

"Find him!" Evander relayed the staff's orders to the skeletons. "Find him and tear him apart!"

The skeletons didn't have any trouble following the noise Will made. Dozens of them converged on him, howling at they ate up the distance between them. FOOM! FOOM! Will's scepter cremated one group and then a second. Here in the refinery there were only so many directions enemies could come at him from. Will could deal with one group after another so long as his scepter's power held out.

Evander regenerated his magic cloud and took to the air. Racing down the streets just above roof level, he and the staff came after Will. His skeletal animals gathered together and came in at the same time. Evander lifted the Staff of Skulls above his head and prepared to rain black lightning down on them.

An arrow hit Evander's cloak, tearing a hole in it right between his knees. A crossbow bolt sailed an inch over his head. Shocked by the attack, he backed away, barely dodging a blast of fire from Will's scepter. More attacks followed as London and Brooklyn helped themselves to Vial's bombs. Vial wasn't strong enough to send them far, but the trolls could throw them over a block with excellent accuracy. Bombs hit the buildings around Evander and blasted holes in them. One bomb hit the Staff of Skulls. The explosion did it no harm, but it buffeted Evander and almost tore the staff from his hands.

Evander and the staff fired back. Black lightning arced down onto the street. Will dodged the first volley by trading places with a scarecrow. With a *whoosh* he disappeared and left his empty uniform to get vaporized. Evander spotted him and lashed out again. FOOM! Will countered the next attacks with his fire scepter. All the while, more arrows, crossbow bolts and bombs flew around Evander.

The skeletons tried to attack Will from behind, but Thumac and Thistle stopped them cold with skilled blows that chopped them to pieces. While they kept one street clear, Prince Alexander and his men blocked another street and made short work of any skeleton that dared approach. Evander had already used up much of his skeletal army in his attack on the Goblin City and then in his search for the Bottle of Hope. Now he lost even more. With the skeletons scattered across the refinery there weren't enough of them together to overrun Will and the others.

An arrow took another bite out of Evander's cloak. Cursing, the necromancer fled the battle and soared into the air. Will fired his scepter at Evander, but it only managed a halfhearted blast of yellow fire that didn't come close to its target.

"It's spent," Will said. He saw the tiny salamander huff and puff inside the largest fire opal on the scepter. He tried to turn the scepter on again, but it only spit out wisps of smoke.

"Duck and cover!" Domo yelled.

Black lightning rained down on the refinery from high above. Evander couldn't aim well at this range. He wasn't even trying. Bolt after bolt came down, blowing holes in buildings and streets. The bolts kicked up clouds of dust that obscured the refinery. Firing blindly, Evander brought down three more buildings.

Will and the others ran for their lives. The dust clouds hid them, and Evander wasted minutes destroying empty buildings and blasting deserted streets. Will stopped next to the foundry, the largest building in the refinery.

Vial buttoned his lab coat shut and said in an apologetic tone, "That was every bomb I had."

"Any more bright ideas?" Jarvis asked Will.

"Yes, but most of them involve being somewhere else. I hear Jamaica is nice this time of year."

Jokes aside, Will knew how bad their situation was. It would only take the Staff of Skulls a few minutes to realize it was shooting at nothing. Once that happened it would direct Evander and the skeletons to resume their search of the city.

Worse, Will's scepter was out of power again. It would take hours for it to recover enough for even one blast and days to fully recharge. The tiny salamander inside the scepter looked angry as could be that it was out of the fight.

"Wait a minute," Will said. He looked up from his scepter to Gladys. "You said my scepter has a live fire salamander in it."

"Yeah, so?"

"You said the Bottle of Hope can heal anyone as long as they're alive." Will smiled and set his scepter on the ground. He took the cap off the Bottle of Hope and held it over the scepter. The salamander looked up at him curiously. "I'm sorry. This might not work. It might even hurt you. I wouldn't take the risk, but we're in a lot of trouble and I need you."

Will tipped the Bottle of Hope. He only meant to pour one drop, but five drops of water fell out and landed on the scepter. The water soaked into the scepter as if it were made of paper instead of bronze. A second later the scepter radiated light so bright everyone had to look away. Will staggered back. Gradually the light faded to bearable levels, but the fire opals still glowed like tiny suns. The salamander gasped in amazement, filled with power the likes of which it had never known.

"You okay?" Will asked. The salamander nodded and smiled. "Good. You want to show Evander who's in charge around here?" The salamander grinned wickedly and rubbed its hands together in eager anticipation. "I'll take that as a yes. Come on, guys. If the Staff of Skulls wants the bottle so bad, we'll give it a taste."

The Staff of Skulls was angry. The Bottle of Hope had escaped somewhere in this decrepit blight upon the world. Worse, the vermin the bottle chose as its owners had nearly killed Evander. Admittedly the necromancer was little more than a mindless puppet at this stage, but the staff needed a living person to access its terrible power. Adding insult to injury, the skeletal army was down to less than half its original size. This fight was taking more time and risks than it liked.

"So be it," the staff said through Evander's lips. "If I must bring down every building to crush you then that is what I shall do. You started this war by interfering with my plans, and now you pay the ultimate price for your actions!"

"Good lord, don't you ever shut up?" a voice echoed through the crumbling buildings. The staff recognized it as the King of the Goblins. The staff spotted the fool walking out in the open with the other vermin gathered around him. He had his scepter aimed at the staff and Evander. "It's like you've got a big book of villainous clichés and you've got to use them all."

Annoyed, the staff spoke through its puppet wizard. "One definition of insanity is trying the same thing over and over and expecting a different result. You keep pointing that defective, mass-produced toy at me as if it were a threat, and every time I send you running for your miserable life. This is the last time that happens."

Will smiled. "Well what do you know? The staff is actually right about something."

There was no explosive FOOM when Will turned on the scepter. Instead it roared like a dragon, shaking nearby buildings and making rubble dance across the street. The fire was so bright it hurt to look at it. Scrap metal melted and concrete exploded under the assault. The blast filled the entire street and shot toward Evander and the Staff of Skulls. The staff fired black lighting at the oncoming firestorm, and watched in horror as the bolt was obliterated without slowing the fire, much less stopping it. Evander and the staff flew higher, barely dodging the attack, only to find two equally massive blasts following close on the heels of the first. Desperate, the staff and Evander flew between buildings. A fourth blast of fire hit the building they were hiding behind and brought it down. The staff and Evander edged away from Will.

"I'm a reasonable man," Will began. "I don't like hurting people. So I'm giving you a once in a lifetime chance. Surrender and you get to live. I'll put you somewhere nobody can find you. You won't get your empire, but you'll be alive. The wizard gets to leave under his own free will after he's gotten rid of the skeletons and sent away the pixies. I think you can figure out what's going to happen if you say no."

Evander chuckled and relayed the staff's hateful words. "You would imprison me? Many others stronger and smarter than you have tried to restrain me. They failed. I have been locked away in treasure vaults, buried deep underground, thrown into the ocean, even entombed in solid rock. I always escape. All it takes is one person who craves the power I offer to find and free me for my plans to begin again. Your punishment is meaningless."

"Maybe," Will said, "but at least you'll be out of action for a while. I don't know if it will be for centuries or just a few years. Either way is victory enough for me."

Evander sneered. Through him, the staff said, "Ah, that's how you did it. You used the bottle on that cheap scepter to empower it. You're a clever little rat. In hundreds of years none have used the bottle's power as wantonly as you. It seems wasting its potential is a valid strategy. You almost impress me. But you made one mistake."

"One mistake?" Will shouted. "Hey, I've made thousands of mistakes!"

"I can vouch for that," Domo added.

Slyly, Evander asked, "Did you never wonder why I blasted so many holes into the ground when I flew over this wretched place?"

Will looked around at the devastated refinery. Fully a third of the buildings were down and the streets were torn up. Soil began to stir in those holes, moving like slithering serpents.

Evander continued to relay the staff's words. "I magnify the magic power of my holder ten times. He is quite proficient at controlling the elements, particularly earth. When the ground was covered, his power couldn't reach it even with my aid. But now there are so many lovely holes in the rock, and beneath them is dirt."

Giant hands made of rocks and dirt shot up from the ground, each one thirty feet high, ten feet across and weighing tons. Several were close enough to attack Will. He turned his scepter on them, vaporizing the nearest ones.

More giant hands rose up across the city. Wherever the staff's attacks had broken through the rocks, giant hands of earth and stone rose up and attacked. Many of them were too far away from Will to attack directly, but they could still hurt him.

Three giant earthen hands attacked an ore silo. The towering silo was a cylinder fifty feet tall and twenty feet in diameter made of crumbling concrete. The hands pushed against its base until the silo fell toward Will.

Will saw it coming and blasted it. His scepter roared as it laid into the silo with fire hot as a blast furnace. The blast hit the silo, pushing it aside and shattering it. The half-molten remains landed well clear of Will and his friends.

This meant he was so busy he missed the real threat entirely.

Five giant earth hands formed on the opposite side of the foundry Will and his friends were standing next to. They pressed against it and exerted all their force on a building that was poorly made to begin with and hadn't been repaired for decades. The walls of the huge building cracked and then buckled under their attack, until the foundry came apart and fell on Will and his friends.

Will turned just in time to see the foundry coming down on them. Forty feet high and made of thick concrete, the building splintered apart as it fell. Will didn't have time to shout a warning or to fire his scepter at the wall.

His new allies were fast enough to avoid the threat. The goblins weren't, and neither was Gladys or the trolls. The goblins took what cover they could behind lampposts or in holes in the street. In the last seconds before the wall came down on them, London set Gladys on the ground and covered her with his body. Brooklyn was standing close to Will. He grabbed Will by the wrist and threw him clear just before the wall buried him. The broken concrete wall came down on his friends with a deafening crash, covering them entirely.

"No!" Will screamed. He ran back and clawed through the rubble.

"Come on, we have to get out of here!" Jarvis told him. "Evander's coming!"

Sure enough, the necromancer floated lazily towards them on his magic cloud, snickering. Will shot a hateful glance at the necromancer and staff before aiming his scepter at them. It fired with a roar, forcing Evander to flee high into the sky. More blasts followed until Evander quit the refinery altogether.

Will hung the scepter on his belt and got back to digging. Prince Alexander came to help and was soon followed by the others. They pushed aside the rubble, working around the heavier slabs of concrete. They were still digging when London pulled himself free. The troll staggered a few steps before falling into Will's arms.

"Sorry, boss, didn't see that one coming," London mumbled.

"It's okay, I got you." Will struggled to support his wounded friend, barely managing to set the troll down gently. Brooklyn was knocked unconscious by the rocks and they had to pull him out. Mr. Niff was stuck between two large slabs of concrete and was the only one of Will's friends moving under his own power. Vial was battered, but he'd survived largely because he didn't have any bombs left that could have been set off. Domo looked the worst, moaning and gripping his legs, his walking stick snapped in half. All of them were badly hurt. Only their innate toughness and good luck had kept them alive. Will and his allies laid out the wounded in the shadow of an ore silo.

Tears streamed down Will's face. These people were his friends. They'd followed him through thick and thin, even when it would have been safer and smarter to abandon him. Now they were hurt, maybe dying, because of decisions he'd made.

"Get me out of here!" Gladys shouted from under the rubble. Will dug her out and set her next to the others. She looked at them and the color drained from her face. "Oh, they look awful."

"Naw, it's just like a cave in," Mr. Niff said and gripped his left arm. "Ooh, a little worse I suppose. Hey, boss, do we get health insurance?"

"You do today," he said. Will pulled the stopper from the Bottle of Hope. Before he could use it, he heard skeletons shrieking in the distance. They'd come to finish their master's work. Will glanced at his allies and said, "I need a minute here. Keep them off me and I'll help you when I'm done."

"We'll handle this," Jarvis said menacingly. He led his adventurers along with Thistle, Prince Alexander and his men out to face the oncoming skeletons.

"I'm so sorry," Will told Mr. Niff.

"Hey, it happens to the best of us. Which means it happens to goofs like me even more often. You just got to shrug and move on. One day we'll look back on this and wince painfully."

Will held the Bottle of Hope to Mr. Niff's lips. "Take a sip, it'll help."

"He just needs a drop," Gladys said.

"He's hurt bad," Will protested as Mr. Niff drank.

"That's potent stuff you're using. One drop does the job."

Will walked over to London and opened his mouth. He poured in a little water and then did the same for Brooklyn. "I'm not taking chances. These are my friends."

Gladys rolled her eyes and threw up her hands. "Fine, what do I know?"

Will gave Domo and Vial a sip of water as well. Once he was done, he capped the bottle and stood up. "Stay with them until they recover. I'm going after the staff, and this time I'm not asking for surrender."

Will marched off in the direction of the oncoming skeleton horde. Gladys waddled closer to the others on the bronze eagle feet of her mirror. Worried, she looked down at them.

"Guys, you have to get up. The boss is going up against Evander, and those idiots he's with won't be enough help. The bottle's power should've kicked in by now." The goblins and troll brothers remained on the ground, no longer moaning but not getting up. She nudged London with the edge of the mirror. "Come on, he needs you. He's the only King we've had smarter than a doorstop. We can't let him get killed!"

Mr. Niff smacked his lips and climbed to his feet. "It's okay, I'm up. The stuff works fast. Wow, I feel—"

A skeletal elk with a full rack of antlers trotted around a corner and saw wounded prey laid out in front of it. It charged with an ear-piercing shriek. Mr. Niff pulled out his knife and threw it so fast that both his hand and knife were blurred. The knife made a whistling sound as it cut through the air and hit the elk. One second the elk was charging and shrieking, the next it was cut in half down the middle. After bisecting the skeleton, the knife hit a concrete wall and went in up to the hilt.

"Great," Mr. Niff finished. He hurried over to his knife and had to pull hard to free it. "Double wow."

London and Brooklyn got up next. Grumbling, London said, "That no good cheating wizard whumped me good, and I aim to give him one back."

Brooklyn helped up Domo and Vial. Both goblins were healed of their injuries, and Vial dusted himself off. Domo looked at the troll and said, "Uh, Brooklyn, your eyes are glowing."

Sure enough, a pale blue light spilled from the troll's eyes, and it grew in intensity with each passing second. Brooklyn rubbed his chin and grunted. He grabbed a concrete slab weighing a thousand pounds, lifted it over his head and hurled it fifty feet into a guard tower, destroying it utterly. As the others watched in astonishment, Brooklyn said, "Don't know what's going on, but I like it."

The eyes of everyone who drank from the Bottle of Hope began to glow. They felt incredible, fairly bursting with power. Vial looked at Mr. Niff and asked, "Exactly how much water did the King give us?"

"A sip each. Maybe thirty drops."

Water from the Bottle of Hope was enormously powerful. One drop could heal any injury and cure any illness. The first drop of water they'd drank did just that and restored them to full health. The other twenty-nine drops poured their strength into already healthy bodies. Will had effectively overdosed them on hope, and all that power had to go somewhere.

"Oh, this is going to be sweet," London said, and cracked his knuckles. Smiling, he and the others went looking for Will.

Chapter Fifteen

For over a hundred years the dwarf refinery was a symphony of sound as miners dug ore from the ground, refined it, shaped it and shipped it off to markets across the world. For ninety years after its abandonment the refinery lay silent, its workers gone and all life stripped from the land around it. Now the refinery was again inhabited, and the sounds of war sang from every corner as buildings fell, skeletons shrieked, black lightning thundered and fires roared in reply.

Half the buildings in the refinery were destroyed, with most of them falling in the last few hours. Evander Hollow, holder and slave of the Staff of Skulls, took responsibility for most of the damage. He flew at the edge of the refinery, firing into it and trying not to make himself a target. Another building came down under his assault.

A white-hot jet of fire answered his attack, then three more. Evander ducked under the blasts and wove through the sky to avoid them. One blast took off the top floor of dormitory and a set a warehouse on fire. Evander went between two buildings, cursing under his breath.

For a second fear overcame him and he tried to flee, but the insidious voices of the Staff of Skulls overcame him and forced him back into the fight. The staff had waited centuries for this battle. Never before had it found such an opportunity to finish its brutal war with the Bottle of Hope. It would destroy the bottle no matter the cost.

Focusing its fury on Will Bradshaw, the current owner of the Bottle of Hope, the Staff of Skulls missed the new threat rising up against it.

London cracked his knuckles as he marched down a street in the refinery. Light poured from his eyes and those of his brother Brooklyn and the goblins Domo, Vial and Mr. Niff. Fearlessly they headed toward the sound of battle, confident that their King was in the middle of it.

Will had given them water from the Bottle of Hope, too much of it, really. Each of them was overdosed with power from the bottle, and under its influence they were far more dangerous than normal.

"How long do you figure this is going to last?" London asked. Pavement cracked under his feet as he walked.

"Thirty-one minutes of heavy use," Vial answered. His mind was working faster and more efficiently than ever.

Brooklyn smiled. "A guy can do a lot of damage in half an hour with this much power."

London ripped a concrete lamppost out of the street and pointed it at a horde of skeletal animals hurrying after Will. The skeletons saw the trolls and goblins, and ran shrieking after them.

"Lucky us," London said. "We've got enemies to use it on."

The skeletons charged the trolls head on, which was arguably the *stupidest* thing they could have done. With their already impressive strength boosted by the bottle, the trolls tore through the skeletons like a chainsaw cutting through paper. London battered skeletons aside with his makeshift club until it crumbled apart in his hands. Brooklyn ground his enemies into powder with his fists. The few skeletons that survived the onslaught ran into Mr. Niff. His knife was a blur of steel as he cut apart the few survivors of the doomed charge.

Grinning maniacally, London lumbered off after Will. "Come on, brother, let's get these jerks off the King."

"If you'll excuse me, there's something I need to do," Vial said. He walked off into the war ravaged streets and picked up a rusty iron pail off the ground. "I should be back soon."

Domo grabbed Mr. Niff's shoulder before he could run off after the trolls. "Hold up. The skeletons and giant hands are just a symptom. The problem is the staff. It can replace whatever we destroy. If we're going to end this we have to take the staff out of the fight."

"How?" Mr. Niff asked.

"Come on, I have an idea."

Will stood in the center of the refinery, a section now clear of standing buildings after he and Evander had exchanged fire. With him was Thistle the elf, Sam Jarvis and his crew of adventurers, and Prince Alexander and his three swordsmen. Between them they had already destroyed a hundred skeletons in the last ten minutes.

More animal skeletons came racing down streets and stumbling over the wrecked remains of buildings. Will pointed his fire scepter at a group and turned it on. The scepter roared, sending out a blast of fire many times stronger than normal. The fire washed over the skeletons and burned them up. It also melted bits of scrap metal and caused concrete to explode from thermal stress. The little wood remaining in the refinery was burning and sent up a pall of smoke.

Will's fury matched the intensity of his scepter. The Staff of Skulls had hurt his friends badly. He'd healed them with the Bottle of Hope, but they'd come close to death. The Staff of Skulls was rumored to be immortal. Will was going to put that theory to the test.

"I appreciate the firepower, but can you dial that thing back a bit?" Jarvis asked between coughs. He was covered in sweat from hard fighting and from standing close to the scepter's blazing infernos.

"Can't," Will said through gritted teeth, "and don't want to."

A black cloud rose up from the city. Will spotted it and fired five times in rapid succession. The cloud whizzed through the air, dodging the attacks and fleeing the refinery. Instead of circling around and coming back as it had before, it continued away from them.

"Where's he headed?" Jarvis asked.

"Maybe he went for more skeletons?" Prince Alexander suggested.

Will shielded his eyes from the sun and tried to spot the necromancer. "I think he already brought his entire army."

"Is there anywhere he can go for assistance?" Thistle asked.

"There's nothing around us for miles," Will replied. "Besides, it's not like anyone's going to help him. He's a...oh no."

Jarvis grabbed Will's arm. "What? What is it?"

"There's a cemetery outside the refinery, and he's heading straight for it! We have to stop him before he makes more skeletons!"

Will started to run after Evander when ten giant hands of rock and dirt reached out of the rubble and tried to grab him. He destroyed the nearest ones with a blast from his scepter while his allies cut another one apart. More hands rose up to take their place.

Evander and the Staff of Skulls floated over the weed filled cemetery. Under the staff's direction, Evander summoned the swarm of pixies flying high in the sky. They fluttered over his head, cackling and giggling.

"You've been patient," the staff told them through Evander's lips. "I promised you power and strength, and now I keep that promise. Serve me without question and all shall be yours."

Evander raised the staff over his head. Black lightning shot from it and into the pixie swarm. The lightning arced between the pixies and the cemetery, slowly drawing them to the ground. The weeds that overran the cemetery blackened and died as the pixies were pulled down into the dirt. In seconds all but eight pixies were gone.

"I'm waiting," the staff said through Evander.

A skeletal hand punched up through the dirt. A skull burst from the ground. The ground cracked and lifted as more bones jutted up. Headstones toppled, pushed over as the bones underneath them merged with the pixie swarm. First in ones and twos, then in dozens, skeletal men and short, broad shouldered skeletal dwarfs clawed their way to the surface. Dozens became hundreds, until nearly a thousand skeletons stood at attention, their eyes blazing red in hatred.

Evander and the staff drifted down to inspect their latest army. The skeletons were in poor shape. Most of them had died in cave-ins or industrial accidents. Some were missing legs and arms, while others had broken ribs or fractured skulls, and all the bones were quite old.

"Not my best work," the staff admitted through Evander, "but suitable for the short term."

"What does our creator ask of us?" a skeletal dwarf asked. This skeleton was missing its right arm and most of its teeth.

Under the staff's direction, Evander pointed at the refinery. "My enemy, the Bottle of Hope, is in those ruins. Find it, destroy it and destroy those who claim it as their own."

The skeleton casually asked, "And we're getting *what* in return?"

Evander and the staff stared hard at the skeleton. "Excuse me?"

"What does the job pay?" the skeletal dwarf clarified. "If we're risking our necks then we're getting something for it. And is this an hourly rate or a lump sum payout at the end of the job?"

Another skeleton raised its hand. "Is there a pension, or do you offer stock options?"

"What's your business plan?" another asked. "Do you have a secured line of credit?"

Evander looked at the refinery, where the Bottle of Hope was again driving the skeletons into revolt. "Didn't waste any time, did you?" the staff said through Evander. He raised the staff as its many voices grew louder. "This didn't stop me last time, and it won't stop me now."

The staff's malignant voices spread madness and hatred into the minds of the skeletons. For a second they resisted its power, and one of them managed to shout, "The labor review board will hear of this!" The staff overcame their minds, and soon they were driven into a mindless fury and ran for the refinery.

Evander and the staff flew back into the refinery, confident of victory despite Evander's increased twitching and drooling. With these skeletons plus the survivors from its last army, there could be no doubt how the battle would end.

Strength. Strength was one of the defining features of a troll. London and Brooklyn were mere adolescents by troll standards, but like all trolls they were still incredibly strong for their size. Under the influence of the Bottle of Hope their strength was magnified many times over. They might be youngsters, but the brothers now possessed the strength of adult trolls.

The brothers walked calmly into a courtyard bordered by a huge fallen crane that had once brought ore carts to the surface. Hundreds of skeletal animals gathered in the courtyard to join Evander's new army when it arrived. Large as this group was, more skeletons were filtering in from other parts of the refinery to join their ranks. The skeletal animals saw the grinning trolls and charged.

London grabbed the crane's rusted steel frame and ripped off a bar five feet long and three inches thick. He hit it against the ground to shake off the rust and test its strength. The bar didn't bend. Brooklyn tore off a section of chain, each link two feet long and two inches thick. He swung it in a circle over his head and shook off most of the rust.

"You get the ones on the left, I get the ones on the right," London said as the skeletons closed on them.

"Who gets the ones in the middle?" Brooklyn asked.

"Whoever finishes first."

London stood his ground and let the skeletons come to him. They came packed together, a veritable wall of snapping jaws and scratching claws. He swung the steel bar and stopped the attack with his first swing, sending bone shards a hundred feet into the air to rain down across the refinery. More skeletons poured in and were caught by his next swing. A skeletal hound snuck in under the third swing and lunged at London's throat. He head butted the hound and smashed it.

Brooklyn ran into the oncoming mob, dragging the length of chain behind him. Three skeletons were in his way, and he knocked them over and crushed them underfoot. Once Brooklyn was deep inside the mob, he skidded to a halt and swung the chain in a circle. The thick chain crushed every skeleton around him. He swung the chain down on a skeletal bear and pulverized it, breaking the paved street below it as well. More skeletons attacked him, but any that came within the reach of the chain were swiftly reduced to so many broken bones.

The battle lasted less than a minute and ended with every skeleton in the courtyard destroyed. London laughed, "I'm not even breathing hard!"

"Yeah, wait until we get a hold of the necromancer," Brooklyn said. "He—"

Two giant hands of rock and dirt rose up from holes in the pavement and swung down on the trolls. London stepped out from under the first while Brooklyn was caught by the second and driven into the ground like a nail. London swung his steel bar at the giant hand attacking him and destroyed it. He whirled around to strike the second hand, only to see his brother's hands punch up from the ground and grab it by the sides. Brooklyn squeezed until the giant hand crumbled apart.

London helped his brother out of the ground and handed him back the chain. "That guy doesn't know when to quit."

"We got twenty more minutes to track him down before we're back to normal," Brooklyn replied.

"We don't need half that long."

Intelligence. Vial was smart enough he could have been a wizard. Unfortunately he'd never found a willing teacher, so he went into alchemy instead. He'd mastered the trade as much as anyone could and played a major role in saving the kingdom, first from King Kervol Ket and now from

Evander and the Staff of Skulls. The Bottle of Hope worked with that intelligence and boosted it.

Vial's brain was now working with the speed and precision of a computer. More than mere speed, he understood how everything fit together. It was like he'd been wearing blinders all his life until this point. The world was now one giant laboratory, and a surprisingly well stocked one at that.

Vial ran through the refinery, looting any building not already destroyed for ingredients. A pinch of coal dust, half a cup of black paint, a tablespoon of soap, all this and more went into the rusted pail he carried with him. Bird droppings, bat guano, dried weeds and industrial solvents well past their expiration dates went in along with even stranger things. Bone shards fell from the sky (courtesy of the troll brothers), and he added them to the mix. When he reached the bathhouse and its cornucopia of molds and fungi, he cried out in joy at finding so many supplies.

After adding samples of the wide variety of fungi, Vial mixed the unwholesome concoction together with a rusty spoon he'd found in a cafeteria. He watched as the goop blended together and began to steam. The pail grew painfully hot to the touch. He tossed in wood chips as the final ingredient and capped the pail with a chipped ceramic plate. Vial tied the plate down with wire and ran off to find Will.

The bomb he'd made was dangerously unstable and would go off on its own in a few minutes if he didn't set it off first. It was also as potent a weapon as any he'd made. When it went off the explosion would be a thing of beauty, provided the viewer was standing far enough back.

Happily, he could hear the sounds of battle not far off. Time to test his latest creation.

Will blasted his way through another giant hand, but Evander and the staff made them as fast as he could destroy them. He and his allies only managed to get a hundred yards through the refinery in fifteen minutes. Increasingly deep piles of rubble from buildings collapsed onto the roads caused more delay.

"I notice our esteemed enemy is no longer sending skeletons after us," Thistle observed. "Has he exhausted his supply, or are they going somewhere else?"

"If he's smart he's getting them together for one big push," Jarvis said. He climbed over the rubble pile from a collapsed ore silo.

Another giant hand shot up, this one just three feet from Jarvis. It punched through the rubble and knocked him on his back. The hand tried to swat Jarvis like a bug, but Thumac and Helena dragged him out of the way. Will blasted the giant hand with his scepter and destroyed it.

"Thanks," Jarvis said. He stood up and pointed at Will's scepter. "How much longer can you keep that up?"

Will studied his scepter for a second. It still shined like the sun, which was really no surprise. Will had given it five drops from the Bottle of Hope and overdosed it the same way he had his friends. The change wasn't permanent, but until the bottle's power was spent Will's scepter was working well beyond its manufacturers' expectations. "I think he's good for the duration."

"We can't get anywhere with these enormous hands slowing us," Prince Alexander said.

"I would think you'd be accustomed to feeling useless," a slurred voice replied.

They whirled around and saw Evander on his magic cloud, the necromancer and staff floating over a warehouse fifty feet away. Evander's movements were jerkier than before, his breathing ragged and irregular. Drool dribbled down his chin.

"Good lord," Prince Alexander whispered.

Will stared at Evander in horror that had nothing to do with the danger the man posed. They'd been fighting him only a few hours and he'd degenerated so much? Feeling a touch of pity for the man who'd tried to kill him, Will managed to say, "You don't look so good."

Evander swayed from side to side as the staff spoke through him. "An unfortunate consequence of controlling my *owner* directly is that they deteriorate quite rapidly. He was reaching the end of his value to me, anyway. He shall last a few more hours, which is longer than any of you have."

"You're insane!" Will shouted at the staff. "Even if you kill us and destroy the bottle, you'll be stuck out here in the middle of the wastelands when Evander dies. No one's going to come here. You'll be trapped the same as if you lost."

Evander jerked his head around as the staff studied the wastelands and ruined refinery through his eyes. Slurring Evander's speech even worse than before, it said, "This is just another prison. I'm good at getting out of those. It may take hundreds of years for a new owner to find me, but sooner or later someone will pick me up. Someone always does. One of the many advantages of immortality is that I can afford to be patient.

Maybe one of your goblins shall find me and have the honor of holding me…for a little while."

Will fired his scepter. Evander and the staff flew away before the blast of fire took the roof off the warehouse. More blasts followed the necromancer, taking the front wall off another warehouse and completely destroying a third. When that warehouse fell it cleared a view out of the refinery to the wastelands, and to the cemetery.

"Oh no," Will said.

They saw Evander's new army running toward the refinery, and if anything they were more revolting than the skeletal animals. These skeletons were made from people, men and dwarfs who'd had hopes and dreams and families who missed them. They'd died and were laid to rest, only to have their bones turned into these abominations.

And there were a lot of them. Will guessed the crowd's size at roughly a thousand strong, and they were running as fast as they could. They'd spread out so Will's scepter couldn't destroy more than a dozen at a time. The skeletons were unarmed except for their teeth and nails, but their sheer numbers made up for their deficit in weapons.

More skeletons came at them from within the refinery. Two mobs of skeletal animals, each hundreds strong, came running down the streets at Will and his allies. Adding to the odds against them, Evander directed eight pixies across the refinery and struck them with black lightning. Bone shards whirled together around the pixies, forming eight monster skeletons identical to the ones he'd used at the Goblin City. Lastly, dozens of giant hands made from rock and dirt erupted from the ground.

"I believe the chess term is checkmate," the staff said through Evander as they floated inches over a warehouse.

"No," Domo said from behind the necromancer. "It's check, and you can get out of check."

Evander spun around and saw Domo running across the roof of the warehouse, his yellow robes whipping around him and light pouring from his eyes. Evander tried to fly away, but before he could Domo threw himself at the necromancer and grabbed the Staff of Skulls.

"Wretch!" Evander gurgled. He spun round, trying to shake Domo loose. "Get off me!"

Domo leaned in and bit Evander's hand. Evander cried out in pain and let go of the staff. Breaking contact with it stunned him and he fell to the roof. Domo dropped down next to Evander and ran to Will.

Willpower. Domo was the closest the goblins had ever come to having a leader of their own. They never followed him or listened to him, but they were mildly proud of him. He'd once been a builder goblin, but he had the willpower to say 'I don't want to do this', and broke away from the builder guild. With the power of the Bottle of Hope coursing through him, his willpower was even greater than before.

Once he had the Staff of Skulls in his hands, it began to whisper to him. It promised riches and power the likes of which he'd never known. Why shouldn't he have the finer things in life? Why shouldn't he be a real ruler? Was it fair that a human was King of the Goblins and not a goblin? He could be king. The goblins would bow before him and obey his every order. He could get even with all the people who'd ever insulted him, mistreated him or ignored him. Not just goblins, he could make others obey his orders. Men, elves, dwarfs, trolls, they'd all bow before him. And if they didn't, he could destroy them and use their bones to make new followers, obedient followers. Anything was possible with the staff.

Domo heard all these lies, and he ignored them.

Running across the warehouse roof, he came to the edge and looked down. The battle was no longer so one sided. The giant hands of rock and earth crumbled away now that Evander lost the staff. Without the staff bolstering his strength he had only his own power, and that wasn't enough to maintain so many of the hands. The skeletons were still coming, but they were about to get a very nasty surprise.

Domo dropped to the ground. A fall like that would normally hurt him, but the Bottle of Hope's power kept him going. He hit the ground running and went straight for Will. A horde of skeletal animals was hot on his heels as he ran around the warehouse that Will had blasted the front off of. Mr. Niff was waiting for them.

Bravery. Mr. Niff was a hero. He'd known it ever since he helped a little girl lost in the woods. Heroes don't back down no matter how ridiculous the odds against them. They keep fighting until they win. Mr. Niff had people who were counting on him, a King who trusted him and an enemy that had to be stopped. What more could a hero ask for?

Mr. Niff stood in a warehouse, the only one in the city with anything in it. It contained forty wooden crates filled with nails, each nail four inches long, sharp and in excellent condition. They weren't exactly knives, but Mr. Niff wasn't fussy. He arranged the crates in a line and opened them. Standing at the first crate in the row, he waited for Domo's signal.

He was surprised when the front of the building disappeared in a blast of fire, but soon realized how lucky he was. He'd been planning to stand at the warehouse door and fight from there, but with the wall gone he had a much better field of fire.

Domo ran past him holding the Staff of Skulls. "Niff, now!"

A horde of skeletal animals ran after Domo. They were faster than he was and would catch the little goblin before he got fifty yards.

Mr. Niff picked up a nail and threw it. With accuracy developed by years of practice, and speed and power provided by the Bottle of Hope, he hit the lead skeleton. Traveling at 180 miles per hour and whistling as it cut through the air, the nail was as dangerous as a bullet. The first nail hit a skeletal wolf and shattered one of its legs, sending it tumbling to the ground. The dozen nails that followed like a blinding flash of steel finished it off. Mr. Niff threw a stream of nails through the skeletal horde like a machinegun. When the first crate was empty he moved to the second one and continued throwing. Dozens and then hundreds of skeletons fell under the rain of nails. The few skeletons that changed course and went after Mr. Niff didn't get within fifty feet of him before they were shredded.

Domo reached Will and his allies while Mr. Niff reduced one of the skeletal hordes to bone fragments. He dropped the staff at Will's feet. "We got it, now we have to get rid of it. Just don't touch it, trust me."

Up close the Staff of Skulls was even more loathsome to behold. Will recognized the skulls that it was made from. Rat, bat, lizard and snake skulls were fused together to make the handle. Raven skulls made up the top, with the skull of a man at the end. The staff glistened like it was slick with grease, and even out of Evander's hands it continued issuing orders to the skeletons with its many voices.

"Stand back," Will said. Everyone got behind Will as he pointed his scepter at the staff. The scepter roared and poured out fire, keeping up the blast for five seconds. When the fire died down the staff remained without so much as a scorch mark on it.

"Hotter!" Will ordered the scepter. The scepter rattled angrily and released a billowing cloud of white-hot fire of such incredible intensity that everyone behind Will was forced back. Will covered his eyes with his left arm to protect himself from the glare. Rock melted and then evaporated under the intense flames.

The fire ended, and the staff remained untouched by the inferno. Its many voices laughed in reply to his attack. This had been tried before. Thousands of heroes, wizards and holy men had tried for centuries to destroy the staff. They'd all failed. It laughed at Will's audacity to think he'd succeed.

The second horde of skeletal animals was almost upon them when London and Brooklyn stepped in their way. Grinning, London asked, "Same as with the last bunch?"

"I want to get the ones on the right!" Brooklyn protested. "That's where the big ones are!"

London frowned. "Fine, but you have to write the letter to mom this time. Use big words, she likes that."

The skeletons crashed into the trolls and suffered for it. Brooklyn swung his chain through them and London batted skeletons to powder with his steel bar. The skeletons should have backed down and looked for a way around the trolls, but they were driven to a mindless fury by the staff. They went straight at the brothers, ignoring the fate of those who went before them. When the fight was over only one got through, and Thistle cut it down.

Evander recovered from losing the staff and floated overhead. He searched desperately for the Staff of Skulls until saw Will pointing his scepter at it. Now that Evander was no longer in contact with the staff it couldn't dominate him, but the wizard's mind had been poisoned by it for years. He screamed, "No! Get away from it. You don't deserve it!"

"You idiot, it's killing you!" Will shouted back.

"Lies!" Evander pointed at Will and screamed, "Kill him! Kill him and bring the staff back to me!"

The last and largest horde of skeletons approached the refinery. This newest army of skeletal men and dwarfs shrieked their hatred. They were a formidable threat even without the staff supporting them, and they'd be on Will and his friends soon.

While the skeletons were still half a mile away, Vial hurried over to Brooklyn and tugged on his arm. The troll bent down and saw Vial holding a rusty steel pail with a ceramic plate wired over it. Smoke wafted out around the edge of the plate, and the pail was vibrating.

Vial held up the pail and asked, "Brooklyn, if you would be so kind as to assist me with an experiment? I need this," he pointed at the pail, "over there," he said, and pointed at the skeletal army.

Brooklyn took the pail and hurled it with his enhanced strength. As it flew through the air, Vial added, "It would be advisable to seek cover."

Will knew what that meant. "Get down!"

The bomb landed as Will and the others laid flat on the ground. It detonated with a deafening explosion, taking out half the army. The explosion tore up a huge section of the rocky wasteland and sent pieces of stone sharp as razors flying through the air. Stone shrapnel scythed through the remaining skeletons and left not a single one standing. A shock wave followed by high winds hit the refinery, forcing Evander and his magic cloud to the ground.

The last line of Evander's army attacked. Eight monstrous skeletons lumbered into battle, each one ten feet tall and made from fused bone shards. London and Brooklyn grabbed the first one and ripped it apart as the rest bore down on Will. Prince Alexander tried to stop one and was kicked over. The skeleton lifted a foot to crush him, but Will burned away the top half, leaving the rest to fall over on its own.

Evander struggled to his feet and pointed at Will. "You can't stop us. Nothing can!"

Will heard the staff laugh louder. Will and his friends had destroyed almost its entire army, and the thing laughed at them. It had committed so many evil deeds over so many years, and here it was, laughing. It had tried to kill his friends. Staring hard at it, Will hung his scepter on his belt and took out the Bottle of Hope. He pulled out the stopper and held the bottle over the staff.

The staff stopped laughing.

"You said the Bottle of Hope was a threat to you," Will said, surprised how calm he sounded with such anger boiling inside him. "You hate it so much you've been trying to kill it for hundreds of years. Let's see if the feeling is mutual."

The staff's many voices fell silent, and for the first time they spoke in unison so Will could understand. "*Wait. We can make a deal.*"

"No," Will said, and poured out the bottle's water onto the staff. "We can't."

Hundreds of drops of water fell onto the Staff of Skulls. The drops tried to heal it, same as they did for everyone. But the Staff of Skulls was made of the skulls of many animals fused together, and like Will's fire scepter, the staff was alive. The healing water tried to make healthy animals out of each of the skulls. The staff shook violently as every part of it grew and tried to rip free from the others. Cracks spread across it and oily black smoke poured out. A high-pitched screech rose up from the staff and grew in volume.

"It's going to blow!" Domo yelled.

Will grabbed the staff and threw it into an empty warehouse. He dove to the ground seconds before the staff detonated and released all its power. Thousands of bolts of black lightning shot into the air, annihilating the warehouse and nearly deafening everyone with the thunderous blast. Over the sound of the explosion they heard the Staff of Skulls scream as it died.

"No!" Evander cried out. He formed a new magic cloud and flew into the air. Snarling like a rabid animal, he shot jets of fire and javelins of ice at Will, missing by inches.

Will's friends and new allies finished off the last of the monstrous skeletons. Cutting them down with streams of nails, a thick length of chain, swords or a simple steel bar, they brought them down one after another. Thistle jumped on top of one monstrous skeleton and took off its head with his two swords. Prince Alexander and his swordsmen cut off another one at the knees and let Thumac and Jarvis finish it. Helena,

Dredmore and Domo took another one apart. When the last monstrous skeleton fell, they turned their attention on the necromancer.

The odds against Evander were so great that running was the only way he could survive. Instead he fought on, spitting and snarling, heedless of the danger.

Evander had clearly gone mad. Will wondered how long the staff had assaulted his mind until he was reduced to this. It could have been years, or even decades. He wondered how many other people had the staff corrupted. Dozens or maybe even hundreds of people had picked up the staff, only to be taken over and drive mad until it ran them into the ground. Evander was one of the staff's victims just as much as Will and his friends were.

"Boss!" Mr. Niff shouted as he ran up to Will. "We got the last of them! It's just that nasty old man left."

"Niff, I need a scarecrow, fast," Will told him. He shook the Bottle of Hope and heard a faint sloshing sound. There was only a little water left.

"I'll get it, but it's our last one."

Mr. Niff ran off while the others formed a circle around Evander. Christina Dredmore loaded her crossbow and Jarvis took the bow off his back. Staying airborne wouldn't protect Evander for much longer. Will had to move fast.

Evander cast all manner of spells, firing ice javelins and spurts of fire. He even managed to create a single giant hand from rock and dirt. None of it helped. His aim was too wild, and the people standing against him too skilled and determined. It was only a matter of time before they closed in for the kill.

Mr. Niff ran back with the scarecrow. The glow in his eyes was dimming, as were the others who'd drunk from the Bottle of Hope. "Oh no, it's wearing off!"

"You did good, Niff," Will said. He took the scarecrow from him and ran to London. Before he reached the troll, he put the stopper back into the Bottle of Hope and tucked it in his belt. Will handed the scarecrow to the troll and said, "London, I need you to throw this at Evander."

London's strength was returning to normal, which meant he was still extremely strong. He didn't ask why Will wanted this job done, merely taking the scarecrow and nodding. "I can nail him with it."

"Do it."

London threw the scarecrow like a spear. It flew awkwardly through the air but was on target. If Evander was in his right mind he could have dodged the ungainly missile, but in his present state he didn't even see it coming. Half a second before the scarecrow hit, Will fell over backwards.

Whoosh. Will traded places with the scarecrow and slammed into Evander. The necromancer kicked him and tried to claw Will's face. Will stepped onto the black magic cloud, which felt spongy under his feet. He struggled with Evander and got the necromancer in a headlock with his left arm before ripping off the wizard's black mask with his right hand. Will tossed the mask aside as Evander tried to break free.

"I'll kill you!" Evander screamed.

Will took the bottle from his belt. He pulled the stopper out with his teeth and spit it out, then jammed the bottle into Evander's mouth and poured the last of the water in. "Down the hatch!"

Evander's eyes bugged out and he shook uncontrollably, knocking Will off the cloud. Just before Will hit the ground from twenty feet up, he saw Evander throw back his head and scream as blinding bright light poured from his lips.

Evander fell off the cloud and landed next to Will, the fall knocking both of them out. Before he lost consciousness, Will said, "What do you know? I think I saved the bad guy."

Chapter Sixteen

Will woke up and found himself on a street choked with rubble. He rubbed his head and stretched his arms and legs. He felt fine, with his bones intact and in the right place. That was pretty surprising given how far he just fell. Judging by the devastated buildings and bone shards on the ground he was still in the refinery. The sun was still high overhead, so he hadn't been out for long.

"The boss is up!" Mr. Niff shouted.

Will's friends gathered around and helped him to his feet. Their eyes were back to normal, proof that the power from the Bottle of Hope was spent. Will checked his scepter and found it no longer glowed like the sun.

London asked Will, "How do you feel?"

"Pretty good."

"Nothing hurts?" Brooklyn asked.

Will shook his head and put on his hat. "I'm not in any pain."

"Good," London said, and then smacked Will in the back of the head. "What were you thinking? Roughing up a necromancer? That was the dumbest thing I've seen in ten years of living with goblins! The only thing that comes close was the Great Goblin Glue Geyser."

"That was a proud moment for us all," Vial said solemnly.

London grabbed Will's shoulders and shook him. "Brooklyn and me are your bodyguards. If anyone's supposed to do something pointlessly dangerous it's us!"

"Sorry," Will apologized. "It seemed like a good idea at the time."

London let go of Will, and Brooklyn said, "Just remember, you're not as tough as we are. From now on leave roughing people up to us."

"It's a deal. How long was I out?"

"Only a few minutes," Domo said. "You were banged up pretty bad. We were worried, so we used the last drop of water from the Bottle of Hope on you."

Mr. Niff handed the bottle to Will. "It's empty."

"So now what?" Will asked.

Jarvis walked up to Will, frowning. "Now we're screwed. The bottle is empty so it's worthless. Helena says she can't feel anything from it anymore. We tried pouring in more water to see if the bottle would make it magic, but it came out normal water. All that work and money spent, and we get nothing."

"You're not the only one," Thistle said. "I'm not just back to square one in my efforts to become a king. With all the gold I squandered, I'm worse off than when I began. Speaking of which, I would like a refund from your seer."

"That's not happening," Jarvis said.

Will held up the empty bottle. "The bottle has been emptied before and was full when we found it. How long does it take to recharge?"

Jarvis threw up his hands. "Who knows? But it's like you said this morning, other treasure hunters are going to try to steal it from us if we have it. If it was working we could supercharge on it like your trolls and goblins, but since it's empty we're just sitting ducks."

Will set the bottle on the pavement and frowned. "One of the most powerful magic items on the planet, and it's temporarily out of service."

He felt bad about that. He'd expended the bottle's power to save his friends and destroy the Staff of Skulls. That was important, but how long would it take to recharge? Will didn't know, but he suspected it would be a while. He thought about the sick and injured people he could have healed with the bottle. He couldn't help but feel he should have used it better. A wiser man would have found a way to stop the staff without exhausting the bottle in the process.

Prince Alexander hurried over when he saw Will standing again. "You're all right! I was worried when I saw you fall."

"It's okay, I'm good," Will replied. "I figured you would have left by now."

"I didn't want to go until I was sure you didn't need help. After all, you gave me more than enough water to share if you needed it." The Prince pointed to the ruins of the warehouse where Will had thrown the Staff of Skulls. "My men and I dug up the staff to make sure it's truly dead."

Worried, Will asked, "You didn't touch it, did you?"

One of the Prince's swordsmen marched up to Will and dropped a charred piece of garbage at his feet. The Prince pointed at it and said, "No fear. The Staff of Skulls is no longer a threat."

Cautiously, Will picked up the broken piece of trash and slowly realized he was holding the Staff of Skulls, or what was left of it. The staff was blackened and cracked so badly it was hard to tell what it was. The malignant voices were gone, as was its mad dream of destruction.

Will tossed the staff to Jarvis, who caught it easily. "You helped destroy the Staff of Skulls. That has to be worth something."

Jarvis rubbed his chin. "Maybe we can get a round of free drinks somewhere."

Domo took the broken staff from Jarvis and smacked him in the shin with it. While the adventurer was jumping up and down and yelping, the little goblin said, "You moron! You're so fixed on getting the bottle you don't see what's right in front of you. The Guild of Heroes is offering a 5000 gold coin reward for destroying the Staff of Skulls. All you have to do is turn this in and you're rich."

"Really?" Jarvis snatched back the staff and ran his fingers over it. He looked nervously at Will and the others.

Prince Alexander waved him away. "You're welcome to the money. I already have my reward."

"Keep it," Will told Jarvis. "You risked your life for a good cause today. You ought to get rewarded for it."

"And what do I receive for my services?" Thistle asked.

"Fair question," Will said. "Can you guys agree to split the money?"

Jarvis smiled at Thistle. "Sure. That was some impressive work today, Thistle. You're pretty good in a fight. Have you thought about working with a team? It would be a lot easier than trying to become a king on your own."

Thistle frowned. "You propose an alliance?"

"Why not? You wouldn't be out here if things were going well for you on your own."

"It...could work," Thistle agreed. "We'll discuss the matter on the way back."

Jarvis smiled. "Great. The six of us will do wonders."

Confused, Thistle asked, "Six?"

"It's a long story," Jarvis told him.

Prince Alexander stood before Will and bowed. "Sir, I am in your debt, as is my entire kingdom. Your generosity will save my father, King Ethan, and you saved my life as well. Let none say my family does not pay its debts. Name a reward, and if it is within my power you shall have it."

Will thought about the Prince's offer. "I need a bed."

The Prince stared at him. "A bed?"

"Yeah. I've been sleeping on a pile of rags for months. Maybe a table and some chairs, and I can use a dresser. Furniture in general would be good. It doesn't have to be good stuff," Will said hastily. "Anything you have in storage would be fine."

Dumbfounded, the Prince asked, "You have a kingdom in your debt and you ask for furniture?"

Will pulled his king contract out from his belt and showed it to Prince Alexander. *Article 61, subsection 2, paragraph 18, line 4: The King can't seek assistance from other royalty to escape his contract. He also can't seek help from the pope, the King of the Gypsies or Santa Claus.*

"The only other thing I really want is to go home, and you can't help me with that," he told the Prince.

Prince Alexander shook Will's hand. "Furniture it is."

Will's friends and allies were around him and in good health. That left one source of concern. "Where's Evander?"

Domo pointed outside the refinery, where Evander Hollow sat on the flat, rocky ground. "He got up before you did. We weren't sure what to do with him, so we waited until you woke up."

Will walked slowly toward Evander. The man sat quietly, staring off into the sky. As Will approached, Evander picked up a broken rib bone and held it up. He turned around to look at Will. With his mask off, Will saw that Evander was an older man, his black hair streaked with gray. He had pale blue eyes and a lost look on his face.

"I," he began in a soft voice, "I was trying to do good. I traveled from one land to another helping people in need. But, but for every good deed I did it seemed there were a hundred people doing evil. Nothing I did seemed to make a difference. I thought, I thought if I was stronger, I could finally make things better."

Evander studied the bone fragment. "I heard of a magic staff. It was rumored to be hard to control, but if a wizard held it his power was ten times as great. I thought of the good I could do with it. I found it high in the mountains sealed in a block of granite. I freed it and then I, I think I touched it. After that my memories are foggy." Evander looked at the destruction around him. "I've done something terrible, haven't I?"

Will sat down next to Evander. "No. The staff did something evil. It used you. But you're free of it now. If you need a place to rest and get your act together, you can stay with me for a while."

Evander stood up. "No, thank you, but I think it would be best for me to be alone. I need to do some thinking."

Evander whispered magic words, and this time a white cloud formed in front of him. He stepped on it and floated off into the sky.

Domo walked up to Will. "Is he going to be okay?"

"I think so. Come on, let's get out of here and go home."

"What about the bottle?" Mr. Niff asked.

Will looked at the Bottle of Hope on the ground with the stopper missing. It had been here for who knows how long, maybe years, and he'd completely used up its amazing powers in less than a day. "Leave it. It's someone else's turn to use it."

Shocked, Gladys asked, "After all we went through you're just going to walk away from it?"

"I only wanted to get it out of the kingdom before the Staff of Skulls blew the place up or an army came looking for it," Will replied. "The staff is destroyed, and I don't think armies are coming anymore. Helena said she couldn't feel anything from the bottle, so chances are nobody else can, either. If anyone comes for it we'll tell them exactly where to find it."

Will led his friends and allies out of the refinery and south into the wastelands. "We should be able to get home before our food runs out. Come on, guys, we'll share with you."

"What provisions do you have?" Thistle asked.

Will searched through the remaining packages. "Some nuts, berries, powdered soup mix and a lot of hardtack biscuits."

"In my kingdom, hardtack is considered a lethal weapon," Prince Alexander said.

"Is that from eating it or throwing it at people?" Will asked as they continued walking.

"Both."

Will looked around and saw Mr. Niff wasn't following them. "Niff, we're leaving!"

Mr. Niff stood over Evander's black lacquered mask. The mask was damaged from when it hit the ground. White cracks spread across it like a spider's web, and there was a large chip missing under the right eyehole. Mr. Niff smiled and tucked the mask inside his shirt. "This'll look great in the treasury."

Mr. Niff hurried to catch up with Will. As they walked away from the refinery, Mr. Niff said, "You know, with all this craziness I forgot there's a holiday coming up. I think we'll be back in the Goblin City in time for National Annoy the King Day."

"Annoy the what?" Will screamed. "Hold on, back up a second!"

Once Will and the others were gone, the Bottle of Hope lifted itself upright. The copper stopper rolled through the ruins until it hit the base of the bottle, then rose up and plugged into place.

Things had gone well. The Staff of Skulls was finally destroyed, and the deed was done in a place where its destruction wouldn't harm anyone. Getting rid of that abomination was a major goal for the bottle. In large part that success was because of the people the bottle had called to help it. They were a good bunch. Sure, some of them were a little rough around the edges, but they were working on it.

The Bottle of Hope had tried to accomplish this goal five years earlier, but the elf army arrived too soon. There had been no time to draw worthy owners to it, nor to lure the Staff of Skulls in and destroy it. The bottle had fled from the elves, knowing they would misuse its power. But this time, this time everything worked just fine.

The bottle rotated, taking in the devastation around it. It hadn't been in the refinery for very long, but any time spent here was unpleasant. The refinery and wastelands had never been a pretty sight, and if anything it was worse after the day's battle. Will was right when he said the dwarfs had long ago judged the land and refinery expendable. This land had been left desolate for so many decades because of their greed. That was unacceptable.

The Bottle of Hope rose into the air and flew high above the refinery. The bottle had a long list of people that needed healing, including King Ethan. Why not add the wastelands to the list? That would have the added benefit of rewarding the King of the Goblins for his help. After all, he and his friends had been put in great danger on its account. Surely some form of compensation was due.

The stopper pulled free and floated away, and the bottle began to spin faster and faster. Water shot from it like a fountain, hundreds of gallons every minute. The bottle flew over the ruined refinery and spread its water far and wide. Its drops melted through the rocks like rainfall melting snow, freeing the land trapped under it.

The water didn't stop at dissolving the cover of stone. Even in the wastelands there were seeds. Carried by the wind or deposited in bird droppings, thousands of seeds on the ground were soaked in the Bottle of Hope's water. The results were explosive.

Weeds, creepers, grass and berry bushes sprouted and grew at incredible speed, putting on months and then years of growth in seconds. Cottonwood and willow trees, their seeds blown in on the wind, grew decades in the span of minutes. A few hazelnuts dropped by Will and his friends added to the forest, growing forty, fifty, sixty feet high.

Creepers grappled the remnants of the refinery and pulled buildings down. Trees punched through the few walls still standing. Weeds grew in cracks and tore up the streets. In minutes the refinery was gone, dissolved by the bottle or smashed apart and smothered by the plants.

The bottle stopped spinning. It ended the cascade and plugged its stopper back in place. Below it the refinery was gone along with 5000 acres of the wastelands around it. In its place grasslands surrounded a lush forest. But it wasn't the kind of airy, open forest humans and elves favored. The trees were so large and close together that no light reached the forest floor. Their branches interlocked so thickly that a skilled climber could travel through the canopy from one end of the forest to the other without ever touching the ground. Ferns and mosses choked the forest floor alongside large mushrooms.

It was, in short, exactly the kind of messy, cluttered place goblins like to live in.

The healing effect slowed down. This zone of growth would continue to spread at the rate of a foot an hour in all directions, dissolving the porous rock and speeding plant growth until the wastelands were nothing more than a bad memory. It would take time, but the bottle was satisfied that the process was started.

This would please the bottle's creator, the holy man Nathaniel Lightwell. Nathaniel's patron would be pleased, too. With its work done, the Bottle of Hope disappeared in a flash of light.

Moments later and thousands of miles away, the bottle reappeared in a farmer's fields. The crops were growing well even though the fields were thick with weeds. The bottle caused a large rock to lift up. It plunked down in the hole and the rock gently came down to cover it.

The farmer, a tall and surprisingly pale man named Josiah Stiller, walked tiredly though his fields. There was plenty of rain and it was warm enough for the crops to grow quickly, but he was miserable. How could he not be? He was sick, as was everyone else in his village. A terrible illness was spreading throughout the land, brought in by a merchant ship whose captain had ignored quarantine rules.

Exhausted, Josiah stopped weeding and leaned against a fence post, then started coughing so hard he doubled over. Even light work like this left him tired, and this blasted cough wouldn't leave him. He'd bought this field and cleared it for planting not five months earlier, and soon it would be harvest time. What would happen if he was too weak to bring in the crops?

Josiah wasn't bad off compared to other people in the village, for unlike so many of them he could still stand, but he was worried. He was one of the few men even remotely healthy in the village. He and the other farmers moved slowly through their fields, doing as much work as their tired bodies would allow. The men weren't just responsible for tending their farms, but were also nursing sick relatives back to health. Hundreds of people depended on these poor, sickly men. What would happen to the village, to their families, if their strength finally failed?

Josiah saw a large rock in the middle of his fields. He'd been meaning to get rid of it for a while, and today he felt strong enough to take care of it. He pulled the rock out and began rolling it away, but then he saw a glimmer in the hole it left behind. It was a copper bottle that shined like it was brand new.

"Wonder how long it's been here?" he muttered as he picked it up. It felt like it was full. "Maybe I can sell it and buy some medicine."

He tuned the bottle over in his hands. One side was stamped with the word HOPE. "Wait a minute, this can't be."

Josiah pulled the stopper out. The bottle was filled with water and smelled faintly of peppermint. He dipped his finger in and put it in his mouth. His eyes snapped open as strength flooded back into him and his congestion cleared. He jammed the stopper back in and ran to his neighbors. "Hey! Hey! Look what I found!"

Made in the USA
Monee, IL
31 January 2021

59267255R00168